Study Guide

*for*

Weiten and Lloyd's

# Psychology Applied to Modern Life

# Adjustment in the 21st Century

Eighth Edition

**William E. Addison**
*Eastern Illinois University*

THOMSON

WADSWORTH

Australia • Brazil • Canada • Mexico • Singapore • Spain • United Kingdom • United States

Printed in the United States of America

1 2 3 4 5 6 7 09 08 07 06 05

Printer: Thomson West

0-495-03032-5

Cover Image: "Clock Parts Face," Pete McArthur; "Looking for Solutions" © Pierre-Yves Goavec/Getty Images Inc.

**Thomson Higher Education**
**10 Davis Drive**
**Belmont, CA 94002-3098**
**USA**

For more information about our products, contact us at:
**Thomson Learning Academic Resource Cente**
**1-800-423-0563**

For permission to use material from this text or product, submit a request online at
**http://www.thomsonrights.com.**
Any additional questions about permissions can be submitted by email to **thomsonrights@thomson.com.**

# TABLE OF CONTENTS

# TO THE STUDENT

Reading a college textbook can sometimes be a challenge. At times the ideas all begin to merge together, and the terms and definitions seem to be just a jumble of words. How do you sort it all out? How do you tell what's important and what isn't? And how do you know if you've got a good understanding of the important points?

A study guide can help you answer these questions. I wrote this study guide to help you understand and learn the material presented in your textbook, *Psychology Applied to Modern Life: Adjustment in the 21st Century*, by Wayne Weiten and Margaret Lloyd. In the study guide, I've highlighted the main points in each chapter, and provided exercises designed to help you learn the material. Specifically, each chapter of the study guide includes three different exercises:

1. **Programmed Review.** The programmed review is designed to provide you with a thorough review of the chapter. In each chapter, I've Included (and highlighted) the learning objectives. These objectives are the points identified as the most important by the authors of your textbook. The statements in the programmed review have key words missing, and in each case the correct word or words can be found along the left side of the page. To do the review, you should cover the answers on the left and try to complete the sentences on your own with the choices provided. Then check your answers. If you didn't get the right answer, it would be a good idea to go to the appropriate page(s) in the textbook (listed in parentheses after the statement), review the relevant material, and then try the statement again.

   This exercise works best if you can do it without looking at the correct answer until you're done; in other words, **no peeking!** If you can answer most of these questions on your own, you probably have a fairly solid understanding of the material. In general, the programmed review is a good way to find out if you understand and remember what you read in the book.

   An important piece of advice when using this review: you should avoid simply memorizing the statements and the correct responses. Using this exercise will be much more beneficial if you take some time to think about the correct responses. For instance, if you choose the correct alternative for a particular statement, take a few seconds to ask yourself why this alternative makes the most sense (i.e., what is it about this response that makes it the correct answer?). On the other hand, if you choose an incorrect alternative, think about why the correct answer is a better choice. This approach won't take a lot of extra time, and it will likely enhance your understanding of the material –and probably improve your course grade!

2. **Quiz Boxes.** The "quiz boxes" contain the key terms (and names) that are highlighted in your textbook and listed at the end of each chapter. I designed the boxes to be used like "flash cards" to help you learn the key terms or concepts. One way to use the boxes is to make photocopies of the pages from the study guide, cut the boxes apart, and then try to match the definitions with the appropriate terms. You can also use the quiz boxes in the same way that you use the programmed review; that is, you can cover the terms on the left, then try to identify the correct term after reading the definition (or vice versa). You should note that the terms appear in the same order that they're covered in the textbook chapter, not in the order they're listed at the end of the chapter (which is alphabetical). There are also quiz boxes for key people in the chapter. Believe it or not, using the quiz boxes with a friend or classmate can actually be kind of fun, and it's a good way for both of you to learn the material. Again, please remember that it's more important to understand the general concepts than it is to simply memorize the definitions.

3. **Self-Test.** The self-test is an opportunity to evaluate what you've learned from reading the textbook and completing the previous exercises. Each test consists of 20 multiple-choice items and 10-15 true/false items. The answers (with brief explanations) can be found at the end of the chapter. Again, page numbers are provided so that if you don't get the correct answer you can go back to the textbook and review the relevant material. When you take the self-test, it's a good idea to think of a rationale for your answer, <u>before</u> you consult the answer key. Then, you can compare your rationale to the brief explanation provided in the key. As with the programmed review, using the self-test will be much more beneficial if you take some time to <u>think</u> about the correct response, as well as to question why the other alternatives are <u>not</u> good choices.

If you use the study guide as I've recommended, I think you'll find it to be a useful supplement to your textbook. I hope your use of the study guide enhances your experience with this course. If you have any suggestions or recommendations for improving the study guide, please do not hesitate to contact me.

## ABOUT THE AUTHOR

William Addison, Professor and Chair of Psychology at Eastern Illinois University, earned his B.A. from Shippensburg University, his M.A. from Marshall University, and his Ph.D. from Miami University. He has published a number of articles, several of which have appeared in the journal *Teaching of Psychology*. He has given over 60 presentations at regional and national conferences, and authored more than 10 textbook ancillaries. He is currently serving as President of Division Two of the American Psychological Association – The Society for the Teaching of Psychology, and as a Faculty Consultant for the Advanced Placement Exam in Psychology.

## ACKNOWLEDGMENTS

I am grateful to a number of people who contributed to the preparation of the study guide. First and foremost, I want to thank Wayne Weiten and Marky Lloyd for writing an outstanding textbook that is truly "student-friendly." Jennifer Keever at Wadsworth/ITP did an excellent job of providing me with necessary materials as quickly as possible, and offering friendly reminders about upcoming deadlines. Pam Gutowski did her usual outstanding job of formatting and proofreading. Kaitlin, Will, and James Addison all provided much-needed support and understanding throughout the project, particularly when my work prevented me from spending as much time with them as they and I would like. Kaitlin also contributed her expertise as an editorial assistant during the final stages of the project. As always, I am especially grateful to Jayne L. Addison, the love of my life and my best friend. This edition of the study guide is dedicated to the memory of Betty M. Addison, beloved mother and grandmother.

William Addison
Psychology Department
Eastern Illinois University
600 Lincoln Avenue
Charleston, IL  61920
217-581-2127
weaddison@eiu.edu

# Chapter 1
## ADJUSTING TO MODERN LIFE

### PROGRAMMED REVIEW

**1. Describe four examples of the paradox of progress.**

television

1-1. Recent research suggests that virtually all the additional leisure time gained over the last 30 years has been absorbed by one of technology's most seductive inventions –(the computer/the telephone/television). (2)

lower

1-2. Research shows that people who are especially concerned with money and possessions tend to report (lower/higher) levels of happiness than others. (2)

material

1-3. Studies find that the gap between what people have and what they desire is greater in the (material/occupational/social) domain than in other areas of life. (2)

increased

1-4. Studies have found that the incidence of depressive disorders has (increased/decreased) over the last 50 years. (3)

behavioral

1-5. To most people, crises such as global warming, deforestation, and widespread air and water pollution sound like technical problems that call for technological answers, but they are also (behavioral/ecological/geographical) problems in that they are fueled by overpopulation and overconsumption. (4)

**2. Explain what is meant by the paradox of progress and how theorists have explained it.**

have not

2-1. The technological advances of the 20th century (have/have not) led to perceptible improvement in our collective health and happiness. (4)

direction

2-2. Many theorists agree that the basic challenge of modern life has become the search for meaning or a sense of (belonging/direction/social awareness). (4)

**3. Provide some examples of people's search for direction.**

bankrupt

3-1. Most experts characterize "self-realization" programs such as est training, Scientology, and Silva Mind Control as intellectually (bankrupt/fulfilling/stimulating). (5)

normal

3-2. In reality, converts to religious cults are a diverse array of (deviant/emotionally needy/normal) people who are swayed by remarkably ordinary social influence strategies. (5)

moral

3-3. Dr. Laura, who is not a psychologist or psychiatrist (her degree is in physiology), analyzes callers' problems in more of a(n) (emotional/moral/sociological) than psychological framework. (6)

**4.    Describe three problems that are common in popular self-help books.**

encourage

4.1.    Many psychotherapists (encourage/do not encourage) their patients to read selected self-help books. (7)

psychobabble

4-2.    Self-help books tend to be dominated by "hip" but hopelessly vague language known as _____. (8)

the authors' intuition

4-3.    The advice offered in self-help books is frequently based on (scientific research/the authors' intuition). (8)

don't provide

4-4.    Self-help books usually (provide/don't provide) explicit directions about how to change your behavior. (8)

**5.    Summarize advice about what to look for in quality self-help books.**

Clarity

5-1.    (Ambiguity/Clarity) in communication is essential for a genuinely helpful book. (9)

cautious

5-2.    The truly useful self-help books tend to be appropriately (cautious/ enthusiastic/open-minded) in their promises. (9)

references

5-3.    Self-help books that are based on more than personal anecdotes and speculation should include a list of (examples/key terms/references) in the back, or at the end of each chapter. (9)

a particular problem

5-4.    More often than not, useful self-help books tend to focus on (a particular problem/a variety of problems). (9)

**6.    Summarize the philosophy underlying this textbook.**

scientific research

6-1.    This textbook summarizes the (anecdotal evidence/scientific research/self-help literature) on human behavior that appears relevant to the challenge of living life effectively in contemporary society. (10)

critical thinking

6-2.    This text attempts to foster a critical attitude about psychological issues and to enhance your (critical thinking/social/writing) skills. (10)

emotional

6-3.    An important guideline for thinking critically is to avoid (emotional/ psychological/scientific) reasoning. (11)

uncertainty

6-4.    Perhaps the hardest step in becoming a critical thinker is to tolerate (emotional reasoning/simplification/uncertainty). (11)

take charge of

6-5.    This text assumes that the key to effective adjustment is to (meditate on/reject your perception of/take charge of) your own life. (11)

**7.    Describe the two key facets of psychology.**

| | |
|---|---|
| science | 7-1. Psychology leads a complex dual existence as both a(n) (art/college course/science) and a profession. (11) |
| Behavior | 7-2. _____ is any overt (observable) response or activity by an organism. (11) |
| does not | 7-3. Psychology (confines/does not confine) itself to the study of human behavior. (11) |
| physiological | 7-4. Psychology includes the study of the (philosophical/physiological) processes that underlie behavior. (12) |
| Clinical | 7-5. (Clinical/Developmental/Social) psychology is the branch of psychology concerned with the diagnosis and treatment of psychological problems and disorders. (12) |

**8.     Explain the concept of adjustment.**

| | |
|---|---|
| biology | 8-1. The concept of adjustment was originally borrowed from (biology/philosophy/ sociology). (12) |
| adaptation | 8-2. The concept of adjustment was modeled after the biological term adaptation/evolution/modification), which refers to efforts by a species to adjust to changes in its environment. (12) |

**9.     Explain the nature of empiricism.**

| | |
|---|---|
| empiricism | 9-1. The premise that knowledge should be acquired through observation is known as _____. (13) |
| systematic observation | 9-2. When we say that scientific psychology is empirical, we mean that its conclusions are based on (common sense/speculation/systematic observation). (13) |

**10.     Explain two advantages of the scientific approach to understanding behavior.**

| | |
|---|---|
| precision | 10-1. The first advantage of the scientific method is its clarity and (applicability/ precision/subjectivity). (13) |
| error | 10-2. The second advantage of the scientific approach is its relative intolerance of (diverse viewpoints/error/objectivity). (13) |

**11.     Describe the experimental method, distinguishing between independent and dependent variables and between experimental and control groups.**

| | |
|---|---|
| experiment | 11-1. A research method in which the investigator manipulates one variable under carefully controlled conditions and observes whether any changes occur in a second variable as a result is known as a(n) (correlational study/experiment/survey). (13) |
| independent | 11-2. A condition or event that an experimenter varies in order to see its impact on another variable is called a(n) (dependent/empirical/independent) variable. (13) |
| dependent; independent | 11-3. The (dependent/independent) variable is the variable that is thought to be affected by the manipulations of the (dependent/independent) variable. (14) |
| experimental control | 11-4. The (control/experimental) group consists of the subjects who receive some special treatment in regard to the independent variable, whereas the (control/experimental) group consists of similar subjects who do not receive the special treatment. (14) |
| independent | 11-5. It is crucial that the experimental and control groups be very similar, except for the different treatment they receive in regard to the (dependent/independent) variable. (14) |
| cause and effect | 11-6. The principal advantage of the experiment is that it allows scientists to draw conclusions about (cause and effect/correlational/empirical) relationships between variables. (14) |

**12.   Distinguish between positive and negative correlation and explain what the size of a correlation coefficient means.**

| | |
|---|---|
| correlation coefficient | 12-1. A numerical index of the degree of relationship that exists between two variables is called a(n) (causal estimate/correlation coefficient/empirical indicator). (15) |
| positive | 12-2. A (positive/negative/normal) correlation means that high scores on variable $x$ are associated with high scores on variable $y$ and that low scores on variable $x$ are associated with low scores on variable $y$. (15) |
| negative | 12-3. A (positive/negative/normal) correlation indicates that two variables covary in the opposite direction. (15) |
| size | 12-4. The (sign/size) of the correlation coefficient indicates the strength of the association between two variables. (15) |
| zero | 12-5. A correlation coefficient near (negative one/zero/positive one) tells us there is no relationship between the variables. (15) |

**13.   Describe three correlational research methods.**

| | |
|---|---|
| naturalistic | 13-1. When researchers engage in careful observation of behavior without intervening directly with their subjects, they are using (experimental/naturalistic/psychological) observation. (16) |

| | |
|---|---|
| case study | 13-2.  A _____ is an in-depth investigation of an individual participant. (17) |
| clinical | 13-3.  Psychologists typically assemble case studies in (classroom/clinical/laboratory) settings. (17) |
| survey | 13-4.  A _____ is a structured questionnaire designed to solicit information about specific aspects of participants' behavior. (17) |

**14.  Compare the advantages and disadvantages of experimental versus correlational research.**

| | |
|---|---|
| cannot | 14-1.  Correlational research (can/cannot) demonstrate conclusively that two variables are causally related. (18) |
| correlational | 14-2.  The "third-variable problem" occurs frequently in (correlational/experimental) research. (19) |

**15.  Discuss the prevalence of reported happiness in modern society.**

| | |
|---|---|
| below | 15-1.  When people are asked to rate their happiness, only a small minority place themselves (above/below) the neutral point on the various scales used. (19) |
| positive | 15-2.  When the average subjective well-being of entire nations is computed, based on almost 1000 surveys, the means cluster toward the (middle/positive/negative end of the scale. (19) |

**16.  List the various factors that are surprisingly unrelated to happiness.**

| | |
|---|---|
| weak | 16-1.  There is a (moderate/strong/weak), positive correlation between income and subjective feelings of happiness. (20) |
| unrelated | 16-2.  Age and happiness are consistently found to be (strongly related/moderately related/unrelated). (20) |
| twice as | 16-3.  Women are treated for depressive disorders about (as/half as/twice as) often as men. (20) |
| neither more nor less | 16-4.  The evidence indicates that people who have children are (more/less/neither more nor less) happy than people without children. (20) |
| have not | 16-5.  Researchers (have/have not) found an association between IQ scores and happiness. (20) |
| negligible | 16-6.  The correlation between physical attractiveness and happiness is (negligible/moderate/strong). (20) |

**17.  Explain how health, social activity, and religion are related to happiness.**

| | |
|---|---|
| moderate | 17-1.   In general, research indicates that there is a (weak/moderate/strong) positive correlation between health status and subjective well-being. (21) |
| above-average | 17-2.   People who are satisfied with their friendship networks and who are socially active report (below-average/average/above-average) levels of happiness. (21) |
| more | 17-3.   A number of surveys suggest that people with heartfelt religious convictions are (more/less) likely to be happy than people who characterize themselves as nonreligious. (21) |

**18.    Discuss how love, work, and personality are related to happiness.**

| | |
|---|---|
| happier | 18-1.   Among both men and women, married people are (happier/less happy) than people who are single or divorced. (21) |
| strongly | 18-2.   Job satisfaction is (not/moderately/strongly) associated with general happiness. (21) |
| past happiness | 18-3.   The best predictor of individuals' future happiness is their (marital status/past happiness/spouse's happiness). (21) |
| does not | 18-4.   Several lines of evidence suggest that happiness (does/does not) depend on external circumstances (e.g., getting promoted, buying a nice house). (22) |
| extraversion | 18-5.   Positive emotionality, also sometimes referred to as (empiricism/ extraversion/introversion), is one of the better predictors of happiness. (22) |

**19.    Summarize the conclusions drawn about the determinants of happiness.**

| | |
|---|---|
| are not | 19-1.   When it comes to happiness, objective realities (are/are not) as important as subjective feelings. (22) |
| people around them | 19-2.   People tend to evaluate what they have relative to what (people around them/people on television/very wealthy people) have. (22) |
| Hedonic | 19-3.   _____ adaptation occurs when the mental scale that people use to judge the pleasantness-unpleasantness of their experiences shifts so that their neutral point, or baseline for comparison, is changed. (23) |

**20.    List three steps for developing sound study habits.**

| | |
|---|---|
| write down | 20-1.   It's important to (constantly modify/memorize/write down) your study schedule. (24) |
| cannot | 20-2.   Most people (can/cannot) study effectively while watching TV, listening to loud music, or overhearing conversations. (24) |

immediate

20-3. It helps to give yourself (long-term/short-term/immediate) rewards for studying. (25)

behavior modification

20-4. The systematic manipulation of rewards involves harnessing the principles of (behavior modification/SQ3R/management theory). (25)

**21. Describe the SQ3R method of effective reading.**

survey

21-1. The first step in the SQ3R method is (simplify/study/survey). (25)

question

21-2. The second step in the SQ3R method is to take each section of a reading assignment, and turn it into a(n) (question/story/outline heading). (25)

third

21-3. Reading is the (first/second/third/last) step in the SQ3R system. (25)

does not

21-4. The SQ3R method (does/does not) have to be applied rigidly to be effective. (26)

**22. Summarize advice on how to get more out of lectures.**

is

22-1. Poor class attendance (is/is not) associated with poor grades. (26)

active

22-2. In trying to get the most out of class lectures, it is a good idea to use (active/passive/unfocused) listening procedures. (27)

should not

22-3. In trying to take class notes effectively, you (should/should not) try to be a human tape recorder. (27)

is

22-4. In trying to get the most out of class lectures, it (is/is not) a good idea to ask questions during the lecture. (27)

**23. Summarize how memory is influenced by practice, interference, depth of processing, and organization.**

retention

23-1. Repeatedly reviewing information usually leads to improved (class attendance/self-esteem/retention). (27)

overlearning

23-2. The continued rehearsal of material after you have first appeared to master it is known as _____. (27)

pays

23-3. Evidence suggests that it (pays/does not pay) to overlearn material. (27)

distributed; massed

23-4. Evidence indicates that retention tends to be greater after (distributed/massed) practice than (distributed/massed) practice. (27)

Interference

23-5. _____ occurs when people forget information because of competition from other learned material. (27)

greater

23-6. Retention tends to be (less/greater/unaffected) when information is well organized. (28)

less

23-7.  Research suggest that how often you go over material is (more/less) critical than the depth of processing that you engage in. (28)

**24.    *Describe several verbal and visual mnemonic devices.***

acrostic

24-1.  "Every good boy does fine" is an example of a(n) (acrostic/narrative/visual) mnemonic device. (28)

narrative

24-2.  A useful way to remember a list of words in a certain order is to use the (acrostic/narrative/link) method, which involves creating a story that includes each of the words in the right order. (28)

visual imagery

24-3.  Both the link method and the method of loci depend on the use of (acronyms/rhymes/visual imagery). (29)

method of loci

24-4.  The (acrostic method/narrative method/method of loci) involves taking an imaginary walk along a familiar path where you have placed mental images of items you want to remember at certain locations. (29)

## QUIZ BOXES

*KEY TERMS*

| | |
|---|---|
| **Psychology** | The science that studies behavior and the physiological and mental processes that underlie it, and the profession that applies the accumulated knowledge of this science to practical problems. |
| **Behavior** | Any overt (observable) response or activity by an organism. |
| **Clinical psychology** | The branch of psychology concerned with the diagnosis and treatment of psychological problems and disorders. |
| **Adjustment** | The psychological processes through which people manage or cope with the demands and challenges of everyday life. |
| **Empiricism** | The premise that knowledge should be acquired through observation. |
| **Experiment** | A research method in which the investigator manipulates one (independent) variable under carefully controlled conditions and observes whether any changes occur in a second (dependent) variable as a result. |
| **Independent variable** | A condition or event that an experimenter varies in order to see its impact on another variable. |
| **Dependent variable** | The variable that is thought to be affected by the manipulations of the independent variable. |
| **Experimental group** | Consists of the subjects who receive some special treatment in regard to the independent variable. |
| **Control group** | Consists of similar subjects (to those in the experimental group) who do not receive the special treatment given to the experimental group. |
| **Correlation** | Exists when two variables are related to each other. |
| **Correlation coefficient** | A numerical index of the degree of relationship that exists between two variables. |
| **Naturalistic observation** | A research method in which a researcher engages in careful observation of behavior without intervening directly with the subjects. |
| **Case study** | An in-depth investigation of an individual participant. |

| Surveys | Structured questionnaires designed to solicit information about specific aspects of participants' behavior. |
|---|---|
| Hedonic adaptation | Occurs when the mental scale that people use to judge the pleasantness-unpleasantness of their experiences shifts so that their neutral point, or baseline for comparison, is changed. |
| SQ3R | A study system designed to promote effective reading that includes five steps: survey, question, read, recite, and review. |
| Overlearning | The continued rehearsal of material after you have first appeared to master it. |
| Interference | Occurs when people forget information because of competition from other learned material. |
| Mnemonic devices | Strategies for enhancing memory. |

## KEY PEOPLE

| David Myers | Emphasized the finding that objective circumstances have limited impact on happiness. Wrote the book *The Pursuit of Happiness: Who Is Happy – and Why*. |
|---|---|
| Barry Schwartz | Suggested that the malaise associated with choice overload undermines individuals' happiness and contributes to depression. Wrote the book *The Paradox of Choice: Why More is Less*. |
| Martin Seligman | Conducted influential research on learned helplessness, attributional style, optimism, depression, and phobias. Wrote the book *What You Can Change & What You Can't*. |

## SELF-TEST

*Multiple Choice Items*

1.   In spite of our great technological progress, social problems and personal difficulties seem more prevalent than ever before.  This issue is known as the
     a.   approach-avoidance conflict          c.   self-realization dilemma
     b.   paradox of progress                  d.   paradox of paradoxes

2.   Which of the following statements regarding cults is <u>not</u> true?
     a.   Cults have attracted hundreds of thousands of converts.
     b.   Most cults flourish in obscurity, unless bizarre incidents attract public attention.
     c.   Cults generally use brainwashing and mind control to seduce lonely outsiders.
     d.   People join cults because these groups appear to provide simple solutions to complex problems.

3.   According to your textbook, one of the major problems with self-help books is that they are dominated by
     a.   psychobabble                         c.   research results
     b.   graphs and tables                    d.   complicated mathematical models

4.   "Subjecting ideas to systematic, skeptical scrutiny" best describes which of the following processes?
     a.   self-realization                     c.   self-actualization
     b.   critical thinking                    d.   psychological adjustment

5.   The branch of psychology concerned with the diagnosis and treatment of psychological problems and disorders is called _____ psychology.
     a.   social                               c.   cognitive
     b.   clinical                             d.   physiological

6.   The emphasis of psychological science on systematic observation best illustrates which of the following concepts?
     a.   empiricism                           c.   determinism
     b.   correlation                          d.   self-realization

7.   Which of the following is <u>not</u> a characteristic of scientists' investigations?
     a.   formal                               c.   subjective
     b.   systematic                           d.   empirical

8.   Which of the following is <u>most</u> likely to be used as an independent variable in a psychological experiment?
     a.   reaction time                        c.   level of noise
     b.   desire to affiliate                  d.   aggression

9.   Which of the following is <u>most</u> likely to be used as a dependent variable in a psychological study?
     a.   age of participants                  c.   instructions to participants
     b.   time of day                          d.   problem solving ability

10.  A psychological researcher will most likely be able to draw conclusions about cause-and-effect relationships by using which of the following research methods?
     a.   survey                               c.   experiment
     b.   case study                           d.   naturalistic observation

11.  The correlation coefficient measuring the relationship between time spent studying and percent correct on a psychology exam is likely to be
     a.  zero
     b.  positive
     c.  negative
     d.  subjective

12.  Which of the following correlation coefficients indicates the strongest relationship between two variables?
     a.  -0.75
     b.  -3.28
     c.  0.16
     d.  0.50

13.  An in-depth investigation of an individual participant is called a(n)
     a.  case study
     b.  experiment
     c.  correlational study
     d.  naturalistic observation

14.  A survey is most likely to be used to study which of the following behaviors?
     a   helping
     b.  aggressive behavior
     c.  religious attitudes
     d.  reaction time

15.  Which of the following variables is least important in determining an individual's happiness?
     a.  health
     b.  money
     c.  social activity
     d.  job satisfaction

16.  The correlation between physical attractiveness and happiness is
     a.  negative
     b.  moderately positive
     c.  strongly positive
     d.  negligible

17.  The best predictor of individuals' future happiness is their
     a.  IQ score
     b.  past happiness
     c.  marital status
     d.  financial status

18.  An organized study program should include
     a.  a detailed schedule of when and what to study
     b.  a place of your own to study that is free of distractions
     c.  rewards that are immediate and satisfying when goals are attained
     d.  all of the above

19.  Which of the following is the correct order for the five steps in the SQ3R method?
     a.  survey, question, recite, read, review
     b.  question, survey, read, recite, review
     c.  survey, question, review, read, recite
     d.  survey, question, read, recite, review

20.  Forgetting learned material because of competition from other learned material
     a.  is called interference
     b.  is called inhibition
     c.  seldom happens if the material is really learned
     d.  happens only when students use massed practice

## True/False Items

T/F     1.  Studies have shown that the incidence of depressive disorders has increased over the last 50 years.

T/F     2.  Most experts agree that self-realization programs (e.g., Scientology, Silva Mind Control) are effective for people who want to turn their lives around quickly.

T/F    3.    Unorthodox religious groups, or cults, generally use brainwashing and mind control to seduce lonely outsiders.

T/F    4.    Self-help books tend to place more emphasis on sales than on science.

T/F    5.    Basically, psychology confines itself to the study of human behavior.

T/F    6.    In psychological studies, the dependent variable is manipulated or controlled by the experimenter.

T/F    7.    The principal advantage of the experimental method is that it allows us to draw conclusions about cause-and-effect relationships between variables.

T/F    8.    A negative correlation coefficient indicates that there is no relationship between two variables.

T/F    9.    Money is not a very important factor in a person's subjective well-being.

T/F    10.    Reading and absorbing information are most likely to be effective when they are done in an active manner.

T/F    11.    An effective note-taking strategy is to try to be a "human tape recorder."

T/F    12.    Research evidence indicates that retention tends to be greater with distributed practice than with massed practice.

# ANSWER KEY FOR SELF-TEST ITEMS

*Multiple Choice Items*

b     1.   The stem of the question basically defines the paradox of progress. (2)

c     2.   This is a common misconception; in reality, converts are a diverse array of normal people who are swayed by remarkably ordinary social influence strategies. (5)

a     3.   The other alternatives for this question are not likely to be found in a typical self-help book. ( 8)

b     4.   Fostering a critical attitude about psychological issues and enhancing your critical thinking skills are among the main goals of your textbook. (10)

b     5.   Clinical psychology was psychology's first professional specialty.  During World War II, a multitude of academic psychologists were pressed into service as clinicians to screen military recruits and treat soldiers suffering from trauma. (12)

a     6.   Empiricism emphasizes the importance of observable evidence. (13)

c     7.   Science emphasizes an *objective* rather than a *subjective* approach. (13)

c     8.   The other alternatives are all examples of behavior, which is typically the focus of the *dependent* variable. (14)

d     9.   In psychological research, the dependent variable is typically a measure of *behavior*. (14)

c     10.  The main advantage of the experimental method is the ability to identify cause-and-effect relationships between variables, something correlational methods (i.e., the other alternatives to this question) generally cannot do. (14)

b     11.  This correlation is likely to be positive because students who spend more time studying tend to score higher on an exam. (15)

a     12.  The strength of a correlation is indicated by the absolute value of the coefficient (not the sign of the number), and it must be between -1.00 and +1.00. (15)

a     13.  Case studies are typically used in clinical settings to learn as much as possible about a particular individual who may be suffering from a psychological problem or disorder. (17)

c     14.  Surveys are commonly used to assess people's attitudes regarding a given issue, or aspects of their behavior that are difficult to observe directly. (17)

b     15.  There is a positive correlation between income and subjective feelings of happiness, but the relationship is surprisingly weak.  The other items listed among the alternatives are all somewhat, or very important factors in happiness. (20)

d     16.  Believe it or not, the available data indicate that there is not much of a relationship between attractiveness and happiness. (20)

b     17.  This finding supports the notion that life events have limited influence on feelings of happiness. (21)

| | | |
|---|---|---|
| d | 18. | All of these are characteristics of an organized and effective study program. (24-25) |
| d | 19. | The order of the letters should give you a clue, but you should note that the reading component of the system is the middle step, and review is the final step. (25-26) |
| a | 20. | Research suggests that interference is one of the major causes of forgetting. (27) |

## True/False Items

| | | |
|---|---|---|
| True | 1. | Researchers like Barry Schwartz suggest that the increased freedom of choice people have may contribute to depression. (3) |
| False | 2. | Actually, most experts characterize these programs as intellectually bankrupt, and suggest that they are basically lucrative money-making schemes. (5) |
| False | 3. | In reality, converts are a diverse array of normal people who are swayed by remarkably ordinary social influence strategies. (5) |
| True | 4. | The advice offered in these books is far too rarely based on solid, scientific research. (8) |
| False | 5. | Many psychologists believe that the principles of behavior are much the same for animals as they are for humans. (11) |
| False | 6. | It is the independent variable that is generally manipulated by the experimenter. (14) |
| True | 7. | However, the ability to establish cause and effect does not apply to correlational research. (14) |
| False | 8. | A negative correlation means that scores on the two variables covary inversely: that is, high scores on one variable are associated with low scores on the other, and vice versa. A correlation coefficient of zero indicates no relationship between the variables. (15) |
| True | 9. | Research findings indicate that money is one of the least important ingredients of happiness. (20) |
| True | 10. | Research indicates that active learning is much more effective than passive learning. (25) |
| False | 11. | A much better strategy is to write down the lecturer's main points in your own words. (27) |
| True | 12. | This is why it's better to distribute your study time over several days rather than to "cram" the night before an exam. (27) |

# Chapter 2
# THEORIES OF PERSONALITY

## PROGRAMMED REVIEW

**1.** **Explain the concepts of personality and traits.**

Personality

1-1. _____ refers to an individual's unique constellation of consistent behavioral traits. (34)

traits

1-2. Adjectives such as honest, dependable, moody, impulsive, suspicious, and friendly describe dispositions that represent personality (constellations/factors/traits). (34)

basic

1-3. Most trait theories of personality assume that some traits are more (basic/beneficial/detrimental) than others. (34)

**2.** **Describe the "Big Five" personality traits.**

extraversion

2-1. People who score high on the trait of _____ are characterized as outgoing, sociable, upbeat, and friendly. (34)

neuroticism

2-2. People who score high on the trait of _____ tend to be anxious, hostile, self-conscious, insecure, and vulnerable. (34-35)

neuroticism

2-3. The trait of _____ is also known as negative emotionality. (35)

openness to experience

2-4. People who score high on the trait of _____ are characterized as curious, flexible, imaginative, and unconventional. (35)

agreeableness

2-5. People who score high in _____ tend to be sympathetic, trusting, cooperative, and modest. (35)

conscientious-ness

2-6. People who score high in _____ tend to be diligent, disciplined, well organized, punctual, and dependable. (35)

**3.** **Describe Freud's three components of personality and how they are distributed across levels of awareness.**

Psychodynamic

3-1. (Behavioral/Psychodynamic/Psychosexual) theories include all the diverse theories descended from the work of Sigmund Freud that focus on unconscious mental forces. (35)

psychoanalysis

3-2. Freud devoted himself to the treatment of mental disorders using an innovative procedure he developed, called (behaviorism/psychoanalysis/psychology). (36)

pleasure

3-3. The id is the primitive, instinctive component of personality that operates according to the (animus/pleasure/reality) principle. (36)

| | |
|---|---|
| ego | 3-4. The (id/ego/superego) is the decision-making component of personality that operates according to the reality principle. (36) |
| superego | 3-5. The (id/ego/superego) is the moral component of personality that incorporates social standards about what represents right and wrong. (36) |
| conscious | 3-6. The (conscious/preconscious/unconscious) consists of whatever you are aware of at a particular point in time. (36) |
| unconscious | 3-7. The (preconscious/subconscious/unconscious) contains thoughts, memories, and desires that are well below the surface of conscious awareness but that nonetheless exert great influence on one's behavior. (37) |

**4.    Explain the importance of sexual and aggressive conflicts in Freud's theory.**

| | |
|---|---|
| conflicts | 4-1. Freud believed that (conflicts/sexual fantasies) dominate people's lives. (37) |
| more | 4-2. Freud thought that sex and aggression are subject to (more/less) complex and ambiguous social controls than other basic motives. (38) |
| more | 4-3. Freud noted that sexual and aggressive drives are thwarted (more/less) often than other basic biological drives. (38) |

**5.    Describe seven defense mechanisms identified by Freud.**

| | |
|---|---|
| anxiety | 5-1. The arousal of (anxiety/hostility/jealousy) is a crucial event in Freud's theory of personality functioning. (38) |
| Defense | 5-2. _____ mechanisms are largely unconscious reactions that protect a person from painful emotions such as anxiety and guilt. (38) |
| rationalization | 5-3. The defense mechanism called _____ involves creating false but plausible excuses to justify unacceptable behavior. (39) |
| unconscious | 5-4. Repression involves keeping distressing thoughts and feelings buried in the (preconscious/subconscious/unconscious). (39) |
| Projection | 5-5. (Projection/Reaction Formation/Repression) involves attributing one's own thoughts, feelings, or motives to another person. (39) |
| Displacement | 5-6. (Displacement/Projection/Reaction Formation) involves diverting emotional feelings (usually anger) from their original source to a substitute target. (39) |
| Reaction formation | 5-7. (Displacement/Projection/Reaction formation) involves behaving in a way that is exactly the opposite of one's true feelings. (39) |
| immature | 5-8. Regression involves a reversion to (higher-order/immature/habitual) patterns of behavior. (39) |

| | |
|---|---|
| Identification | 5-9. (Displacement/Identification/Projection) involves bolstering self-esteem by forming an imaginary or real alliance with some person or group. (39) |
| | **6.** ***Outline Freud's stages of psychosexual development and their theorized relations to adult personality.*** |
| psychosexual | 6-1. The (psychoanalytic/psychodynamic/psychosexual) stages are developmental periods with a characteristic sexual focus that leave their mark on adult personality. (40) |
| fixation | 6-2. A failure to move forward from one psychosexual stage to another as expected is called _____. (40) |
| mouth | 6-3. During the oral stage of development, the main source of erotic stimulation is the _____. (40) |
| oral | 6-4. Fixation at the _____ stage could form the basis for excessive eating or smoking later in life. (40) |
| anal | 6-5. During the _____ stage, children supposedly get erotic pleasure from their bowel movements. (40) |
| phallic | 6-6. During the _____ stage, the genitals become the focus for the child's erotic energy. (40) |
| Oedipal | 6-7. In the (inferiority/superiority/Oedipal) complex, children manifest erotically tinged desires for their other-gender parent, accompanied by feelings of hostility toward their same-gender parent. (40) |
| latency | 6-8. Important developmental events during the (phallic/latency/genital) stage center on expanding social contacts beyond the immediate family. (41) |
| genital | 6-9. With the advent of puberty, the child evolves into the (phallic/latency/genital) stage of psychosexual development. (41) |
| | **7.** ***Summarize Jung's views on the unconscious.*** |
| collective unconscious | 7-1. In Jung's theory, the _____ is a storehouse of latent memories inherited from people's ancestral past that is shared with the entire human race. (41) |
| archetypes | 7-2. In Jung's theory, emotionally charged images and thought forms that have universal meaning are called _____. (41-42) |
| dreams | 7-3. Jung believed that an understanding of archetypal symbols helped him make sense of his patients' (dreams/sexual urges/conscious desires). (42) |
| introverted extraverted | 7-4. Jung was the first to describe the _____ (inner-directed) and _____ (outer-directed) personality types. (42) |
| | **8.** ***Summarize Adler's views on key issues relating to personality.*** |

superiority

Compensation

social

birth order

does

do;
do

often

difficult

inadequate

women

Behaviorism

behavior

development

Ivan Pavlov

8-1.   According to Adler, the foremost human drive is a striving for (sexual fulfillment/self-actualization/superiority). (42)

8-2.   (Actualization/Compensation/Fixation) involves efforts to overcome imagined or real inferiorities by developing one's abilities. (42)

8-3.   Adler's theory stressed the (biological/sexual/social/) context of personality development. (42)

8-4.   Adler was among the first theorists to focus attention on the possible importance of (birth order/introversion/sexuality) as a factor governing personality. (42)

8-5.   In recent years, Frank Sulloway has argued that birth order (does/does not) have an impact on personality development. (42)

**9.    Evaluate the strengths and weaknesses of psychodynamic theories of personality.**

9-1.   Research has demonstrated that unconscious forces (do/do not) influence behavior, and that early childhood experiences (do/do not) exert significant influence over adult personality. (43)

9-2.   Research has demonstrated that internal conflict (often/rarely) plays a role in generating psychological distress. (43)

9-3.   Concepts such as the superego, the preconscious, and collective unconscious are (easy/difficult) to measure. (43)

9-4.   The empirical evidence on psychodynamic theories has often been characterized as (supportive/adequate/inadequate). (43)

9-5.   Many critics have argued that psychodynamic theories are biased against (adolescents/men/women). (43)

**10.   Describe Pavlov's classical conditioning and its contribution to understanding personality.**

10-1.  _____ is a theoretical orientation based on the premise that scientific psychology should study observable behavior. (44)

10-2.  John Watson argued that psychology should abandon its focus on mental processes and focus exclusively on the study of overt (behavior/emotions/sexuality). (44)

10-3.  Although behaviorists have shown relatively little interest in personality structure, they have focused extensively on personality (development/disorders/traits). (44)

10-4.  The process of classical conditioning was first described in 1903 by (Sigmund Freud/Ivan Pavlov/John Watson). (45)

| | |
|---|---|
| unlearned | 10-5. The unconditioned response (UCR) is a(n) (learned/unlearned) reaction to an unconditioned stimulus. (45) |
| neutral | 10-6. The conditioned stimulus is a previously (aversive/learned/neutral) stimulus that has acquired the capacity to evoke a conditioned response through conditioning. (45) |
| often | 10-7. The unconditioned response and the conditioned response (never/occasionally/often) involve the same behavior. (45) |
| emotional responses | 10-8. In everyday life, classical conditioning contributes to the acquisition of (emotional responses/reasoning skills/interpersonal skills). (46) |
| extinction | 10-9. The gradual weakening and disappearance of a conditioned response tendency is known as _____. (46) |

**11. Discuss how Skinner's principles of operant conditioning can be applied to personality development.**

| | |
|---|---|
| consequences | 11-1. Operant conditioning is a form of learning in which voluntary responses come to be controlled by their (antecedents/consequences). (47) |
| favorable | 11-2. Skinner demonstrated that organisms tend to repeat those responses that are followed by (favorable/unfavorable) consequences. (47) |
| punishment | 11-3. In Skinner's model, unfavorable consequences correspond to (reinforcement/extinction/punishment). (47) |
| Positive | 11-4. (Positive/Negative/Neutral) reinforcement occurs when a response is strengthened (increases in frequency) because it is followed by the arrival of a pleasant stimulus. (47) |
| strengthened | 11-5. Negative reinforcement occurs when a response is (strengthened/weakened) because it is followed by the removal of an unpleasant stimulus. (47) |
| extinction | 11-6. In both classical and operant conditioning, (acquisition/extinction/fixation) refers to the gradual weakening and disappearance of a response. (48) |
| Punishment | 11-7. (Negative reinforcement/Punishment/Extinction) occurs when a response is weakened (decreases in frequency) because it is followed by the arrival of an unpleasant stimulus. (48) |

**12. Describe Bandura's social learning theory and his concept of self-efficacy.**

| | |
|---|---|
| cognitive | 12-1. Although Bandura originally called his modified brand of behaviorism social learning theory, today he refers to his model as social (behavioral/cognitive/relationship) theory. (49) |

| | |
|---|---|
| models | 12-2. Observational learning occurs when an organism's responding is influenced by the observation of others, called (conditioners/models/targets). (49) |
| does not view | 12-3. Bandura (views/does not view) observational learning as entirely separate from classical and operant conditioning. (49) |
| consequences | 12-4. Observational learning requires that you pay attention to behavior, that you understand its (causes/consequences/precursors), and that you store this information in memory. (49) |
| Self-efficacy | 12-5. _____ is one's belief about one's ability to perform behaviors that should lead to expected outcomes. (49-50) |
| higher; greater | 12-6. Studies have found that feelings of greater self-efficacy are associated with (lower/higher) levels of academic performance and (greater/less) resistance to stress. (50) |

**13.    Evaluate the strengths and weaknesses of behavioral theories of personality.**

| | |
|---|---|
| emotional | 13-1. Pavlov's model of behavior has shed light on how conditioning can explain people's sometimes troublesome (emotional/sexual/social) responses. (50) |
| consequences | 13-2. Skinner's work has demonstrated how personality is shaped by the (antecedents/consequences) of behavior. (50) |
| observations | 13-3. Bandura's social cognitive theory has shown how people's (observations/unconscious desires/reinforcement histories) mold their characteristic behavior. (50) |
| observable | 13-4. Social learning theory undermines the foundation on which behaviorism was built —the idea that psychologists should study only (observable/sexual/unconscious) behavior. (51) |
| animal | 13-5. Some critics of behavioral theories, especially humanistic theorists, argue that behaviorists depend too much on (anecdotal/animal/correlational) research. (51) |

**14.    Discuss humanism as a school of thought in psychology.**

| | |
|---|---|
| dehumanizing | 14-1. Historically, the principal charge hurled at behavioral and psychodynamic theories of personality was that they were (dehumanizing/unscientific/untestable). (51) |
| personal growth | 14-2. Humanism is a theoretical orientation that emphasizes the unique qualities of humans, especially their free will and potential for (personal growth/social relationships/unselfish behavior). (51) |
| optimistic | 14-3. Humanistic theorists generally take a(n) (optimistic/pessimistic/mechanistic) view of human nature. (51) |

**15.    Explain Rogers's views on self-concept, development, and defensive behavior.**

person

15-1.    Carl Rogers called his approach to personality a(n) (intuition/person/research)-centered theory. (51)

self

15-2.    A collection of beliefs about one's own nature, unique qualities, and typical behavior is called a _____-concept. (51-52)

Incongruence

15.3    (Fixation/Incongruence/Transference) refers to the disparity between one's self-concept and one's actual experience. (52)

unconditional
conditional

15-4.    Rogers believed that (conditional/unconditional) love from parents fosters congruence, and that (conditional/unconditional) love fosters incongruence. (52)

congruent

15-5.    Rogers held that psychological health is rooted in a(n) (ambiguous/congruent/incongruent) self-concept. (53)

**16.    Describe Maslow's hierarchy of needs and summarize his findings on self-actualizing persons.**

healthy

16-1.    Like Rogers, Maslow argued that psychology should take a greater interest in the nature of the (healthy/unhealthy) personality. (53)

basic

16-2.    According to Maslow's hierarchy of needs, higher levels consist of progressively less (basic/important/social) needs. (53)

actualization

16-3.    The highest need in Maslow's hierarchy, which is the need to fulfill one's potential, is the need for self- (actualization/esteem/realization). (53-54)

sensitive

16-4.    Self-actualized people tend to be (sensitive/insensitive) to the needs of others. (54)

are not

16-5.    Self-actualized people (are/are not) dependent on others for approval. (54)

**17.    Evaluate the strengths and weaknesses of humanistic theories of personality.**

positive

17-1.    One could argue that the humanists' optimistic, growth-and-health-oriented approach laid the foundation for the emergence of the (clinical/ positive/ social) psychology movement. (55)

difficult

17-2.    Humanistic concepts such as personal growth and self-actualization are (easy/difficult) to define and measure. (55)

optimistic

17-3.    Critics charge that the humanists have been overly (optimistic/pessimistic/mechanistic) in their assumptions about human nature. (55)

clinical

17-4. Humanistic theories are based primarily on discerning but uncontrolled observations in (academic/clinical/laboratory) settings. (55)

**18.    *Describe Eysenck's views on personality structure and development.***

heredity

18-1. According to Hans Eysenck, personality is determined largely by a person's (heredity/social environment/unconscious desires). (56)

traits

18-2. Eysenck views personality structure as a hierarchy of (needs/traits/urges). (56)

extraversion-
introversion

18-3. Eysenck has shown a special interest in explaining variations in (agreeableness/extraversion-introversion/conscientiousness). (56)

**19.    *Summarize recent twin studies that support the idea that personality is largely inherited.***

100;
50

19-1. The genetic overlap in identical twins is (50/75/100) percent, whereas the genetic overlap in fraternal twins is (50/75/100) percent. (57)

heritability

19-2. A (heritability/genetic/trait) ratio is an estimate of the proportion of trait variability in a population that is determined by variations in genetic inheritance. (57)

considerable

19-3. The accumulating evidence from twin studies suggests that heredity exerts (little/a moderate amount of/considerable) influence over many personality traits. (57)

little

19-4. A number of recent studies have found that shared family environment has (little/moderate/considerable) impact on personality. (58)

**20.    *Summarize evolutionary analyses of why certain personality traits appear to be important.***

natural selection

20-1. The basic premise of evolutionary psychology is that (natural selection/society/Western culture) favors behaviors that enhance organisms' reproductive success. (58)

adaptive

20-2. David Buss has argued that the Big Five personality traits stand out as important dimensions of personality in a variety of cultures because those traits have had significant (adaptive/behavioral/sexual) implications. (58)

**21.    *Evaluate the strengths and weaknesses of biological theories of personality.***

convincing

21-1. Recent research in behavioral genetics has provided (convincing/little) evidence that biological factors help shape personality. (59)

| | |
|---|---|
| can't | 21-2.  The effects of heredity and environment on personality (can/can't) be separated cleanly. (59) |
| theory | 21-3.  A major criticism of the biological perspective is that there is currently a lack of adequate (research/theory/understanding). (59) |

**22.    Explain the chief concepts and hypotheses of terror management theory.**

| | |
|---|---|
| self-esteem | 22-1.  One of the chief goals of terror management theory is to explain why people need (a self-concept/self-esteem/social interaction). (59) |
| a cultural worldview | 22-2.  According to terror management theory, faith in (a cultural worldview/an all-powerful creator/our cognitive abilities) can give people a sense of order, meaning and context that can soothe humans' fear of death. (59) |
| anxiety | 22-3.  According to terror management theory, self-esteem serves as a buffer against (anxiety/death/social failure). (60) |

**23.    Describe how reminders of death influence people's behavior.**

| | |
|---|---|
| more; larger | 23-1.  After briefly pondering their mortality, research participants respond (more/less) negatively to people who criticize their country, and give (smaller/larger) rewards to people who uphold cultural standards. (60) |
| neuroticism | 23-2.  Terror management theorists suggest that people high in (agreeableness/conscientiousness/neuroticism) tend to be especially uptight about sex. (60) |
| narrower | 23-3.  Terror management theory is (broader/narrower) in scope than psychoanalytic, behavioral, and humanistic theories. (62) |

**24.    Discuss why the subject of personality has generated so much theoretical diversity.**

| | |
|---|---|
| cannot | 24-1.  A single theory (can/cannot) adequately explain everything that we know about personality. (62) |
| complementary | 24-2.  It is probably best to think of the various theoretical orientations in psychology as (competing/complementary/opposing) viewpoints. (62) |
| strength; weakness | 24-3.  Modern psychologists increasingly recognize that theoretical diversity is a (strength/weakness) rather than a (strength/weakness). (63) |

**25.    Compare and contrast the personality theories of Freud, Skinner, Rogers, and Eysenck.**

| | |
|---|---|
| stimulus | 25-1.  According to Skinner's theory, personality is a collection of response tendencies tied to specific (childhood/social/stimulus) situations. (63) |

genetic

25-2. According to Eysenck's theory of personality, psychological disorders have their roots in (genetic/sexual/unconscious) vulnerability activated in part by environmental factors. (63)

concept

25-3. Carl Rogers' model of personality structure is based on the notion of self-(actualization/concept/esteem), which may or may not be congruent with actual experience. (63)

case studies

25-4. The source of data and observations for Freud's view of personality is (case studies/laboratory experiments/twin studies). (63)

behavioral

25-5. A strong emphasis on learning and the role of experience is closely associated with the (behavioral/biological/humanistic/psychodynamic) view of personality. (63)

psychodynamic

25-6. An emphasis on fixation or progress through psychosexual stages is associated with the (behavioral/biological/humanistic/psychodynamic) view of personality. (63)

biological

25-7. Twin, family, and adoption studies provide the source of data and observations for the (behavioral/biological/humanistic/psychodynamic) view of personality. (63)

humanistic

25-8. The actualizing or self-actualizing tendency is the key motivational force for the _____ model of personality. (63)

**26.** ***Explain the concepts of standardization, test norms, reliability, and validity.***

standardized

26-1. A psychological test is a(n) (individualized/normalized/standardized) measure of a sample of a person's behavior. (64)

mental ability

26-2. An achievement test is considered a (mental ability/personality) test. (64)

Standardization

26-3. _____ refers to the uniform procedures used to administer and score a test. (64)

norms

26-4. Test (norms/samples/standards) provide information about where a score on a psychological test ranks in relation to other scores on that test. (64)

similar

26-5. A reliable test is one that yields (different/similar/standardized) results for people on repetition of the test. (65)

Validity

26-6. _____ is the ability of a test to measure what it was designed to measure. (65)

**27.** ***Discuss the value and limitations of self-report inventories.***

personality scales

27-1. Self-report inventories are (aptitude inventories/achievement tests/personality scales) that ask individuals to answer a series of questions about their characteristic behavior. (65)

the Big Five

27-2.  The NEO Personality Inventory is designed to measure (the Big Five/ social/ unconscious) personality traits. (66)

desirability

27-3.  In responding to self-report inventories, some people endorse only those statements that make them look good; that is, they are influenced by the social (desirability/meaning/standards) of the statements. (66)

**28.    *Discuss the value and limitations of projective tests.***

clinical

28-1.  Projective tests, which take an indirect approach to the assessment of personality, are used extensively in (academic/clinical/work) settings. (66)

ambiguous

28-2.  The assumption underlying projective testing is that (ambiguous/sexually oriented/work-related) materials can serve as a blank screen onto which people project their characteristic concerns, conflicts, and desires. (67)

difficult

28-3.  With projective tests, it is (easy/difficult) for people to engage in intentional deception. (67)

inadequate

28-4.  There is (adequate/inadequate) evidence for the reliability and validity of projective measures. (67)

# QUIZ BOXES

## KEY TERMS

| | |
|---|---|
| **Personality** | An individual's unique constellation of consistent behavioral traits. |
| **Personality trait** | A durable disposition to behave in a particular way in a variety of situations. |
| **Psychodynamic theories** | Include all the diverse theories descended from the work of Sigmund Freud, that focus on unconscious mental forces. |
| **Id** | In Freud's theory, the primitive, instinctive component of personality that operates according to the pleasure principle. |
| **Ego** | In Freud's theory, the decision-making component of personality that operates according to the reality principle. |
| **Superego** | In Freud's theory, the moral component of personality that incorporates social standards about what represents right and wrong. |
| **Conscious** | This level of awareness consists of whatever one is aware of at a particular point in time. |
| **Preconscious** | According to Freud, this level of awareness contains material just beneath the surface of awareness that can be easily retrieved. |
| **Unconscious** | According to Freud, this level of awareness contains thoughts, memories, and desires that are well below the surface of conscious awareness, but that nonetheless exert great influence on behavior. |
| **Defense mechanisms** | According to Freud, these are largely unconscious reactions that protect a person from painful emotions such as anxiety and guilt. |
| **Rationalization** | This defense mechanism involves creating false but plausible excuses to justify unacceptable behavior. |
| **Repression** | This defense mechanism involves keeping distressing thoughts and feelings buried in the unconscious. |
| **Projection** | This defense mechanism involves attributing one's own thoughts, feelings, or motives to another person. |

| Displacement | This defense mechanism involves diverting emotional feelings (usually anger) from their original source to a substitute target. |
|---|---|
| Reaction formation | This defense mechanism involves behaving in a way that is exactly the opposite of one's true feelings. |
| Regression | This defense mechanism involves a reversion to immature patterns of behavior. |
| Identification | This defense mechanism involves bolstering self-esteem by forming an imaginary or real alliance with some person or group. |
| Psychosexual stages | Developmental periods with a characteristic sexual focus that leave their mark on adult personality. |
| Fixation | A failure to move forward from one psychosexual stage to another as expected. |
| Oedipal complex | Emerges during the phallic stage when children manifest erotically tinged desires for their other-gender parent, accompanied by feelings of hostility toward their same-gender parent. |
| Collective unconscious | According to Jung, this level of the unconscious consists of a storehouse of latent memory traces inherited from people's ancestral past that is shared with the entire human race. |
| Archetypes | According to Jung, these memories are emotionally charged images and thought forms that have universal meaning. |
| Compensation | According to Adler, this process involves efforts to overcome imagined or real inferiorities by developing one's abilities. |
| Behaviorism | A theoretical orientation based on the premise that scientific psychology should study observable behavior. |
| Classical conditioning | A type of learning in which a neutral stimulus acquires the capacity to evoke a response that was originally evoked by another stimulus. |
| Unconditioned stimulus (UCS) | A stimulus that evokes an unconditioned response without previous conditioning. |
| Unconditioned response (UCR) | An unlearned reaction to an unconditioned stimulus that occurs without previous conditioning. |

| Conditioned stimulus (CS) | A previously neutral stimulus that has acquired the capacity to evoke a conditioned response through conditioning. |
|---|---|
| Conditioned response (CR) | A learned reaction to a conditioned stimulus that occurs because of previous conditioning. |
| Extinction | The gradual weakening and disappearance of a conditioned response tendency. |
| Operant conditioning | A form of learning in which voluntary responses come to be controlled by their consequences. |
| Positive reinforcement | Reinforcement that occurs when a response is strengthened (increases in frequency) because it is followed by the arrival of a (presumably) pleasant stimulus. |
| Negative reinforcement | Reinforcement that occurs when a response is strengthened (increases in frequency) because it is followed by the removal of a (presumably) unpleasant stimulus. |
| Punishment | Occurs when a response is weakened (decreases in frequency) because it is followed by the arrival of a (presumably) unpleasant stimulus. |
| Observational learning | This type of learning occurs when an organism's responding is influenced by the observation of others, who are called models. |
| Self-efficacy | One's belief about one's ability to perform behaviors that should lead to expected outcomes. |
| Humanism | A theoretical orientation that emphasizes the unique qualities of humans, especially their free will and their potential for personal growth. |
| Self-concept | A collection of beliefs about one's own nature, unique qualities, and typical behavior. |
| Incongruence | According to Rogers, this refers to the disparity between one's self-concept and one's actual experience. |
| Hierarchy of needs | According to Maslow, this is a systematic arrangement of needs, according to priority, in which basic needs must be met before less basic needs are aroused. |
| Need for self-actualization | The need to fulfill one's potential; it is the highest need in Maslow's motivational hierarchy. |

| Heritability ratio | An estimate of the proportion of trait variability in a population that is determined by variations in genetic inheritance. |
|---|---|
| Evolutionary psychology | A theoretical orientation that examines behavioral processes in terms of their adaptive value for members of a species over the course of many generations. |
| Psychological test | A standardized measure of a sample of a person's behavior. |
| Standardization | The uniform procedures used to administer and score a test. |
| Test norms | They provide information about where a score on a psychological test ranks in relation to other scores on that test. |
| Reliability | The measurement consistency of a test. |
| Validity | The ability of a test to measure what it was designed to measure. |
| Self-report inventories | Personality scales that ask individuals to answer a series of questions about their characteristic behavior. |
| Projective tests | Tests that ask people to respond to vague, ambiguous stimuli in ways that may reveal the respondents' needs, feelings, and personality traits. |

## KEY PEOPLE

| Alfred Adler | Developed a psychodynamic theory of personality called individual psychology, which emphasized a striving for superiority as the foremost human drive. |
|---|---|
| Albert Bandura | Added a cognitive flavor to traditional behaviorism with his social learning theory, now called social cognitive theory; described the process of observational learning. |
| Hans Eysenck | Suggested that personality is determined to a large extent by a person's genes; views personality structure as a hierarchy of traits. |
| Sigmund Freud | Developed the theory of psychoanalysis, a model of personality that emphasizes the role of unconscious motivation, the importance of childhood experiences, and the influence of sexual urges. |

| Carl Jung | Developed a psychodynamic theory of personality called analytical psychology, which includes the collective unconscious, archetypes.  Described introverted and extraverted personality types. |
|---|---|
| Abraham Maslow | Humanistic theorist who proposed the notion of self-actualization, and the hierarchy of needs. |
| Ivan Pavlov | First described the process of classical conditioning, and its role in learning. |
| Carl Rogers | Humanistic theorist who developed the person-centered theory of personality, based on the notion of self-concept. |
| B. F. Skinner | Led the study of operant conditioning, which focuses on how responses come to be controlled by their consequences (i.e., reward and punishment). |

# SELF-TEST

*Multiple Choice Items*

1.  Which of the following is <u>not</u> one of the "Big Five" personality traits in the five-factor model of personality?
    a.  consistency                             c.  agreeableness
    b.  neuroticism                             d.  conscientiousness

2.  Most of Sigmund Freud's contemporaries were uncomfortable with his theory of personality because he suggested that
    a.  unconscious forces govern our behavior
    b.  childhood experiences strongly determine adult personality
    c.  our personalities are shaped by how we cope with our sexual urges
    d.  all of the above

3.  According to Freud, the decision-making component of personality that operates according to the reality principle is called the
    a.  id                                      c.  superego
    b   ego                                     d.  preconscious

4.  After a child is scolded by her parents, she takes her anger out on her younger brother by yelling at him.  In this example, the girl is using which of the following defense mechanisms?
    a.  projection                              c.  rationalization
    b.  displacement                            d.  reaction formation

5.  In which of the following psychosexual stages does the Oedipal complex occur?
    a.  oral                                    c.  phallic
    b.  anal                                    d.  latency

6.  According to Alfred Adler, the foremost human drive is a striving for
    a.  sexuality                               c.  superiority
    b.  aggression                              d.  self-actualization

7.  Ivan Pavlov discovered that if the sound of a tone were paired with meat powder over a number of trials, dogs would learn to salivate to the sound of the tone alone.  In this example, the conditioned stimulus (CS) is the
    a.  tone                                    c.  salivation to the tone
    b.  meat powder                             d.  salivation to the meat powder

8.  Which of the following behaviors is most likely to be acquired through classical conditioning?
    a.  phobia                                  c.  driving a car
    b.  study habits                            d.  playing tennis

9.  Negative reinforcement plays a major role in the development of _____ tendencies.
    a.  sexual                                  c.  emotional
    b.  avoidance                               d.  aggressive

10. Which of the following concepts is <u>least</u> likely to be emphasized in a strict behavioral view of personality?
    a.  response                                c.  cognition
    b.  stimulus                                d.  consequences

11. According to Carl Rogers, which of the following is likely to be the main cause of troublesome anxiety?
   a. childhood trauma
   b. unconscious sexual urges
   c. the inability to achieve self-actualization
   d. experiences that threaten one's self-concept

12. Abraham Maslow argued that humans have an innate drive toward
   a. superiority
   b. personal growth
   c. Oedipal resolution
   d. reproductive fitness

13. Which of the following theoretical orientations is most likely to rely on evidence from twin studies for support?
   a. psychodynamic
   b. behavioral
   c. humanistic
   d. biological

14. Which of the following theoretical orientations is most likely to rely on evidence from research on animal subjects for support?
   a. psychodynamic
   b. behavioral
   c. humanistic
   d. biological

15. Hans Eysenck is most closely associated with which of the following theoretical orientations?
   a. psychodynamic
   b. behavioral
   c. humanistic
   d. biological

16. Which of the following theoretical orientations takes the most optimistic view of human nature?
   a. psychodynamic
   b. behavioral
   c. humanistic
   d. biological

17. The notion of reproductive fitness is most closely associated with which of the following theoretical approaches to personality?
   a. psychodynamic
   b. behavioral
   c. humanistic
   d. biological

18. According to terror management theory, which of the following helps humans reconcile their self-preservation instinct with the notion that death is inevitable?
   a. a cultural worldview
   b. striving for self-actualization
   c. the use of defense mechanisms
   d. the acquisition of material goods

19. Suppose an individual takes an intelligence test on two separate occasions, three years apart. The fact that the two scores are nearly identical is a good indication that the test is
   a. valid
   b. reliable
   c. normalized
   d. standardized

20. A projective test is generally used to measure
   a. attitudes
   b. intelligence
   c. academic achievement
   d. personality traits

## True/False Items

T/F     1. Psychodynamic theories are all descended from the work of Sigmund Freud.

T/F     2. According to Freud, the ego operates according to the pleasure principle.

T/F    3.    Defense mechanisms are largely conscious reactions that protect a person from painful emotions such as anxiety.

T/F    4.    According to Carl Jung, the collective unconscious is a storehouse of memory traces that is shared with the entire human race.

T/F    5.    In classical conditioning, the unconditioned response (UCR) and the conditioned response (CR) often involve the same behavior.

T/F    6.    Once a stimulus-response bond has been formed through classical conditioning, it will generally last indefinitely.

T/F    7.    In operant conditioning, a response is mainly influenced by events that follow it.

T/F    8.    Negative reinforcement and punishment are synonymous.

T/F    9.    According to B. F. Skinner, conditioning in humans operates much as it does in other animals (e.g., rats, pigeons).

T/F    10.    According to Carl Rogers, children who receive conditional affection from their parents tend to develop congruence between their self-concept and their actual experience.

T/F    11.    According to Abraham Maslow's hierarchy of needs, an individual may regress back to lower levels if basic needs cease to be satisfied.

T/F    12.    A number of recent studies have found that shared family environment has surprisingly little impact on personality.

T/F    13.    Terror management theory is narrower in scope than psychoanalytic, behavioral, and humanistic theories.

T/F    14.    In psychological testing, reliability refers to the test's ability to measure what it was designed to measure.

T/F    15.    The vast majority of personality tests are self-report inventories.

# ANSWER KEY FOR SELF-TEST ITEMS

*Multiple Choice Items*

| | | |
|---|---|---|
| a | 1. | Consistency is an important aspect of personality in the sense that behavior patterns tend to be consistent across situations, but it is not actually a personality *trait*. (34-35) |
| | 2. | Freud's contemporaries were uncomfortable with all of these aspects of his theory. (36) |
| b | 3. | The ego considers social realities–society's norms, etiquette, rules, and customs–in deciding how to behave. (36) |
| b | 4. | Displacement involves diverting emotional feelings (usually anger) from their original source to a substitute target. (39) |
| c | 5. | Occurring around age 4, the Oedipal complex is the basis for the child's identification with the same-gender parent, according to Freud. (40) |
| c | 6. | Adler viewed striving for superiority as a universal drive to adapt, improve oneself, and master life's challenges. (42) |
| a | 7. | The tone is the previously neutral stimulus that, through being paired with the meat powder, acquires the capacity to evoke salivation, the conditioned response. (45) |
| a | 8. | Classical conditioning frequently contributes to the acquisition of emotional responses, such as anxieties, fears, and phobias. (46) |
| b | 9. | Many people tend to avoid facing up to awkward situations and sticky personal problems. This personality trait typically develops because avoidance behavior gets rid of anxiety and is therefore negatively reinforced. (48) |
| c | 10. | Although cognition is addressed in Bandura's social cognitive theory, which is considered a behavioral approach, it is not included in the *strict* conditioning models of behavior. (49) |
| d | 11. | This answer should not be too surprising, since self-concept is the single most important element in Carl Rogers' person-centered theory of personality. (52) |
| b | 12. | The need for personal growth is one of the main characteristics of the humanistic approach to personality. This emphasis is reflected in Maslow's hierarchy of needs, which places the *growth needs* in the higher levels of the hierarchy. (54) |
| d | 13. | Researchers frequently study the behavior of identical versus fraternal twins to assess the influence of heredity on personality traits. (57) |
| b | 14. | In fact, critics suggest that behavioral theorists tend to depend too much on animal research in explaining human personality. (59) |
| d | 15. | Eysenck's view of personality is considered a biological approach because he emphasizes the role of genetics in personality. (63) |
| c | 16. | With their emphasis on free will and the potential for personal growth, humanists present a very positive view of human nature. (63) |

d    17.    The concept of reproductive fitness is a major emphasis in evolutionary psychology, which is considered a biological approach to personality. (63)

a    18.    Faith in a cultural worldview can give people a sense of order, meaning, and context that can soothe their fear of death. (60)

b    19.    The concept of reliability deals with the consistency of scores over time. (65)

d    20.    The assumption underlying projective testing is that ambiguous materials can serve as a blank screen onto which people project their characteristic concerns, conflicts, and desires. (66)

## True/False Items

True    1.    The fact that they are descended from Freud's work is what all of the psychodynamic theories have in common. (35)

False    2.    The ego operates according to the reality principle.  It's the id that operates according to the pleasure principle. (36)

False    3.    Defense mechanisms generally operate at the *unconscious* level. (38)

True    4.    Although an interesting concept, this idea had little impact on the mainstream of thinking in psychology. (41)

True    5.    In Pavlov's initial demonstration, salivation was an unconditioned response when evoked by the UCS (meat powder) and a conditioned response when evoked by the CS (the tone). (45)

False    6.    The right circumstances can lead to extinction, the gradual weakening and disappearance of a conditioned response tendency. (46)

True    7.    In operant conditioning, it is the consequences of a response (i.e., reinforcement, punishment) that lead to learning. (47)

False    8.    This is a common misconception.  Negative reinforcement is still reinforcement, which means it results in the strengthening of a response, whereas punishment results in the weakening of a response. (47-48)

True    9.    The principles of conditioning are based largely on research done on animals.  Skinner conducted extensive laboratory research using rats and pigeons as his subjects. (48)

False    10.    Rogers believed that *unconditional* love from parents fosters congruence and that conditional love fosters incongruence. (52)

True    11.    Needs that are unsatisfied and basic tend to be of highest priority. (53)

True    12.    Although for many years social scientists have assumed that the environment shared by children growing up together leads to personality similarities, recent findings seriously undermine this widespread belief. (57-58)

True    13.    However, the theory has wide-ranging implications and it is being applied to more and more aspects of human behavior. (60)

False | 14. Reliability deals with consistency of measurement, whereas validity refers to the test's ability to measure what it was designed to measure. (65)

True | 15. The logic underlying the use of self-report measures is that you know yourself better than anyone else does. (65)

# Chapter 3
# STRESS AND ITS EFFECTS

## PROGRAMMED REVIEW

**1.** *Explain the nature of stress and discuss how common it is.*

| | | |
|---|---|---|
| coping | 1-1. | Stress is any circumstances that threaten or are perceived to threaten one's well-being and thereby tax one's (coping/thinking/writing) abilities. (72) |
| are not | 1-2. | Major and minor stressors (are/are not) entirely independent. (72) |
| mental and physical | 1-3. | Research shows that routine hassles may have significant negative effects on a person's (mental/physical/mental and physical) health. (72) |
| daily hassles | 1-4. | Richard Lazarus and his colleagues devised a scale to measure stress in the form of (daily hassles/life-changing events/traumatic experiences). (72) |
| cumulative | 1-5. | Many theorists believe that stressful events can have a(n) (cumulative/independent/positive) impact. (72) |

**2.** *Distinguish between primary and secondary appraisal of stress.*

| | | |
|---|---|---|
| Primary | 2-1. | (Preliminary/Primary/Secondary) appraisal refers to an initial evaluation of whether an event is irrelevant, relevant, or stressful. (72) |
| coping | 2-2. | When you view an event as stressful, you are likely to make a secondary appraisal, which is an evaluation of your (coping/financial/social) resources and options for dealing with the stress. (72) |
| subjective | 2-3. | That stress lies in the mind of the beholder means that people's appraisals of stressful events are highly (objective/subjective). (73) |

**3.** *Summarize the evidence on ambient stress.*

| | | |
|---|---|---|
| environmental | 3-1. | Ambient stress consists of chronic (emotional/environmental/work-related) conditions that, although not urgent, are negatively valued and that place adaptive demands on people. (73) |
| elevated | 3-2. | Investigators have found an association between exposure to high levels of noise and (decreased/elevated) blood pressure among children attending school near Los Angeles International Airport. (73) |
| increased | 3-3. | Generally, studies find an association between high residential density and (increased/decreased) physiological arousal. (73) |
| modestly | 3-4. | Research has shown that scores on the City Stress Index are (not/modestly/strongly) correlated with measures of subjects' depressive symptoms, hostility, and irritability. (74) |
| more | 3-5. | Because stress is often self-imposed, people have (more/less) control over their stress than they probably realize. (74) |

**4.** *Explain how culture and ethnicity are related to stress.*

vary greatly

4-1.   Cultures (are similar/vary greatly) in the predominant forms of stress their people experience. (74)

day-to-day living

4-2.   In recent years, social scientists interested in ethnicity have been shifting their focus to the effects of subtle discrimination in (day-to-day living/health care/hiring practices). (75)

ambiguous

4-3.   According to researchers, acts of everyday discrimination are often (ambiguous/reinforced/obvious). (75)

confirmation

4-4.   The threat of stereotype (bias/confirmation/discrimination) can become a source of chronic apprehension for members of ethnic minorities. (75)

**5.** *Distinguish between acute and chronic stressors.*

Acute; chronic

5-1.   _____ stressors are threatening events that have a relatively short duration and a clear endpoint, whereas _____ stressors are threatening events that have a relatively long duration and no readily apparent time limit. (75).

acute

5-2.   Waiting for the results of a medical test would be an example of a(n) (acute/ambient/chronic) stressor. (75)

chronic

5-3.   Ongoing pressures from a hostile boss at work would be an example of a(n) (acute/ambient/chronic) stressor. (76)

virtually impossible

5-4.   Classifying stressful events into nonintersecting categories is (fairly common/virtually impossible). (76)

**6.** *Describe frustration as a form of stress.*

Frustration

6-1.   _____ occurs in any situation in which the pursuit of some goal is thwarted. (76)

unrealistic

6-2.   Some people make frustration due to failure almost inevitable by setting (too many/too few/unrealistic) goals for themselves. (76)

frustration

6-3.   More often than not, (failure/frustration/loss) appears to be responsible when people feel troubled by environmental stress. (76)

**7.** *Outline the three types of conflict and discuss typical reactions to conflicts.*

Conflict

7-1.   (Conflict/Frustration/Aggression) occurs when two or more incompatible motivations or behavioral impulses compete for expression. (76)

approach-approach

7-2.   In an (approach-approach/avoidance-avoidance/approach-avoidance) conflict a choice must be made between two attractive goals. (76)

| | | |
|---|---|---|
| approach-approach | 7-3. | If you are torn between two appealing college majors, you are experiencing (approach-approach/avoidance-avoidance/approach-avoidance) conflict. (77) |
| unattractive | 7-4. | An avoidance-avoidance conflict involves a choice between two (attractive/unattractive) goals. (77) |
| avoidance-avoidance | 7-5. | If you are "caught between a rock and a hard place," you are experiencing (approach-approach/avoidance-avoidance/approach-avoidance) conflict. (77) |
| approach-avoidance | 7-6. | If you must make a choice about whether to pursue a single goal that has both attractive and unattractive aspects, you are experiencing a(n) (approach-approach/avoidance-avoidance/approach-avoidance) conflict. (77) |
| vacillation | 7-7. | Approach-avoidance conflicts often produce (aggression/vacillation/withdrawal). (77) |

**8.    Summarize evidence on life change as a form of stress.**

| | | |
|---|---|---|
| life changes | 8-1. | Any noticeable alterations in one's living circumstances that require readjustment are called (life changes/stressors/vacillators). (78) |
| stressful | 8-2. | From their research on the relation between stressful life events and physical illness, Holmes and Rahe concluded that disruptions in our daily routines are (rejuvenating/stressful/self-actualizing). (78) |
| more | 8-3. | Research on the Social Readjustment Rating Scale (SRRS) and similar scales has shown that people with higher scores on the SRRS tend to be (more/less) vulnerable to physical illness. (79) |
| methods | 8-4. | Recently, experts have criticized research using the SRRS, citing problems with the (methods/sample sizes/subjects) used in the research. (79) |
| most | 8-5. | Research findings suggest that undesirable or negative life events cause (little/only some/most) of the stress tapped by the SRRS. (80) |

**9.    Summarize evidence on pressure as a form of stress.**

| | | |
|---|---|---|
| Pressure | 9-1. | (Conflict/Pressure/Readjustment) involves expectations or demands that one behave in a certain way. (80) |
| perform; conform | 9-2. | Pressure can be divided into two subtypes: the pressure to _____ and the pressure to _____. (80) |
| perform | 9-3. | You are under pressure to (conform/perform) when you are expected to execute tasks and responsibilities quickly, efficiently, and successfully. (80) |
| conform | 9-4. | Young adults are expected to get married by the time they are 30. That is, there is pressure for them to (adjust/conform/perform). (81) |

**10.    List three categories of negative emotions commonly elicited by stress.**

physiological

10-1.    When your pulse quickens and your stomach knots up during a stressful event, you are experiencing a(n) (behavioral/emotional/physiological) response. (81)

uncontrollable

10-2.    Emotions are powerful, largely (controllable/uncontrollable) feelings, accompanied by physiological changes. (82)

anger

10-3.    As a stressor, frustration is particularly likely to generate feelings of (anger/anxiety/dejection). (83)

anxiety

10-4.    Freudian theory has long recognized the link between conflict and (anger/anxiety/depression). (83)

dejection

10-5.    Routine setbacks, such as traffic tickets and poor grades, often produce feelings of (dejection/fear/rage). (83)

**11.    Discuss the role of positive emotions in the stress process.**

may

11-1.    Research shows that positive emotions (may/do not) occur during periods of stress. (83)

positively;
negatively

11-2.    In a study that examined subjects' emotional functioning early in 2001 and again in the weeks following the 9/11 terrorist attacks, researchers found that the frequency of positive emotions correlated (positively/negatively) with a measure of subjects' resilience, whereas unpleasant emotions correlated (positively/negatively) with resilience. (83)

reduce

11-3.    Research findings indicate that positive emotions associated with stress may (increase/reduce) the adverse physiological effects of stress. (83)

enhance

11-4.    Research evidence suggests that positive emotions associated with stress can (diminish/enhance) immune system functioning. (84)

**12.    Explain the effects of emotional arousal on coping efforts and describe the inverted-U hypothesis.**

both facilitate and
hamper

12-1.    Strong emotional arousal can (facilitate/hamper/both facilitate and hamper) efforts to cope with stress. (84)

low

12-2.    Students who show high test anxiety tend to score (high/low) on exams. (84)

performance

12-3.    The inverted-U hypothesis is based on the relationship between arousal and (coping/emotion/performance). (84)

optimal

12-4.    The level of arousal at which performance peaks is called the (necessary/optimal/variable) level of arousal for a task. (84).

decrease

12-5.    As tasks become more complex, the optimal level of arousal (for peak performance) tends to (decrease/increase). (84)

| | |
|---|---|
| high;<br>lower | 12-6. A fairly (high/low) level of arousal should be optimal for simple tasks and a (higher/lower) level of arousal should be optimal for complex tasks. (84) |

**13.    Describe the fight-or-flight response and the three stages of the general adaptation syndrome.**

| | |
|---|---|
| physiological | 13-1. The fight-or-flight syndrome is a(n) (cognitive/emotional/physiological) reaction that mobilizes an organism for attacking (fight) or fleeing (flight) an enemy. (85) |
| autonomic | 13-2. The (autonomic/central/peripheral) nervous system is made up of the nerves that connect to the heart, blood vessels, smooth muscles, and glands. (85) |
| sympathetic | 13-3. The fight-or-flight response is mediated by the (central/sympathetic/ parasympathetic) division of the autonomic nervous system. (85) |
| tend-and-befriend | 13.4 Shelley Taylor and her colleagues maintain that evolutionary processes have fostered a (lock-and-load/tend-and-befriend/turn-and-run) response to stress in females. (85) |
| alarm | 13-5. When an organism recognizes the existence of a threat, it exhibits a(n) (alarm/resistance/exhaustion) reaction. (86) |
| coping | 13-6. In the resistance stage of the general adaptation syndrome, physiological changes stabilize as (coping/escape) efforts get underway. (87) |
| exhaustion | 13-7. During the stage of (alarm/resistance/exhaustion), the body's resources may be depleted, causing decreased arousal and sometimes collapse. (87) |
| diseases | 13-8. Selye's theory showed how prolonged physical arousal could lead to (coping/diseases/personality disorders). (87) |

**14.    Describe the two major pathways along which the brain sends signals to the endocrine system in response to stress.**

| | |
|---|---|
| hormones | 14-1. The endocrine system consists of glands that secrete chemicals called (enzymes/hormones/neurotransmitters) into the bloodstream. (87) |
| hypothalamus | 14-2. The (cortex/hypothalamus/thalamus), a small structure near the base of the brain, appears to initiate action along both major pathways to the endocrine system. (87) |
| adrenal | 14-3. In one pathway, the hypothalamus activates the sympathetic division of the autonomic system, which stimulates the (adrenal/pineal/thyroid) glands to release large amounts of catecholamines into the bloodstream. (87-88) |
| increase | 14-4. The release of catecholamines from the adrenal glands produces a(n) (decrease/increase) in heart rate and blood flow. (88) |
| pituitary | 14-5. In the second major pathway, the hypothalamus sends signals to the so-called master gland of the endocrine system, the (adrenal/pineal/pituitary) gland. (88) |

corticosteroids

14-6.  Hormones called (androgens/catecholamines/corticosteroids) stimulate the release of chemicals that help inhibit tissue inflammation in case of injury. (88)

immune

14-7.  Evidence indicates that stress can suppress certain aspects of the (digestive/immune/respiratory) system. (88)

greater

14-8.  Long-lasting stressors, such as caring for a seriously ill spouse, are associated with (greater/less) immune suppression than relatively brief stressors. (88)

**15.  *Explain the concept of coping.***

behavioral

15-1.  Coping involves (behavioral/physiological) responses to stress. (88)

stress

15-2.  Coping refers to active efforts to master, reduce, or tolerate the demands created by _____. (88-89)

unhealthy

15-3.  Coping efforts may range from healthy to _____. (89)

**16.  *Explain the phenomenon of choking under pressure.***

disrupts

16-1.  Baumeister's theory assumes that pressure to perform often makes people self-conscious and that this elevated self-consciousness (disrupts/focuses) their attention. (89)

common

16-2.  Laboratory research on "normal" subjects suggests that choking under pressure is fairly (common/uncommon). (89)

**17.  *Summarize evidence of how stress can affect cognitive functioning.***

attention

17-1.  Keinan's research suggests that Baumeister is on the right track in looking to (attention/emotions/memory) to explain how stress impairs task performance. (89)

disrupted

17-2.  Keinan found that stress (disrupted/enhanced) two out of three aspects of attention measured in a study. (89)

shock

17-3.  Severe stress may leave people dazed and confused, in a state of (heightened anxiety/mania/shock). (89)

**18.  *Describe the symptoms and causes of burnout.***

work

18-1.  Burnout involves physical and emotional exhaustion, cynicism and a lowered sense of self-efficacy that is attributable to (family/work)-related stress. (90)

cumulative

18-2.  According to researchers, burnout is a(n) (acute/cumulative) stress reaction to ongoing occupational stressors. (90)

| | |
|---|---|
| increased; decreased | 18-3.  Burnout is associated with (increased/decreased) absenteeism and (increased/decreased) productivity at work. (90) |

**19.    Discuss the prevalence, symptoms, and causes of posttraumatic stress disorder.**

| | |
|---|---|
| the Vietnam war | 19-1.  Researchers began to appreciate the frequency and severity of posttraumatic stress disorders after (the Korean war/the Vietnam war/World War II) ended. (90) |
| more | 19-2.  Posttraumatic stress disorders are much (more/less) common than originally believed. (90) |
| more | 19-3.  Research suggests that the various types of traumatic events that can cause PTSD are (more/less) common than most people realize. (91) |
| higher | 19-4.  PTSD is associated with a (higher/lower) risk for substance abuse, depression, and anxiety disorders. (91) |
| decrease | 19-5.  The frequency and severity of posttraumatic symptoms usually (increase/decrease) over time. (91) |
| do not develop | 19-6.  The vast majority of people who experience traumatic events (develop/do not develop) PTSD. (91) |
| intense | 19-7.  Vulnerability to PTSD seems to be greatest among people whose reactions at the time of the traumatic event were very (intense/mild). (91) |

**20.    Discuss the potential impact of stress on mental and physical health.**

| | |
|---|---|
| Chronic | 20-1.  (Acute/Ambient/Chronic) stress contributes to many types of psychological problems and mental disorders. (92) |
| often | 20-2.  Stress (often/rarely) contributes to the onset of full-fledged psychological disorders. (92) |
| psychosomatic | 20-3.  Genuine physical ailments thought to be caused in part by stress and other psychological factors were known as _____ diseases. (92) |
| fallen into disuse | 20-4.  Since the 1970s, the concept of psychosomatic disease has (become widely accepted/fallen into disuse/grown in popularity). (92) |

**21.    Describe positive psychology and three ways in which stress might lead to beneficial effects.**

| | |
|---|---|
| are not | 21-1.  The effects of stress (are/are not) entirely negative. (93) |
| negative | 21-2.  The positive psychology movement seeks to shift the field's focus away from (childhood/negative/observable) experiences. (93) |
| stimulation | 21-3.  Stressful events can help satisfy the need for (affiliation/social support/stimulation). (93) |

improvement

21-4. Stressful events sometimes force people to develop new skills and acquire new strengths. In other words, stress can promote self-(concept/esteem/improvement). (93)

tolerance

21-5. Some studies suggest that exposure to stress can increase (sensitivity/tolerance) to stress. (93)

**22.    Explain how social support moderates the impact of stress.**

moderator

22-1. The impact of stress on physical and mental health can be softened by a number of (mediator/moderator/intervening) variables. (94)

social

22-2. A moderator variable involving aid and succor provided by members of one's social networks is called (emotional/psychodynamic/social) support. (94)

decreases

22-3. Social support (increases/decreases) the negative impact of stressful events. (95)

beneficial

22-4. Recent research suggests that providing social support to others can be (beneficial/detrimental) to mental and physical health. (95)

**23.    Describe the hardiness syndrome and how it influences stress tolerance.**

Hardiness

23-1. (Conscientiousness/Hardiness/Optimism) is a syndrome marked by commitment, challenge, and control that is purportedly associated with strong resistance to stress. (95)

active

23-2. Hardiness may reduce the effects of stress by fostering more (active/passive/optimistic) coping. (95)

lower

23-3. A study of Vietnam veterans found that higher hardiness was related to a (higher/lower) likelihood of developing posttraumatic stress disorders. (95-96)

**24.    Discuss how optimism is related to stress tolerance.**

optimists

24-1. Those who have a general tendency to expect good outcomes are called _____. (96)

better

24-2. Research with the Life Orientation Test has consistently shown that optimism is associated with (better/worse/average) mental and physical health. (96)

explanatory

24-3. Many studies have linked the optimistic (explanatory/interactive/writing) style to superior physical health. (96)

adaptive

24-4. Research suggests that optimists cope with stress in more (adaptive/conscientious/passive) ways than pessimists. (97)

**25.    List five problems with the SRRS.**

change

**25-1.** Holmes and Rahe designed the Social Readjustment Rating Scale (SRRS) to measure the amount of (change/family/work)-related) stress that people experience. (97)

inaccurate

**25-2.** The assumption that the SRRS measures change exclusively has been shown to be (accurate/inaccurate). (97)

subjective

**25-3.** The SRRS fails to take into account differences among people in their (subjective/unconscious) perception of how stressful an event is. (98)

ambiguous

**25-4.** Many of the events listed on the SRRS and similar scales are highly (ambiguous/empirical/selective), leading people to be inconsistent as to which events they report experiencing. (98)

many

**25-5.** Studies examining the thoroughness of stressful events included on the SRRS have found (relatively few/some/many) significant omissions. (98)

neuroticism

**25-6.** The correlation between SRRS scores and health outcomes may be inflated because subjects' (neuroticism/optimism/hardiness) affects both their responses to stress scales and their self-reports of health problems. (98)

**26.** *Summarize how the LES corrects some of the problems that are characteristic of the SRRS.*

respondent

**26-1.** The LES takes into consideration differences among people in their appraisal of stress, by dropping the normative weights and replacing them with weightings assigned by the (administrator/manual/respondent). (98)

allows

**26-2.** The LES (allows/does not allow) the respondent to write in personal events that are not included on the scale. (98)

negative; positive

**26-3.** Research to date suggests that the (positive/negative) change score on the LES is the crucial one; (positive/negative) change has not been found to be a good predictor of adaptational outcomes. (100)

**27.** *Explain why one should be cautious in interpreting scores on stress scales.*

relatively low

**27-1.** Most of the correlations observed between stress scores and illness have been (relatively low/relatively high/very high). (101)

Many

**27-2.** (Many/Some/Very few) people endure high levels of stress without developing significant problems. (101)

should not

**27-3.** A high score on any measure of stress (should/should not) be viewed as reason for alarm. (101)

## QUIZ BOXES

*KEY TERMS*

| | |
|---|---|
| **Stress** | Any circumstances that threaten or are perceived to threaten one's well-being and thereby tax one's coping abilities. |
| **Primary appraisal** | An initial evaluation of whether an event is (1) irrelevant to you, (2) relevant, but not threatening, or (3) stressful. |
| **Secondary appraisal** | An evaluation of your coping resources and options for dealing with the stress. |
| **Ambient stress** | Chronic environmental conditions that, although not urgent, are negatively valued and that place adaptive demands on people. |
| **Acute stressors** | Threatening events that have a relatively short duration and a clear endpoint. |
| **Chronic stressors** | Threatening events that have a relatively long duration and no readily apparent time limit. |
| **Frustration** | Occurs in any situation in which the pursuit of some goal is thwarted. |
| **Conflict** | Occurs when two or more incompatible motivations or behavioral impulses compete for expression. |
| **Approach-approach conflict** | Type of conflict in which a choice must be made between two attractive goals. |
| **Avoidance-avoidance conflict** | Type of conflict in which a choice must be made between two unattractive goals. |
| **Approach-avoidance conflict** | Type of conflict in which a choice must be made about whether to pursue a single goal that has both attractive and unattractive aspects. |
| **Life changes** | Any noticeable alterations in one's living circumstances that require readjustment. |
| **Pressure** | Involves expectations or demands that one behave in a certain way. |
| **Emotions** | Powerful, largely uncontrollable feelings, accompanied by physiological changes. |

| Fight-or-Flight response | A physiological reaction to threat that mobilizes an organism for attacking (fight) or fleeing (flight) an enemy. |
|---|---|
| General adaptation syndrome | A model of the body's stress response, consisting of three stages: alarm, resistance, and exhaustion. |
| Endocrine system | Consists of glands that secrete chemicals called hormones into the bloodstream. |
| Coping | Active efforts to master, reduce, or tolerate the demands created by stress. |
| Burnout | Physical and emotional exhaustion, cynicism, and a lowered sense of self-efficacy that is attributable to work-related stress. |
| Posttraumatic stress disorder (PTSD) | An enduring psychological disturbance attributed to the experience of a major traumatic event. |
| Psychosomatic diseases | Genuine physical ailments thought to be caused in part by stress and other psychological factors. |
| Social support | Various types of aid and succor provided by members of one's social networks. |
| Hardiness | A syndrome marked by commitment, challenge, and control that is purportedly associated with strong stress resistance. |
| Optimism | A general tendency to expect good outcomes. |

## KEY PEOPLE

| Susan Folkman | Conducted research showing that positive emotions occur about as often as negative emotions during periods of stress. |
|---|---|
| Thomas Holmes and Richard Rahe | Developed the Social Readjustment Rating Scale (SRRS) to measure life change as a form of stress. |
| Suzanne Ouellette (Kobasa) | Described the role of hardiness in moderating the impact of stressful events. |
| Richard Lazurus | Devised a scale to measure stress in the form of everyday hassles; found that scores on the scale were related to subjects' mental health. |

| Neal Miller | Conducted extensive investigation of three types of conflict: approach-approach, avoidance-avoidance, and approach-avoidance. |
|---|---|
| Han Selye | Formulated a theory of stress reactions called the general adaptation syndrome, which consists of three stages: alarm, resistance, and exhaustion. |
| Shelley Taylor | Suggested that evolutionary processes have fostered more of a tend-and-befriend response to stress in females, as opposed to a fight-or-flight response. |

# SELF-TEST

*Multiple Choice Items*

1.    Researchers have found that stress
      a.    is healthy because it presents a challenge to the person
      b.    almost always comes from crises that are overwhelming and traumatic
      c.    leads to poor mental health and an eventual breakdown if it is not resolved
      d.    can come from everyday problems and minor nuisances as well as major crises

2.    Which of the following would not be considered a form of ambient stress?
      a.    crowding                                    c.    excessive heat
      b.    air pollution                               d.    unrealistic expectations

3.    Which of the following statements regarding ethnicity-related sources of stress is not accurate?
      a.    Everyday acts of discrimination are often ambiguous.
      b.    Overt racial discrimination in America has declined in recent decades.
      c.    In recent years, researchers have focused their attention on the causes of institutional racism.
      d.    The threat of stereotype confirmation can be a source of stress for minority group members.

4.    Which of the following would be considered an example of an acute stressor?
      a.    having your home threatened by severe flooding
      b.    ongoing pressures from a hostile boss at work
      c.    persistent financial strains produced by huge credit-card debts
      d.    the demands of caring for a sick family member for an extensive period of time

5.    Research on life change and stress began when Thomas Holmes, Richard Rahe, and their
      colleagues set out to explore the relation between stressful life events and
      a.    frustration                                 c.    physical illness
      b.    aggressive behavior                         d.    schizophrenia

6.    Using a scale to measure pressure as a form of life stress, Weiten was able to demonstrate that
      a.    pressure is not an important source of stress
      b.    there is, at most, a weak relationship between pressure and some psychological problems
      c.    pressure is the leading cause of stress in the lives of Americans today
      d.    there is a strong relationship between pressure and a variety of psychological problems

7.    Which of the following emotions is most likely to be evoked by frustration?
      a.    anger                                       c.    sadness
      b.    anxiety                                     d.    annoyance

8.    According to the inverted-U hypothesis, performance on a task
      a.    usually decreases with emotional arousal
      b.    usually increases with emotional arousal
      c.    peaks at the optimal level of arousal for the particular task
      d.    peaks at about the same level no matter what the task is

9.    A physiological reaction that mobilizes an organism for attacking or fleeing is
      a.    called the fight-or-flight response
      b.    called the autonomic nervous system response
      c.    a function of the parasympathetic nervous system
      d.    seen only in animals, not in humans

10. In contrast to the traditional fight-or-flight model of responding to stress, Shelley Taylor and her colleagues have suggested that females may be more likely to engage in a _____ response.
    a. run-and-hide
    b. tend-and-befriend
    c. lock-and-load
    d. wait-and-see

11. Which of the following is the <u>correct</u> order for the three stages of the general adaptation syndrome?
    a. alarm, resistance, exhaustion
    b. resistance, alarm, exhaustion
    c. exhaustion, resistance, alarm
    d. alarm, exhaustion, resistance

12. When a person experiences stress, the brain sends signals to the endocrine system along two pathways. The structure that appears to initiate action along both pathways is the
    a. adrenal gland
    b. catecholamine
    c. hypothalamus
    d. pituitary gland

13. Laboratory research on "normal" subjects suggests that choking under pressure
    a. is fairly common
    b. occurs only in athletic events
    c. is common only for "high-anxious" individuals
    d. rarely occurs outside of professional sports

14. Burnout is associated with all but which of the following?
    a. increased absenteeism
    b. increased sense of self-efficacy
    c. reduced productivity at work
    d. increased vulnerability to health problems

15. Which of the following experiences is likely to produce posttraumatic stress disorder (PTSD)?
    a. rape
    b. combat
    c. a serious automobile accident
    d. All of the above may produce PTSD.

16. Posttraumatic stress disorder (PTSD) is associated with an elevated risk for which of the following?
    a. depression
    b. anxiety disorders
    c. substance abuse
    d. all of the above

17. Which of the following statements regarding the effects of social support on stress is <u>not</u> accurate?
    a. Social support is favorably related to physical health.
    b. Social support seems to be unrelated to mental health.
    c. Providing social support to others can be beneficial.
    d. Social support may serve as a protective buffer from stress.

18. Hardiness tends to reduce the effects of stress by altering one's
    a. stress appraisals
    b. frustration level
    c. need for sensory stimulation
    d. autonomic reactivity

19. The Social Readjustment Rating Scale was designed to measure the amount of _____ stress that people experience.
    a. ambient
    b. social
    c. physiological
    d. change-related

20.    Which of the following is <u>not</u> one of the main criticisms of the Social Readjustment Rating Scale (SRRS)?
        a.    The list of stressful events on the SRRS is too lengthy.
        b.    Many of the events listed on the SRRS are highly ambiguous.
        c.    The impact of neuroticism is overemphasized on the SRRS.
        d.    The SRRS measures change-related stress exclusively.

## True/False Items

T/F        1.    Minor stresses tend to produce minor effects.

T/F        2.    Some people are more prone to feel threatened by life's difficulties than are others.

T/F        3.    Among the three kinds of conflict, the approach-approach type tends to be the least stressful.

T/F        4.    According to Holmes and Rahe, any life changes, whether they are desirable or undesirable, tend to be stressful.

T/F        5.    Students who display high test anxiety tend to score low on exams.

T/F        6.    Task performance generally improves with emotional arousal.

T/F        7.    Research evidence indicates that stress can suppress the functioning of the immune system.

T/F        8.    Coping responses may be either healthy or unhealthy.

T/F        9.    Cases of posttraumatic stress disorder (PTSD) have been found exclusively in veterans of the Vietnam War.

T/F       10.    Vulnerability to posttraumatic stress disorder (PTSD) seems to be greatest among people whose emotional reactions during the traumatic event were especially intense.

T/F       11.    Stressful events can have positive effects on our lives.

T/F       12.    Recent research suggests that providing social support to others can be beneficial in coping with stress.

T/F       13.    Researchers have found a correlation between optimism and relatively good physical health.

T/F       14.    Many people endure high levels of stress without developing significant problems.

# ANSWER KEY FOR SELF-TEST ITEMS

*Multiple Choice Items*

d | 1. | Contrary to popular belief, routine, minor stresses may produce significant negative effects on one's mental and physical health. (72)

d | 2. | Unrealistic expectations are a form of self-imposed stress; the others are all ambient, or environmental stress. (73)

c | 3. | Although this was the traditional approach to research, the focus in recent years has shifted to studies on the effects of subtle discrimination in day-to-day living. (75)

a | 4. | Although it would certainly be stressful, the threat of a flood would likely have a relatively short duration and a clear endpoint. The other alternatives are all good examples of chronic stressors. (75)

c | 5. | Their research led to the development of the Social Readjustment Rating Scale. (78)

d | 6. | Wayne Weiten (the co-author of your textbook) was one of the first researchers to examine the role of pressure as a factor in stress. (81)

a | 7. | Although all of these emotions can be evoked by stress, the stress that occurs as a result of frustration is particularly likely to generate anger. (83)

c | 8. | The optimal level of arousal appears to depend in part on the complexity of the particular task. On complex tasks, a relatively low level of arousal tends to be optimal. On simple tasks, however, performance may peak at a much higher level of arousal. (84-85)

a | 9. | The fight-or-flight response is defined as a physiological reaction to threat that mobilizes an organism for attacking (fight) or fleeing (flight) an enemy. (85)

b | 10. | According to Taylor et al., in reacting to stress, females are likely to allocate more effort to the care of offspring and seeking help and support. (85-86)

a | 11. | Alarm is the initial recognition of stress, resistance involves coping with the stress, and exhaustion finally occurs if the stress continues over a substantial period of time. (86)

c | 12. | The hypothalamus, a small structure near the base of the brain, is a key component in the physiological response to stress. (87)

a | 13. | These findings support Baumeister's theory that pressure to perform often makes people self-conscious and that this elevated self-consciousness disrupts their attention, resulting in poorer performance (i.e., "choking"). (89)

b | 14. | Burnout is actually associated with a *decreased* sense of self-efficacy, which involves declining feelings of competence at work that give way to feelings of hopelessness and helplessness. (90)

d | 15. | Although posttraumatic stress disorders are widely associated with the experiences of Vietnam veterans, they are seen in response to other cases of traumatic stress, such as the examples in this question. (90)

d | 16. | PTSD is also associated with a great variety of physical health problems. (91)

| b | 17. | Most studies have found an association between social support and mental health. (95) |
|---|---|---|
| a | 18. | Hardiness may also reduce the effects of stress by fostering more active coping. (95) |
| d | 19. | The scale is based on the assumption that major life changes are frequently a source of stress. This is why the correlation between scores on the Social Readjustment Rating Scale and health outcomes may be inflated. (97) |
| a | 20. | Actually, the criticism is that the SRRS does not sample from the domain of stressful events thoroughly enough.  Studies of the major stresses that people typically experience have found many significant omissions on the SRRS. (97-98) |

### True/False Items

| False | 1. | Routine hassles may have significant negative effects on one's mental and physical health. (72) |
|---|---|---|
| True | 2. | This is one reason why stress lies in the eye of the beholder. (73) |
| True | 3. | After all, this is a situation in which both alternatives are desirable. (77) |
| True | 4. | Other researchers have argued this point, suggesting that the desirability of the changes is a factor in our response to them. (78) |
| True | 5. | A critical factor in the effects of test anxiety appears to be the disruption of attention to the test. (84) |
| False | 6. | This is true up to a point.  Once the optimal level of arousal is reached, performance tends to suffer. (84) |
| True | 7. | This is one way stress can produce negative effects on physical health. (84) |
| True | 8. | Most people think of coping as a positive response to stress, but coping strategies can also take negative forms (e.g., giving up). (89) |
| False | 9. | Other cases include victims of rape or serious accidents, and people who see someone die. (91) |
| True | 10. | Recent research suggests that a key predictor of vulnerability to PTSD is the intensity of one's reaction at the time of the traumatic event. (91) |
| True | 11. | Although this is contrary to common sense, your textbook discusses several ways stress can have beneficial effects (e.g., satisfying the need for stimulation and challenge). (93) |
| True | 12. | It appears that the presence of social support is not the only feature of our social relations that may have some bearing on our wellness. (95) |
| True | 13. | Optimism is one of a number of factors than seem to help people withstand the effects of stress. (97) |
| True | 14. | This is one reason why scores on stress scales (e.g., Life Experiences Survey) should be viewed with caution. (101) |

# Chapter 4
# COPING PROCESSES

## PROGRAMMED REVIEW

*1.* ***Discuss the variety of coping strategies that people use.***

Coping

1-1. _____ refers to efforts to master, reduce, or tolerate the demands created by stress. (106)

14

1-2. Carver, Scheier, and Weintraub found that they could sort their participants' coping strategies into (3/8/14) categories. (105)

planning

1-3. Coming up with a strategy to deal with a stressful situation is an example of (acceptance/planning/restraint coping). (106)

denial

1-4. Refusing to believe that a stressful event has happened is an example of (acceptance/active coping/denial). (106)

*2.* ***Discuss whether individuals display distinctive styles of coping.***

flexibility

2-1. The need for (consistency/flexibility/stimulation) may explain why people's coping strategies show only moderate stability across varied situations. (106)

counter-productive

2-2. Coping strategies range from the helpful to the (extremely helpful/moderately helpful/counterproductive). (106)

*3.* ***Analyze the adaptive value of giving up as a response to stress.***

sadness

3-1. The response of apathy and inaction when confronted with stress tends to be associated with the emotional reaction of (anger/relief/sadness). (107)

passive

3-2. Learned helplessness involves (active/passive/coping) behavior produced by exposure to unavoidable aversive events. (107)

cognitive

3-3. Martin Seligman proposed that one's (cognitive/emotional/unconscious) interpretation of aversive events determines whether a person will develop learned helplessness). (107)

increased

3-4. The strategy of behavioral disengagement (i.e., giving up) is associated with (increased/decreased) distress. (108)

*4.* ***Describe the adaptive value of aggression as a response to stress.***

aggression

4-1. Behavior that is intended to hurt someone, either physically or verbally, is called (aggression/hostility/withdrawal). 1087

frustration-aggression

4-2. The _____-_____ hypothesis holds that aggression is always due to frustration. (108)

| | | |
|---|---|---|
| displacement | 4-3. | Lashing out aggressively at others who had nothing to do with one's frustration was called (displacement/projection/regression) by Freud. (108) |
| Catharsis | 4-4. | (Catharsis/Displacement/Projection) refers to the release of emotional tension that may accompany aggressive behavior. (109) |
| has not | 4-5. | Experimental research generally (has/has not) supported the catharsis hypothesis. (109) |
| minimal | 4-6. | The adaptive value of aggressive behavior as a coping strategy tends to be (minimal/significant/situational). (109) |

**5.    Evaluate the adaptive value of indulging yourself as a response to stress.**

| | | |
|---|---|---|
| indulgence | 5-1. | Stress sometimes leads to reduced impulse control, or self-(actualization/ esteem/indulgence). (109) |
| alternative | 5-2. | Researchers Moos and Billings list "developing (alternative/multiple/ negative) rewards" as a common response to stress. (109) |
| Internet | 5-3. | An individual who spends an inordinate amount of time on the Internet and shows an inability to control his/her online use may be suffering from _____ addiction. (109-110) |
| does not | 5-4. | The Internet addiction syndrome (does/does not) appear to be rare. (110) |
| marginal | 5-5. | Self-indulgence has (marginal/moderate/significant) adaptive value. (111) |

**6.    Discuss the adaptive value of negative self-talk as a response to stress.**

| | | |
|---|---|---|
| critical | 6-1. | When confronted by stress (especially frustration and pressure) people often become highly self-(critical/indulgent/reflective). (111) |
| catastrophic | 6-2. | The tendency to engage in "negative self-talk" in response to stress is called (catastrophic/emotive/rational) thinking by Albert Ellis. (111) |
| counter-productive | 6-3. | Researchers agree that self-blame tends to be (adaptive/counterproductive/ useful) as a coping strategy. (111) |

**7.    Explain how defense mechanisms work.**

| | | |
|---|---|---|
| Freud | 7-1. | The concept of defense mechanisms was originally developed by (Bandura/ Ellis/Freud). (111) |
| unconscious | 7-2. | Defense mechanisms are largely (conscious/subconscious/unconscious) reactions that protect a person from unpleasant emotions such as anxiety and guilt. (111) |
| stress | 7-3. | Above all else, defense mechanisms shield the individual from the emotional discomfort elicited by (aggressive impulses/sexual urges/stress). (112) |

deception

7-4.    Defense mechanisms work through the process of self-(actualization/ deception/indulgence). (112)

fantasy

7-5.    An individual who tends to gratify frustrated desires through imaginary achievements is using the defense mechanism called (fantasy/intellectualization/undoing). (112)

normal

7-6.    The use of defense mechanisms is considered a(n) (normal/abnormal) pattern of coping. (112)

**8.    *Evaluate the adaptive value of defense mechanisms, including recent work on healthy illusions.***

poor

8-1.    Generally, defense mechanisms are considered (adequate/appropriate/ healthy/poor) ways of coping. (112)

favorable

8-2.    Research indicates that "normal" people tend to have overly (favorable/ unfavorable) self-images. (113)

overestimate

8-3.    "Normal" subjects tend to (underestimate/overestimate) the degree to which they control chance events. (113)

maladaptive; beneficial

8-4.    According to Roy Baumeister, extreme self-deception is (adaptive/ maladaptive), but small illusions may be (beneficial/harmful). (113)

**9.    *Discuss whether constructive coping is related to intelligence.***

Constructive

9-1.    _____ coping refers to efforts to deal with stressful events that are judged to be relatively healthful. (113)

is

9-2.    Research findings indicate that constructive coping (is/is not) related to measures of "success" in work, love, and social relationships. (113)

weakly related

9-3.    Constructive coping appears to be (weakly related/strongly related/ unrelated) to IQ scores. (113)

**10.    *Describe the nature of constructive coping.***

directly

10-1.    Constructive coping involves confronting problems (directly/indirectly). (114)

realistic

10-2.    Constructive coping is based on relatively (realistic/unrealistic) appraisals of your stress and coping resources. (114)

problem

10-3.    Enhancing time management is an example of a(n) (appraisal/emotion/ problem)-focused coping strategy. (114)

appraisal

10-4.    Rational thinking is an example of a(n) (appraisal/emotion/problem)-focused coping strategy. (115)

emotion

10-5.    Managing hostile feelings is an example of a(n) (appraisal/emotion/ problem)-focused coping strategy. (115)

**11.**    *Explain Ellis's analysis of the causes of maladaptive emotions.*

Rational-emotive

11-1.    (Client-centered/Psychoanalytic/Rational-emotive) therapy focuses on altering clients' patterns of irrational thinking to reduce maladaptive emotions and behavior. (115)

think

11-2.    According to Albert Ellis, you feel the way you (eat/behave/think). (115)

Catastrophic

11-3.    _____ thinking involves unrealistic appraisals of stress that exaggerate the magnitude of one's problems. (115)

activating

11-4.    The "A" in Ellis's system stands for the _____ event that produces the stress. (115)

belief system

11-5.    The (activating event/belief system/consequence) in Ellis's system represents an individual's appraisal of the stress. (115)

consequence

11-6.    The "C" in Ellis's system stands for the (classification/climax/consequence) of one's negative thinking. (115)

B

11-7.    In Ellis's A-B-C model, it's (A/B) that causes C. (116)

**12.**    *Describe some assumptions that contribute to catastrophic thinking.*

irrational

12-1.    According to Ellis, unrealistic appraisals of stress are derived from the (fundamental/irrational/rational) assumptions that people hold. (116)

liked

12-2.    Many people foolishly believe that they should be (despised/liked/revered) by everyone they come into contact with. (116)

win

12-3.    Because we live in a highly competitive society, we feel that we must always (compete/fight/win). (116)

unrealistically

12-4.    Many people go through life (realistically/unrealistically) expecting others' efficiency and kindness. (116)

detect;
dispute

12-5.    In order to reduce your unrealistic appraisals of stress, Ellis suggests that you must learn how to (detect/eliminate/minimize) catastrophic thinking and (detect/dispute/encourage) the irrational assumptions that cause it. (117)

**13.**    *Discuss the merits of positive reinterpretation and humor as coping strategies.*

high

13-1.    Findings from research on humor and coping indicate that increased stress leads to a smaller increase in mood disturbance in the (high/low)-humor group. (117)

increases

13-2.    Research has shown that humor (increases/decreases) the experience of positive emotions. (117)

tougher

13-3.    Comparing your plight with others' (similar/less serious/tougher) struggles can help you put your problems in perspective. (118)

good;
bad

13-4.    One way to use positive reinterpretation to cope with stress is to search for something (bad/good) in a (bad/good) situation. (118)

**14.    List and describe four steps in systematic problem solving.**

problem

14-1.    Making efforts to remedy or conquer the stress-producing problem itself is called (emotion/problem/management)-focused coping. (118)

clarify

14-2.    The first step in any systematic problem-solving effort is to (clarify/rationalize/redefine) the nature of the problem. (118-119)

is not

14-3.    In generating alternative courses of action, it (is/is not) a good idea to go with the first alternative that comes to mind. (119)

brainstorming

14-4.    Generating as many ideas as possible while withholding criticism and evaluation is called (appraisal/brainstorming/clarifying). (119)

evaluating

14-5.    Once you generate as many alternatives as you can, you need to start (eliminating/evaluating/maximizing) the possibilities. (119)

implement

14-6.    The last step in systematic problem-solving is to (discard/evaluate/implement) your chosen course of action. (119)

**15.    Discuss the adaptive value of seeking help as a coping strategy.**

buffer

15-1.    Social support can be a powerful force that helps (increase/reduce/buffer) the deleterious effects of stress. (119)

embarrassment

15-2.    Because of potential (embarrassment/loss of support), many people are reluctant to acknowledge their problems and seek help from others. (119)

**16.    Explain five common causes of wasted time.**

priorities

16-1.    One of the main causes of wasted time is an inability to set or stick to (a schedule/priorities/realistic goals). (121)

no

16-2.    One of the main causes of wasted time is the inability to say (yes/no/I quit). (121)

delegating

16-3.    One reason people waste time is that they have difficulty (accepting/delegating/putting off) work. (121)

wastebaskets

16-4.    According to R. Alec Mackenzie, a prominent time-management researcher, people would save time if they made more use of their (email/file cabinets/wastebaskets). (122)

perfection

16-5.    Some people waste time because they have the inability to accept anything less than (complete delegation/perfection/full responsibility). (122)

**17.    Describe evidence on the causes and consequences of procrastination.**

| | |
|---|---|
| procrastination | 17-1.  The tendency to delay tackling tasks until the last minute is called _____. (122) |
| 20 | 17-2.  Research suggests that about (20/40/75) percent of adults are chronic procrastinators. (122) |
| negative | 17-3.  Studies show that procrastination tends to have a (positive/negative) impact on the quality of task performance. (122) |
| Perfectionism | 17-4.  Among the personality factors that contribute to procrastination is excessive (conscientiousness/perfectionism/self-efficacy). (122) |
| Often | 17.5  People who struggle with procrastination (seldom/often) impose deadlines and penalties on themselves. (122) |
| | **18.    Summarize advice on managing time effectively.** |
| effectiveness | 18-1.  Time management experts emphasize that the key to better time management is increased (effectiveness/efficiency/procrastination). (122) |
| time | 18-2.  The first step toward better time management is to monitor your use of (email/social support/time). (123) |
| goals | 18-3.  One suggestion for using time more effectively is to clarify your (goals/needs/strengths). (124) |
| short-term | 18-4.  At the beginning of each week, you should make up a list of (short-term/long-term) goals. (124) |
| prime | 18-5.  One way to manage time effectively is to protect your (down/prime/work) time. (124) |
| similar | 18-6.  One way to increase your efficiency is to group (similar/different) tasks together. (125) |
| control | 18-7.  Self-discipline and self-(control/esteem/indulgence) are the key to handling many of life's problems effectively. (125) |
| | **19.    Describe the nature and value of emotional intelligence.** |
| emotional | 19-1.  According to some theorists, (emotional/social/verbal) intelligence is the key to being resilient in the face of stress. (125) |
| regulate | 19-2.  People need to be able to (express/regulate) their emotions so that they can dampen negative emotions and use positive emotions effectively. (125) |
| performance | 19-3.  The authors of the Mayer-Salovey-Caruso Emotional Intelligence Test have tried to make their test a (personality/performance/temperament) based measure of the ability to deal effectively with emotions. (125-126) |

| | |
|---|---|
| social interactions | 19-4.  Illustrating the practical importance of emotional intelligence, scores on the Mayer-Salovey-Caruso Emotional Intelligence Test predict the quality of subjects' (reasoning ability/social interactions/verbal intelligence). (126) |

**20.  Analyze the adaptive value of releasing pent-up emotions and distracting yourself.**

| | |
|---|---|
| more | 20-1.  Research suggests that people who inhibit the expression of anger and other emotions are somewhat (more/less) likely than other people to have high blood pressure. (126) |
| increased | 20-2.  Research suggests that efforts to actively suppress emotions result in (increased/decreased) stress and autonomic arousal. (126) |
| detrimental | 20-3.  Research on gay men who conceal their sexual identity suggests that psychological inhibition may be (beneficial/detrimental) to one's health. (126) |
| beneficial | 20-4.  Research has shown that talking or writing about traumatic events can have (beneficial/detrimental) effects on health. (126-127) |

**21.  Discuss the importance of managing hostility and forgiving others' transgressions.**

| | |
|---|---|
| increased | 21-1.  Studies have shown that hostility is related to (increased/decreased) risk for heart attacks and other types of illnesses. (127) |
| anger | 21-2.  The first step in managing hostility is to learn to quickly recognize one's (anger/limitations/motivation). (127) |
| positively; inversely | 21-3.  In one study of divorced or permanently separated women, the extent to which the women had forgiven their former husbands was (inversely/positively) related to several measures of well-being and (inversely/positively) related to measures of anxiety and depression. (128) |

**22.  Summarize the evidence on the effects of meditation.**

| | |
|---|---|
| focus | 22-1.  Meditation refers to a family of mental exercises in which a conscious attempt is made to (focus/monitor) attention in a non-analytical way. (128) |
| decreases | 22-2.  Most studies of meditation find (increases/decreases) in participants' heart rate, respiration rate, and oxygen consumption. (128) |
| high; low | 22-3.  Researchers who have studied brain activity during meditation observed (high/low) activity in the prefrontal cortex, and (high/low) activity in an area in the parietal lobe that is known to process information on the body's location is space. (129) |
| stress | 22-4.  Research suggests that meditation may have some value in reducing the effects of (alcoholism/overeating/stress). (129) |

relaxation

22-5.  At least some of the positive effects of meditation may be just as attainable through systematic (chemical/relaxation/surgical) procedures. (129)

**23.  Describe the requirements and procedure for Benson's relaxation response.**

distraction

23-1.  According to Herbert Benson, it is easiest to induce the relaxation response in a(n) (distraction/emotion/smoke)-free environment. (130)

constant

23-2.  According to Benson's technique, to shift attention inward and keep it there, you need to focus on a (constant/loud/moving) stimulus. (130)

mental device

23-3.  According to Benson's technique, whenever your mind wanders from your attentional focus, you should calmly redirect attention to your (breathing/extremities/mental device). (130)

comfortable

23-4.  To use Benson's technique effectively, it is important to assume a (sitting/ comfortable/standing) position. (130)

daily

23-5.  For full benefit, Benson's relaxation procedure should be practiced (daily/weekly/monthly). (130)

**24.  Explain why traits cannot be target behaviors in self-modification programs.**

conditioning

24-1.  Behavior modification is a systematic approach to changing behavior through the application of the principles of (conditioning/observational learning/positive self-talk). (131)

response

24-2.  Behavior modification can only be applied to a clearly defined, overt (emotion/response/trait). (131)

examples of

24-3.  To identify target responses, you need to ponder past behavior or closely observe future behavior and list specific (examples of/traits associated with) responses. (131)

**25.  Discuss the three kinds of information you should pursue in gathering your baseline data.**

initial

25-1.  The first step in gathering baseline data for a behavior modification program is to determine the (initial/desired) response level of your target behavior. (131)

antecedents

25-2.  Events that typically precede the target response are called (antecedents/ pre-targets/reinforcers). (132)

negative

25-3.  In trying to identify reinforcers, remember that avoidance behavior is usually maintained by (positive/negative) reinforcement. (132)

**26.  Discuss how to use reinforcement to increase the strength of a response.**

| positive | 26-1. | Efforts to increase the frequency of a target response depend largely on the use of (positive/negative) reinforcement. (132) |

positive

26-1. Efforts to increase the frequency of a target response depend largely on the use of (positive/negative) reinforcement. (132)

contingencies

26-2. Once you have chosen your reinforcer, you have to set up reinforcement (contingencies/consequences/schedules). (132)

unrealistically high

26-3. A common mistake in self-modification that may result in discouragement is to set goals that are (too low/unrealistically high). (133)

token

26-4. A _____ economy is a system for doling out symbolic reinforcers that are exchanged later for a variety of genuine reinforcers. (133)

Shaping

26-5. _____ is accomplished by reinforcing closer and closer approximations of the desired response. (133)

**27.    *Explain how to use reinforcement, control of antecedents, and punishment to decrease the strength of a response.***

not emitting

27-1. To use reinforcement to reduce the frequency of an undesirable response such as overeating, you can reinforce yourself for (emitting/not emitting) a response. (134)

avoiding

27-2. One way to decrease responses is to identify the antecedents and (avoid/seek) exposure to them. (134)

should

27-3. If you're going to use punishment in a self-modification program, you (should/should not) use punishment in conjunction with positive reinforcement. (134)

mild

27-4. If you're going to use punishment in a self-modification program, it's a good idea to use a relatively (mild/severe) punishment. (134)

**28.    *Analyze issues related to fine-tuning and ending a self-modification program.***

contract

28-1. A behavioral (consequence/contingency/contract) is a written agreement outlining a promise to adhere to the contingencies of a behavior modification program. (135)

weak

28-2. A common flaw in designing a self-modification program is depending on a (strong/weak) reinforcer. (135)

reinforcers

28-3. Another flaw in designing a self-modification program is permitting lengthy delays between appropriate behavior and delivery of (antecedents/reinforcers/punishment). (135)

gradual

28-4. Often, it is a good idea to phase out a self-modification program by planning a (gradual/rapid) reduction in the frequency or potency of your reinforcement for appropriate behavior. (135)

**QUIZ BOXES**

*KEY TERMS*

| | |
|---|---|
| **Coping** | Efforts to master, reduce, or tolerate the demands created by stress. |
| **Learned helplessness** | Passive behavior produced by exposure to unavoidable aversive events. |
| **Aggression** | Any behavior intended to hurt someone, either physically or verbally. |
| **Catharsis** | A release of emotional tension following aggressive behavior. |
| **Internet addiction** | Spending an inordinate amount of time on the Internet and inability to control online use. |
| **Defense mechanisms** | Largely unconscious reactions that protect a person from unpleasant emotions such as anxiety and guilt. |
| **Constructive coping** | Efforts to deal with stressful events that are judged to be relatively healthful. |
| **Rational-emotive therapy** | An approach to therapy that focuses on altering clients' patterns of irrational thinking to reduce maladaptive emotions and behavior. |
| **Catastrophic thinking** | Unrealistic appraisals of stress that exaggerate the magnitude of one's problems. |
| **Brainstorming** | Generating as many ideas as possible while withholding criticism and evaluation. |
| **Procrastination** | The tendency to delay tackling tasks until the last minute. |
| **Emotional intelligence** | The ability to perceive and express emotion, assimilate emotion in thought, understand and reason with emotion, and regulate emotion. |
| **Meditation** | A family of mental exercises in which a conscious attempt is made to focus attention in a nonanalytical way. |
| **Behavior modification** | A systematic approach to changing behavior through the application of the principles of conditioning. |

| Antecedents | Events that typically precede the target response. |
|---|---|
| Token economy | A system for doling out symbolic reinforcers that are exchanged later for a variety of genuine reinforcers. |
| Shaping | Accomplished by reinforcing closer and closer approximations of a desired response. |
| Behavioral contract | A written agreement outlining a promise to adhere to the contingencies of a behavior modification program. |

## KEY PEOPLE

| Herbert Benson | "Demystified" meditation; developed the "relaxation response," a simple, nonreligious procedure that could provide benefits similar to meditation. |
|---|---|
| Albert Ellis | Devised rational-emotive therapy, based on the notion that catastrophic thinking causes maladaptive behavior. |
| Sigmund Freud | Discussed the diversion of anger to a substitute target (displacement). Coined the term "catharsis" to suggest that behaving aggressively can free pent-up emotion and thus be adaptive. |
| Martin Seligman | Developed a model of the giving-up syndrome, called learned helplessness, based on studies of animal subjects. |
| Shelley Taylor | Reviewed several lines of evidence suggesting that positive "illusions" may be adaptive for mental health and well-being. |

## SELF-TEST

*Multiple Choice Items*

1. If you look for the good in what is happening in a stressful situation, you are using which of the following coping strategies?

   a.  denial
   b.  planning
   c.  restraint coping
   d.  positive reinterpretation

2. Passive behavior produced by exposure to unavoidable aversive events is called

   a.  catharsis
   b.  aggression
   c.  learned helplessness
   d.  irrational self-talk

3. Which of the following conclusions about research on the cathartic value of aggressive behavior is most accurate?

   a.  Aggression reliably produces a cathartic effect.
   b.  The adaptive value of aggressive behavior tends to be minimal.
   c.  Aggression generally results in learned helplessness rather than catharsis.
   d.  Aggression can be cathartic as long as it is directed at a stranger.

4. There is evidence relating stress to increases in which of the following behaviors?

   a.  eating
   b.  smoking
   c.  alcohol consumption
   d.  all of the above

5. Which of the following is least closely associated with the use of defense mechanisms as a coping strategy?

   a.  denial
   b.  reality
   c.  normal
   d.  deception

6. To use constructive coping effectively, a person must

   a.  confront problems directly
   b.  make a realistic appraisal of one's coping resources
   c.  inhibit potentially disruptive emotional reactions
   d.  do all of the above

7. Improving one's self-control is an example of which of the following constructive coping tactics?

   a.  appraisal-focused coping
   b.  problem-focused coping
   c.  emotion-focused coping
   d.  defense-focused coping

8. The tendency to engage in "negative self-talk" in response to stress has been noted by a number of theorists.  Albert Ellis calls this phenomenon _____ thinking.

   a.  defensive
   b.  optimistic
   c.  pessimistic
   d.  catastrophic

9. Which of the following is the correct order for the stages of events in Albert Ellis's explanation of the process of catastrophic thinking?

   a.  activating event, belief system, consequence
   b.  belief system, activating event, consequence
   c.  activating event, consequence, belief system
   d.  belief system, consequence, activating event

10.    Which of the following statements is likely to be considered an irrational assumption?
       a.    It's okay if I don't win all the time.
       b.    Other people are not always considerate.
       c.    Things will not always go the way I want them to.
       d.    I must have love and affection from people who are close to me.

11.    Which of the following has been offered as an explanation for the stress-reducing effects of humor?
       a.    Humor increases the experience of positive emotions.
       b.    Humor positively affects the appraisals of stressful events.
       c.    A good sense of humor promotes social support, which can buffer the effects of stress.
       d.    All of the above have been offered as explanations.

12.    In generating alternative courses of action to solve a problem, it's a good idea to
       a.    go with the first alternative that comes to mind
       b.    use a process like brainstorming to generate alternatives
       c.    focus on the negative feelings associated with the problem
       d.    think of the possible courses of action as alternative *solutions*

13.    Which of the following statements about procrastination is not accurate?
       a.    Personality factors often contribute to procrastination.
       b.    Procrastinators tend to have fewer health problems than non-procrastinators.
       c.    Procrastination tends to have a negative impact on the quality of task performance.
       d.    All of the above statements are accurate.

14.    Experts maintain that the key to better time management is increased
       a.    efficiency
       b.    effectiveness
       c.    emphasis on achieving perfection
       d.    willingness to assume responsibility

15.    As a coping strategy for relieving stress, meditation
       a.    is not recommended, as it has been highly overrated
       b.    has not been demonstrated to be effective in Western cultures
       c.    functions like a variety of other systematic relaxation procedures
       d.    has not been demonstrated to calm inner emotional turmoil

16.    Herbert Benson concluded that the beneficial aspects of meditation come from the
       a.    state of relaxation that it produces in the individual
       b.    heightened spirituality of the person who learns how to meditate
       c.    subtle blending of religion and psychology that brings on the relaxed state
       d.    trance-like state that encourages the person to think of new solutions to personal problems

17.    Which of the following is not considered a critical factor in the effective practice of Benson's relaxation response?
       a.    a mental device                              c.    a passive attitude
       b.    soothing music                               d.    a comfortable position

18.    Advocates of behavior modification assume that
       a.    what is learned can be unlearned
       b.    our behavior is the product of learning
       c.    some behavior patterns are more desirable than others
       d.    all of the above

19.  Having specified a target behavior, the next step in a behavior modification program is to
    a.  gather baseline data
    b.  select a reinforcer
    c.  design the program
    d.  set behavioral goals

20.  A token economy is a system for doling out symbolic reinforcers that are exchanged later for a variety of genuine
    a.  placebos
    b.  reinforcers
    c.  antecedents
    d.  contingencies

## True/False Items

T/F     1.  Research findings indicate that behavioral disengagement (i.e., giving up) is associated with increased distress.

T/F     2.  Carol Tavris and other researchers have concluded that aggression usually leads to catharsis.

T/F     3.  There is evidence relating stress to increases in eating and drug consumption.

T/F     4.  Defense mechanisms can operate at varying levels of awareness.

T/F     5.  Psychologists generally consider the use of defense mechanisms to be an indication of abnormal behavior.

T/F     6.  Recent research suggests that the use of certain illusions may be adaptive for mental health and well-being.

T/F     7.  Recognizing that "things could be worse" is an example of negative self-talk that is likely to result in increased distress.

T/F     8.  Brainstorming involves generating a select number of possible alternatives and evaluating each alternative carefully.

T/F     9.  Research on procrastination indicates that many people do their best work under pressure.

T/F     10.  In the long run, people who tend to discuss their problems with others enjoy better mental and physical health than those who hold back.

T/F     11.  Evidence indicates that meditation may be an effective way to reduce troublesome arousal.

T/F     12.  Advocates of behavior modification assume that what is learned can be unlearned.

T/F     13.  In selecting a reinforcer for a self-modification program, it is a good idea to use a new reinforcer that you've never experienced before.

T/F     14.  A common mistake in self-modification programs is to set unrealistically high goals.

# ANSWER KEY FOR SELF-TEST ITEMS

## *Multiple Choice Items*

d | 1. | Positive reinterpretation, or searching for something good in a bad experience, is one of 14 categories of coping strategies listed in your textbook. (106)

c | 2. | This behavior pattern was first noted by Martin Seligman in his research on animals that were exposed to electric shock that they could not escape. (107)

b | 3. | The research findings on the cathartic value of aggressive behavior are decidedly mixed. Although there is some experimental evidence to support this connection, it is clear that aggression does not *reliably* lead to catharsis. (109)

d | 4. | Increases in all of these behaviors have been found to be associated with stress. (109)

b | 5. | Defense mechanisms accomplish their goals by *distorting* reality so it does not appear to be threatening. (112)

d | 6. | All of these are important elements of constructive coping. (114)

b | 7. | Problem-focused coping strategies focus on efforts to remedy or conquer the stress-producing problem itself. (125)

d | 8. | According to Ellis, this type of thinking is rooted in irrational assumptions and it tends to be counterproductive. (115)

a | 9. | The first letters of the three stages correspond to the "A-B-C" in the sequence. According to Ellis, the order of these events is critical in understanding the role of catastrophic thinking in dealing with stress. (115)

d | 10. | This kind of assumption is likely to make a person depressed if a close relationship comes to an end. (116)

d | 11. | In addition to these explanations, it has been suggested that high-humor people may benefit from not taking themselves as seriously as low-humor people do. (117)

b | 12. | With brainstorming, you generate alternatives without paying any attention to their apparent practicality, which facilitates creative expression of ideas. All the other choices in this question are approaches you should avoid. (119)

b | 13. | In fact, procrastinators tend to experience an increase in health problems as deadlines approach. (122)

b | 14. | Better efficiency may be helpful, but experts generally maintain that efficiency is overrated. They emphasize that the key to better time management is increased *effectiveness* – that is, learning to allocate time to your most important tasks. (122)

c | 15. | Although there is evidence that meditation can lead to a potentially beneficial physiological state, the effect may not be unique to meditation. (129)

c | 16. | After "demystifying" meditation, Benson went on to devise a simple, nonreligious procedure that could provide similar benefits. He called this procedure the "relaxation response." (129-130)

b          17.   In fact, Benson suggests that a quiet environment is best for practicing the relaxation response. (130)

d          18.   All of these are basic assumptions underlying the use of behavior modification. (131)

a          19.   Basically, you need to systematically observe your target behavior for a period of time (usually a week or two) before you work out the details of your program. (131)

b          20.   The fact that the tokens can be exchanged for genuine reinforcers (e.g., compact discs, restaurant meals, etc.) is why the tokens are effective rewards. (133)


**True/False Items**

True       1.    This is one reason why giving up is not a highly regarded method of coping. (108)

False      2.    On the contrary, Tavris concluded that aggressive behavior does *not* reliably lead to catharsis. (109)

True       3.    Stress sometimes leads to self-indulgent behaviors such as increased consumption of food, drugs, or alcohol. Recent research suggests that stress can also result in an increased use of the Internet. (109)

True       4.    Freud originally assumed that defense mechanisms operate entirely at an unconscious level. However, the concept of defense mechanisms has been broadened since Freud's time to include processes that operate at varying levels of awareness. (112)

False      5.    In fact, everyone uses defense mechanisms on a regular basis. (112)

True       6.    Although this claim is somewhat controversial, Taylor and Brown have reviewed several lines of research that provide supportive evidence. (113)

False      7.    In fact, this tactic is a form of positive reinterpretation, a relatively healthful coping strategy. (118)

False      8.    Actually, brainstorming involves generating as many ideas as possible while withholding criticism and evaluation as a way to facilitate the creative expression of ideas. (119)

False      9.    Although people may claim this is the case, the empirical evidence suggests otherwise. (122)

True       10.   Research findings indicate that people who do not talk about traumatic events suffer more health problems than those who tend to confide in others. (127)

True       11.   Although this statement is true, the benefits of meditation may not be as spectacular as supporters claim, and you may be able to attain some of the same benefits through less exotic techniques (i.e., relaxation procedures). (129-130)

True       12.   Otherwise, there would be no point in using behavior modification to eliminate troublesome behaviors such as smoking. (131)

True       13.   An important aspect of selecting a reinforcer is that you can use reinforcers that you are already getting, although you may have to restructure the contingencies under which you get them. (132)

True | 14.  Setting unrealistically high goals often leads to unnecessary discouragement. (133)

# Chapter 5
## THE SELF

**PROGRAMMED REVIEW**

**1.** ***Describe some key aspects of the self-concept.***

Self-concept     1-1.    _____-_____ is an organized collection of beliefs about the self. (140)

schemas     1-2.    The beliefs contained in the self-concept are also called self-(ideas/ interpretations/schemas). (140)

working     1-3.    The self-concept that is accessible at any particular point in time is called the (conscious/schematic/working) self-concept. (140)

Possible     1-4.    "_____ selves" refers to one's conceptions about the kind of person one might become in the future. (141)

are not     1-5.    Individuals' beliefs about themselves (are/are not) easily changed. (141)

**2.** ***Cite two types of self-discrepancies and describe their effects.***

perceptions     2-1.    Self-discrepancy refers to the mismatching of self-(concepts/esteems perceptions). (141)

self-esteem     2-2.    According to Higgins, when people live up to their personal standards, they experience high (energy/motivation/self-esteem). (141)

dejection     2-3.    The self-discrepancy that occurs when the actual self is at odds with the ideal self tends to trigger (agitation/anxiety/dejection)- related emotions. (141)

agitation     2-4.    The mismatch between actual and ought selves is likely to trigger (agitation/ anxiety/dejection)-related emotions. (141-142)

parent-child     2-5.    Self-guide "preferences" are rooted in (parent-child/peer/teacher-pupil) interactions and an individual's temperament. (142)

**3.** ***Describe two ways of coping with self-discrepancies.***

behavior     3-1.    One way people cope with self-discrepancies is to change their (awareness/ behavior/self-concept) to bring it more in line with their ideal or ought selves. (142)

awareness     3-2.    Another way to cope with self-discrepancies is to blunt your self-(awareness/ concept/perceptions). (142)

alcohol     3-3.    Some people use (alcohol/defense mechanisms/meditation) to blunt their self-awareness. (142)

**4.      *Discuss important factors that help form the self-concept.***

comparison

4-1.     Social (comparison/learning/perception) theory proposes that individuals compare themselves with others in order to assess their abilities and opinions. (143)

reference

4-2.     A set of people against whom people compare themselves is called a (comparison/control/reference) group. (143)

positive

4-3.     In making observations of our own behavior, the general tendency is to distort reality in a(n) (positive/negative) direction. (143)

strong

4-4.     There is (little/strong) evidence for a relationship between children's perceptions of their parents' attitudes toward them and their own self-perceptions. (144)

reinforces

4-5.     Feedback from others usually (contradicts/reinforces) one's self-views. (144)

**5.      *Discuss how individualism and collectivism influence self-concept.***

Individualism

5-1.     (Collectivism/Individualism) involves putting personal goals ahead of group goals and defining one's identity in terms of personal attributes rather than group memberships. (145)

higher

5-2.     In comparison to individualistic cultures, collectivist cultures place a (lower/higher) priority on shared values and resources, cooperation, and concern for how one's actions will affect group members. (145)

individualistic;
collectivistic

5-3.     In general, North American and Western European cultures tend to be (collectivistic/individualistic), whereas Asian, African, and Latin American cultures tend to be (collectivistic/individualistic). (145)

independent;
interdependent

5-4.     Individuals reared in individualistic cultures usually have an (independent/interdependent) view of the self, whereas individuals reared in collectivist cultures typically have an (independent/interdependent) view of the self. (145)

more

5-5.     Women usually have (more/less) interdependent self-views than men. (146)

**6.      *Describe some implications of self-concept confusion and self-esteem instability.***

Self-esteem

6-1.     _____-_____ refers to one's overall assessment of one's worth as a person. (146)

confused

6-2.     Individuals with low self-esteem tend to have self-views that are more (confused/positive/negative) than others. (147)

stable

6-3.     Studies generally show self-esteem to be (stable/unstable) over time. (147)

difficult

6-4.     It is (easy/difficult) to obtain accurate measures of self-esteem. (147)

**7.    *Discuss how low and high self-esteem are related to adjustment.***

more

7-1.    Low self-esteem is (more/less) likely than high self-esteem to lead to depression. (148)

has not

7-2.    High self-esteem (has/has not) been shown to be a reliable cause of improvement in academic performance. (148)

more

7-3.    Regarding romantic relationships, those with low self-esteem are (more/less) likely to distrust their partners' expressions of love and support. (148)

themselves

7-4.    When individuals with low self-esteem do poorly, they tend to blame (significant others/strangers/themselves). (148)

**8.    *Distinguish between high self-esteem and narcissism, and discuss narcissism and aggression.***

narcissism

8-1.    The tendency to regard oneself as grandiosely self-important is known as _____. (148)

sensitive

8-2.    Narcissistic individuals passionately want to think well of themselves and are highly (sensitive/insensitive) to criticism. (148)

aggressively

8-3.    Narcissists tend to react (aggressively/excitedly/submissively) when they experience threats to their self-views. (148-149)

equally likely as

8-4.    In the absence of provocation, narcissists are (equally likely as/more likely than/less likely than) non-narcissists to behave aggressively. (149)

higher;
about the same

8-5.    In a study comparing male prisoners and college men on narcissism and self-esteem, violent offenders scored (higher/lower/about the same) on narcissism, and (higher/lower/about the same) on self-esteem. (149)

**9.    *Discuss some key influences in the development of self-esteem.***

very early in life

9-1.    The foundations of self-esteem are laid (very early in life/during adolescence/at around college age). (149)

parenting

9-2.    Psychologists have focused much of their attention on the role of (genetics/parenting/peer relationships) in self-esteem development. (149)

low;
high

9-3.    The authoritarian parenting style is associated with (low/high) acceptance and (low/high) control. (149)

Authoritative

9-4.    (Authoritarian/Authoritative/Permissive) parenting is associated with the highest self-esteem scores. (149)

Neglectful

9-5.    (Authoritative/Neglectful/Permissive) parenting is associated with the lowest self-esteem scores. (149)

| | |
|---|---|
| competition | 9-6. A classic study reported that preadolescents' academic self-esteem was affected by the quality of (competition/requirements/teaching) they faced in school. (151) |

**10.    Summarize the findings on ethnicity and gender regarding self-esteem.**

| | |
|---|---|
| lower; higher | 10-1. The self-esteem of Asians, Hispanics, and Native Americans is (higher/ lower) than that of whites, and the self-esteem of blacks is (higher/lower) than whites. (151) |
| high | 10-2. High individualism is associated with (high/low) self-esteem. (151) |
| lower; less | 10-3. Females resemble ethnic minorities in that they tend to have (higher/lower) status and (more/less) power than males. (151) |
| higher | 10-4. Research on gender differences in self-esteem has generally found that males have (higher/lower) self-esteem than females. (151) |
| lower | 10-5. White adolescent girls have (higher/lower) self-esteem than do minority girls. (151) |

**11.    Distinguish between automatic and controlled processing.**

| | |
|---|---|
| mindlessness; mindfulness | 11-1. Automatic processing is also known as (mindlessness/mindfulness), and controlled processing is also known as (mindlessness/mindfulness). (152) |
| the self | 11-2. Another way that cognitive resources are protected is through selective attention, with high priority given to information pertaining to (decision making/one's immediate surroundings/the self). (152) |

**12.    Define self-attributions and identify the key dimensions of attributions.**

| | |
|---|---|
| Self-attributions | 12-1. _____-_____ are inferences that people draw about the causes of their own behavior. (152) |
| Internal | 12-2. (External/Internal) attributions ascribe the causes of behavior to personal dispositions, traits, abilities, and feelings. (152) |
| External | 12-3. (External/Internal) attributions ascribe the causes of behavior to situational demands and environmental constraints. (152) |
| stable; internal | 12-4. Intelligence would be considered a(n) (stable/unstable) (internal/external) cause of behavior. (153) |
| unstable; internal | 12-5. A bad mood would be considered a(n) (stable/unstable) (internal/external) cause of behavior. (153) |
| controllable | 12-6. The amount of effort you expend on a task would be considered a(n) (controllable/uncontrollable) cause of behavior. (153) |

**13. Explain how optimistic and pessimistic explanatory styles are related to adjustment.**

optimistic

13-1. A person with a(n) (optimistic/pessimistic) explanatory style has a tendency to attribute setbacks to external, unstable, and specific factors. (153)

pessimistic

13-2. A person with a(n) (optimistic/pessimistic) explanatory style has a tendency to attribute setbacks to internal, stable, and global factors. (153)

passive;
more

13-3. A pessimistic explanatory style can foster (active/passive) behavior and make people (more/less) vulnerable to learned helplessness and depression. (154)

**14. Discuss four motives that guide self-understanding.**

assessment

14-1. The self-(assessment/improvement/verification) motive is reflected in people's desire for truthful information about themselves. (154)

verification

14-2. The (assessment/improvement/verification) motive drives people toward information that matches what they already know about themselves. (154)

stable

14-3. The tendency to strive for a consistent self-image ensures that individuals' self-concepts are relatively (stable/unstable). (154)

consistent

14-4. According to William Swann's self-verification theory, people prefer to receive feedback from others that is (consistent/inconsistent) with their own self-views. (155)

successful others

14-5. In trying to improve, individuals typically look to (family members/significant others/successful others) for inspiration. (155)

enhancement

14-6. The tendency to hold flattering views of one's personal qualities is an example of the self-(enhancement/improvement/verification) motive. (155)

is not

14-7. Self-enhancement (is/is not) universal. (155)

**15. Describe four strategies individuals use to maintain positive feelings about the self.**

social comparison

15-1. The defensive tendency to compare oneself with someone whose troubles are more serious than one's own is termed downward (enhancement/social comparison/assessment). (155)

self-serving

15-2. The tendency to attribute one's successes to personal factors and one's failures to situational factors is called (comparison/enhancement/self-serving) bias. (156)

self-serving

15-3. A person with a (comparison/attributional/self-serving) bias will probably attribute a failure to "bad luck." (156)

basking

15-4. The tendency to enhance one's image by publicly announcing one's association with those who are successful is called (basking/comparing/living) in reflected glory. (157)

| | |
|---|---|
| handicapping | 15-5. The tendency to sabotage one's performance to provide an excuse for possible failure is called self-(basking/comparing/handicapping). (157) |
| poor | 15-6. Self-handicapping will likely result in (better/excellent/poor) performance. (157) |

**16.  Define self-regulation and explain the ego-depletion model of self-regulation.**

| | |
|---|---|
| regulation | 16-1. The work of directing and controlling one's behavior is termed self-(attribution/efficacy/regulation). (158) |
| limited | 16-2. The idea behind the ego-depletion model of self-regulation is that people have a(n) (limited/unlimited) amount of self-control resources. (158) |
| early; stable | 16-3. Self-regulation seems to develop (early/late) in life and remain relatively (stable/unstable). (158) |

**17.  Explain why self-efficacy is important to psychological adjustment.**

| | |
|---|---|
| efficacy | 17 1. Sclf-(attribution/efficacy/regulation) refers to people's conviction that they can achieve specific goals. (158) |
| success | 17-2. People with high self-efficacy tend to anticipate (failure/success) in future outcomes. (159) |
| learned; can | 17-3. Self-efficacy is (innate/learned) and (can/cannot) be changed. (159) |

**18.  Describe how individuals develop self-efficacy.**

| | |
|---|---|
| mastering | 18-1. The most important path to self-efficacy is through (mastering/practicing) new skills. (159) |
| Vicarious | 18-2. _____ experiences involve watching others perform a skill you want to learn. (159-160) |
| less | 18-3. Persuasion and encouragement are (more/less) effective than mastery experiences and vicarious experiences in developing self-efficacy. (160) |
| physiological | 18-4. The (behavioral/emotional/physiological) responses that accompany feelings and one's interpretations of these responses are another source of self-efficacy. (160) |

**19.  Describe the three categories of self-defeating behavior.**

| | |
|---|---|
| intentional | 19-1. Self-defeating behaviors are seemingly (intentional/unintentional) actions that thwart a person's self-interest. (160) |
| destruction | 19-2. In deliberate self-(destruction/indulgence/reflection), people want to harm themselves and they choose courses of action that will forseeably lead to that result. (160) |

| | |
|---|---|
| infrequent | 19-3.  Deliberate self-destruction appears to be (frequent/infrequent) in normal populations. (160) |
| tradeoffs | 19-4.  Overeating, smoking, and drinking to excess are all examples of (deliberate self-destruction/counterproductive strategies/tradeoffs). (160) |
| judgement | 19-5.  One factor that underlies most self-defeating tradeoffs is poor (judgement/ planning/social skills). (160) |
| counter-productive strategies | 19-6.  In (deliberate self-destruction/counterproductive strategies/tradeoffs), a person pursues a desirable outcome but misguidedly uses an approach that is bound to fail. (160) |

**20.    Explain why and when individuals engage in impression management.**

| | |
|---|---|
| public | 20-1.  Your (other/public/rational) self involves how you want others to see you. (162) |
| a number of | 20-2.  Typically, people have (only one or two/a number of) public selves. (162) |
| better | 20-3.  People who seem themselves as being similar across different social roles are (better/less well) adjusted than those who perceive less integration in their self-views across different roles. (162) |
| conscious | 20-4.  Impression management refers to usually (conscious/unconscious) efforts by people to influence how others think of them. (162) |

**21.    Cite some strategies people use to make positive impressions on others.**

| | |
|---|---|
| Ingratiation | 21-1.  _____ is the most fundamental and most frequently used self-presentation strategy. (163) |
| ingratiation | 21-2.  Giving compliments to others in an effort to make oneself likable is a common form of (ingratiation/intimidation/supplication). (163) |
| promotion | 21-3.  To get others to respect them, people are likely to use self-(indulgence/ ingratiation/promotion). (163) |
| intimidation | 21-4.  The self-presentation strategy that sends the message, "Don't mess with me," is (ingratiation/intimidation/supplication). (163) |
| supplication | 21-5.  The self-presentation strategy of presenting oneself as weak and dependent is called _____. (163) |
| less | 21-6.  People are (more/less) likely to strive to make positive impressions with their friends than they are with strangers. (164) |

**22.    Describe how high self-monitors are different from low self-monitors.**

| | |
|---|---|
| high;<br>low | 22-1.  People who are (low/high) self-monitors seem to be sensitive to their impact on others, while those who are (low/high) in self-monitoring are less concerned about impression management. (164) |
| High | 22-2.  (Low/High) self-monitors are concerned about making a favorable impression. (164) |
| Low | 22-3.  (Low/High) self-monitors are more likely than others to express their true beliefs. (164) |
| decrease | 22-4.  Self-monitoring scores tend to (increase/decrease) as people age. (164) |

**23.    *Explain when it is inadvisable to increase self-esteem, and why this is so.***

| | |
|---|---|
| possible | 23-1.  It is (possible/impossible) for self-esteem to be too high. (165) |
| realistically | 23-2.  Better adjustment is associated with (extremely/realistically) high self-esteem. (165) |

**24.    *Describe seven ways to build self-esteem.***

| | |
|---|---|
| has | 24-1.  A person (has/does not have) the power to change his/her self-image. (165) |
| learn | 24-2.  One way to boost your self-esteem is to (learn/talk/think) more about yourself. (165) |
| not let | 24-3.  In building your self-esteem, it's important to (let/not let) others set your goals. (165) |
| Unrealistic | 24-4.  (Realistic/Unrealistic) comparisons tend to undermine self-esteem. (166) |
| talk | 24-5.  In building self-esteem, it's important to recognize the destructive potential of negative self-(enhancement/monitoring/talk) and bring it to a halt. (167) |
| little | 24-6.  People with low self-esteem often derive (great/little) satisfaction from their accomplishments and virtues. (167) |
| positive | 24-7.  A (positive/negative) outlook will promote rewarding interactions and help one to gain acceptance. (167) |

## QUIZ BOXES

*KEY TERMS*

| | |
|---|---|
| **Self-concept** | An organized collection of beliefs about the self. |
| **Possible selves** | One's conceptions about the kind of person one might become in the future. |
| **Self-discrepancy** | A mismatching of self-perceptions. |
| **Social comparison theory** | Theory that proposes that individuals compare themselves with others in order to assess their abilities and opinions. |
| **Reference group** | A set of people against whom individuals compare themselves. |
| **Individualism** | Involves putting personal goals ahead of group goals and defining one's identity in terms of personal attributes rather than group memberships. |
| **Collectivism** | Involves putting group goals ahead of personal goals and defining one's identity in terms of the groups one belongs to. |
| **Self-esteem** | One's overall assessment of one's worth as a person; the evaluative component of the self-concept. |
| **Narcissism** | The tendency to regard oneself as grandiosely self-important. |
| **Self-attributions** | Inferences that people draw about the causes of their own behavior. |
| **Internal attributions** | Ascribe the causes of behavior to personal dispositions, traits, abilities, and feelings. |
| **External attributions** | Ascribe the causes of behavior to situational demands and environmental constraints. |
| **Explanatory style** | The tendency to use similar causal attributions for a wide variety of events in one's life. |
| **Self-verification theory** | Theory that proposes that people prefer to receive feedback from others that is consistent with their own self-views. |
| **Self-enhancement** | The tendency to maintain positive feelings about the self. |
| **Downward social** | The defensive tendency to compare oneself with someone |

| comparison | whose troubles are more serious than one's own. |
| --- | --- |
| **Self-serving bias** | The tendency to attribute one's successes to personal factors and one's failures to situational factors. |
| **Basking in reflected glory** | The tendency to enhance one's image by publicly announcing one's association with those who are successful. |
| **Self-handicapping** | The tendency to sabotage one's performance to provide an excuse for possible failure. |
| **Self-regulation** | The work of directing and controlling one's behavior. |
| **Self-efficacy** | People's conviction that they can achieve specific goals. |
| **Self-defeating behaviors** | Seemingly intentional actions that thwart a person's self-interest. |
| **Public self** | An image presented to others in social interactions. |
| **Impression management** | Usually conscious efforts by people to influence how others think of them. |
| **Ingratiation** | Behaving in ways to make oneself likable to others. |
| **Self-monitoring** | The degree to which people attend to and control the impressions they make on others. |

## *KEY PEOPLE*

| **Albert Bandura** | Described four sources of self-efficacy: mastery experiences, vicarious experiences, persuasion and encouragement, and interpretation of emotional arousal. |
| --- | --- |
| **Roy Baumeister** | Suggested a connection between "self-concept confusion" and lower scores on self-esteem tests; proposed the ego-depletion model of self-regulation. |
| **Hazel Markus** | Coined the term "working self-concept," which is the self-concept that is currently accessible. |
| **Mark Snyder** | Conducted a number of studies on self-monitoring; suggested that people vary in their awareness of how they are perceived by others. |

# SELF-TEST

*Multiple Choice Items*

1. Which of the following is <u>not</u> one of the main types of self-perceptions, according to E. Tory Higgins?
   - a. ideal self
   - b. other self
   - c. actual self
   - d. ought self

2. Kaitlin believes that she is outgoing and fun to be around. This belief is most likely to change under which of the following conditions?
   - a. She takes a college class in psychology.
   - b. She leaves college to take a job in another state.
   - c. Her parents suggest that she is actually quite shy.
   - d. She reads a book that suggests that shy people are seen as attractive by others.

3. Which of the following sources influences the development of one's self-concept?
   - a. one's own observations
   - b. feedback from others
   - c. cultural guidelines
   - d. all of the above

4. If you want to improve your academic performance, which of the following reference groups would you be likely to compare yourself to?
   - a. students who get higher grades than you
   - b. students who get lower grades than you
   - c. students who get grades that are similar to yours
   - d. people with good jobs who were successful as students

5. People with an independent view of the self are most likely to engage in which of the following behaviors?
   - a. see themselves as responsible for group failures
   - b. place great importance on social duties and obligations
   - c. claim more than their share of credit for group successes
   - d. adjust themselves to the needs of the groups to which they belong

6. A critical childhood determinant of self-esteem appears to be the parents'
   - a. genetic makeup
   - b. use of disciplinary techniques
   - c. conditional love for the child
   - d. approach to acceptance and control

7. Research has shown that academic self-esteem is boosted by being a
   - a. "small fish in a big pond"
   - b. "big fish in a small pond"
   - c. "fish out of water"
   - d. "fish in an aquarium"

8. The "cocktail party effect" (the ability to pick out one's name in a roomful of chattering people) illustrates the concept of
   - a. internal attribution
   - b. external attribution
   - c. selective attention
   - d. controlled processing

9. Suppose you explain your good grade on a psychology test by the fact that you studied particularly hard. This explanation is an example of a(n) _____ attribution.
   - a. stable internal
   - b. stable external
   - c. unstable internal
   - d. unstable external

10. According to Martin Seligman, people with a pessimistic explanatory style tend to attribute their setbacks to which of the following combinations of factors?
    a. internal, stable, and global
    b. internal, unstable, and specific
    c. external, stable, and global
    d. external, unstable, and specific

11. The tendency to maintain positive feelings about the self is called
    a. self-complexity
    b. self-attribution
    c. self-enhancement
    d. self-verification

12. Psychologists have found that when people are threatened, they frequently choose to compare themselves to someone who is
    a. in similar circumstances
    b. worse off than they are
    c. better off than they are
    d. a member of their immediate family

13. The self-serving bias is the tendency to attribute one's successes to _____ factors and one's failures to _____ factors.
    a. external; stable
    b. stable; unstable
    c. situational; personal
    d. personal; situational

14. The notion of "basking in reflected glory" is most closely associated with which of the following researchers?
    a. Robert Cialdini
    b. Albert Bandura
    c. Erik Erikson
    d. Roy Baumeister

15. A person who says, "I probably won't play very well because my ankle hurts," just before the beginning of a tennis match is engaging in which of the following?
    a. ingratiation
    b. self-monitoring
    c. self-handicapping
    d. basking in reflected glory

16. Research has demonstrated that self-efficacy is related to all but which of the following?
    a. career choice
    b. academic success
    c. job performance
    d. marital satisfaction

17. Your textbook suggests that parents, teachers, and coaches should set high but attainable goals for children, encourage them to learn from their mistakes, and inspire them to persevere until they succeed. This advice is most closely associated with which of the following sources of self-efficacy?
    a. mastery experiences
    b. vicarious experiences
    c. persuasion and encouragement
    d. interpretation of emotional arousal

18. Which of the following statements concerning the presentation of a public self is not true?
    a. Everyone presents a public self.
    b. Your public self is based on how you see yourself.
    c. It is perfectly normal to present a public self.
    d. Typically, individuals have a number of public selves.

19. Doing favors for others in order to get them to like you is a form of
    a. ingratiation
    b. self-monitoring
    c. self-handicapping
    d. basking in reflected glory

20. Which of the following is not good advice for building self-esteem?
    a. Emphasize your strengths.
    b. Don't let others set your goals.
    c. Always compare yourself to the best.
    d. Recognize and eliminate negative self-talk.

*True/False Items*

T/F     1.   According to your textbook, everyone experiences self-discrepancies.

T/F     2.   The finding that a close partner's support and affirmation can bring a loved one's actual self-views and behavior more in line with his or her ideal self has been called the Michelangelo phenomenon.

T/F     3.   Members of minority groups generally have lower self-esteem than members of the dominant majority group.

T/F     4.   People tend to erase past memories that conflict with present behavior.

T/F     5.   When people feel threatened, they frequently choose to compare themselves with someone who is better off than they are.

T/F     6.   Self-handicapping usually occurs after the outcome of a task is known.

T/F     7.   Self-regulation seems to develop early and remain stable.

T/F     8.   It's possible for a person to have high self-efficacy in one area (e.g., making friends) and low self-efficacy in another area (e.g., athletics).

T/F     9.   Impression management is generally an unconscious process whereby we try to influence how others think of us.

T/F     10.  All self-presentation strategies carry risks.

T/F     11.  In building your self-esteem, it's best to let others help set your goals.

T/F     12.  In building self-esteem, a good strategy is to downplay your accomplishments and recognize your shortcomings.

# ANSWER KEY FOR SELF-TEST ITEMS

## *Multiple Choice Items*

b     1.     Because the question deals with *self*-perception, the term "other self" (whatever *that* might mean) isn't relevant. (141)

b     2.     Individuals' beliefs about themselves seem to be most susceptible to change when they shift from an important and familiar social setting to an unfamiliar one. (141)

d     3.     Your textbook discusses all three of these influences on the development of self-concept. (143)

a     4.     If you want to improve in some way, it's a good idea to use a reference group that is at a higher level than you, because this gives you something to strive for. (143)

c     5.     This is one way these individuals can "look out for number one." The other three alternatives are associated with individuals who have an *interdependent* view of the self. (145)

d     6.     Diana Baumrind identified four distinct parenting styles as interactions between the two dimensions of acceptance and control. These interactions (e.g., high acceptance, high control) seem to have a marked influence on children's self-esteem. (149)

b     7.     In one study, children in low-quality schools tended to display greater academic self-esteem than children of similar academic ability enrolled in high-quality schools. (151)

c     8.     Selective attention is one way cognitive resources can be protected. According to this notion, high priority is given to information pertaining to the self. (152)

c     9.     It's unstable because your study habits are variable and subject to change, and it's internal because it has to do with your own dispositions and abilities. (153)

a     10.     These attributions make them feel bad about themselves and pessimistic about their ability to handle future challenges. (154)

c     11.     This strategy is consistent with the notion that self-perceptions tend to be biased in the positive direction. (155)

b     12.     This defensive strategy is called downward social comparison. (155)

d     13.     Self-serving bias is one of several cognitive strategies used for self-enhancement. (156)

a     14.     Basking in reflected glory, which is the tendency to enhance one's image by publicly announcing one's association with successful individuals, is a concept proposed by Robert Cialdini and his colleagues. (157)

c     15.     The idea of self-handicapping is to have a ready-made excuse for failure, should it occur. (157)

d     16.     According to your textbook, self-efficacy is related to all of these except marital satisfaction. (159)

a     17.     This approach provides the mastery experiences children need to build self-efficacy and will enable them to approach future challenges with confidence. (159)

b      18.   Your public self involves how you want *others* to see you; self-concept deals with how you see yourself. (162)

a      19.   Through the use of ingratiation, people hope to receive favorable evaluations from others. (163)

c      20.   This is definitely *not* good advice for building self-esteem.  If you consistently compare yourself to the best, you will generally be disappointed, thus undermining your self-esteem. (166)

### True/False Items

True    1.    Although everyone does experience self-discrepancies, most people still manage to feel good about themselves. (141)

True    2.    Researchers have used this term to reflect the partner's role in "sculpting" into reality the ideal self of a loved one. (145)

False   3.    Although this has generally been assumed, there is a good deal of evidence to the contrary. (151)

True    4.    This tendency, called "self-verification," is a function of the desire to maintain a consistent self-image. (154)

False   5.    In fact, in this situation people will generally compare themselves to someone who is worse off in order to maintain their self-esteem.  This strategy is called downward social comparison. (155)

False   6.    Self-handicapping is used *before* an outcome is known.  That way, the person has a ready-made excuse for failure, should it occur. (157)

True    7.    One study found that 4-year-olds who were better at delaying gratification did better both in terms of academic performance and social competence some 10 years later. (158)

True    8.    According to Albert Bandura, efficacy beliefs vary according to one's skills. (158-159)

False   9.    Impression management strategies are usually *conscious*. (163)

True    10.   For example, if you use ingratiation, you may be viewed as a "boot-licker," or conformist.  This is why it's important to use the strategies skillfully if you want to make a good impression. (163)

False   11.   It's important to make your own decisions about what you will do and what you will believe in. (165)

False   12.   Although you should accept your shortcomings, it's a good idea to emphasize your strengths. (167)

# Chapter 6
# SOCIAL THINKING AND SOCIAL INFLUENCE

## PROGRAMMED REVIEW

**1. Cite the five sources of information people use to form impressions of others.**

are

1-1. Physical features such as height, weight, skin color, and hair color (are/are not) frequently used to form impressions of others. (172)

content

1-2. In using verbal behavior to form impressions, people generally focus on the (content/intensity/tone) of conversations for information about others. (172)

behavior

1-3. Because people don't always tell the truth, one must rely heavily on their (behavior/hair color/friends) to provide insights about them. (172)

nonverbal

1-4. A key source of information about others is _____ communication: facial expressions, eye contact, body language, and gestures. (172)

situational

1-5. Without (nonverbal/situational) cues, it would be hard to know whether a crying person is happy or sad. (172)

**2. Describe the key differences between snap judgements and systematic judgements**

Snap

2-1. (Snap/Systematic) judgements about others are those made quickly and on the basis of only a few bits of information and preconceived notions. (172)

systematic

2-2. In forming impressions of those who can affect their welfare and happiness, people tend to make (snap/systematic) judgements. (173)

**3. Define attributions and explain when people are likely to make them.**

causes

3-1. Attributions are inferences that people draw about the (causes/effects) of their own behavior, others' behavior, and events. (173)

internal

3-2. When people ascribe the causes of someone's behavior to personal dispositions, traits, abilities, or feelings, they are making (internal/external) attributions. (173)

external

3-3. When people attribute the causes of a person's behavior to situational demands and environmental constraints, they are making (internal/external) attributions. (173)

unexpected

3-4. People are most likely to make attributions when others behave in (expected/unexpected) ways. (174)

relevant

3-5. People are most likely to make attributions when events are personally (relevant/irrelevant). (174)

**4.    *Describe two expectancies that can distort observers' perceptions.***

confirmation

4-1.    The tendency to behave toward others in ways that confirm your expectations about them is termed (confirmation/self-fulfilling/self-serving) bias. (155)

less;
more

4-2.    When people have a high need for accuracy in their impression of someone, they are (more/less) likely to engage in selective questioning and (more/less) likely to ask diagnostic questions. (174)

fulfilling

4-3.    The process whereby expectations about a person cause the person to behave in ways that confirm the expectations is termed the self- (fulfilling/ confirming/reflective) prophecy. (175)

less

4-4.    Self-fulfilling prophecies are (more/less) likely to operate if perceivers are motivated to form accurate impressions of others. (175)

less

4-5.    When target persons are confident about their self-views, they are (more/ less) likely to be influenced by a perceiver with different perceptions. (176)

**5.    *Describe four important cognitive distortions and how they operate.***

ingroup; outgroup

5-1.    Individuals perceive individuals similar to themselves to be members of the (ingroup/outgroup) and those who are dissimilar to be in the (ingroup/ outgroup). (176)

homogeneity

5-2.    The tendency to explain the behavior of outgroup members on the basis of the characteristic that sets them apart but attribute the same behavior by an ingroup member to individual personality traits is known as the outgroup (homogeneity/heterogeneity/attribution) effect. (176)

Stereotypes

5-3.    _____ are widely held beliefs that people have certain characteristics because of their membership in a particular group. (176)

do

5-4.    Attractive people (do/do not) have an advantage in the social arena. (176)

functional

5-5.    Stereotypes are considered cognitively (functional/dysfunctional). (177)

personal;
situational

5-6.    The fundamental attribution error refers to the tendency to explain other people's behavior as the result of (personal/situational), rather than (personal/situational), factors. (177)

actual

5-7.    The fundamental attribution error is different from stereotyping in that inferences are based on (actual/predicted) behavior. (177)

defensive

5-8.    The tendency to blame victims for their misfortune, so that one feels less likely to be victimized in a similar way, is called (defensive/fundamental/ stereotypic) attribution. (178)

**6.    *Describe some ways in which perceptions of others are efficient, selective, and consistent.***

| | | |
|---|---|---|
| little | 6-1. | In forming impressions of others, people prefer to exert as (much/little) effort as is necessary. (179) |
| fits | 6-2. | Especially if someone's behavior is ambiguous, people are likely to interpret what they see in a way that (fits/does not fit) their expectations. (180) |
| primacy | 6-3. | A (primacy/recency) effect occurs when initial information carries more weight than subsequent information. (180) |
| comparable to | 6-4. | In one study, researchers found that the accuracy of Web-based impressions was (less than/greater than/comparable to) the accuracy of impressions based on face-to-face encounters. (180) |
| subjective | 6-5. | The process of person perception is (objective/subjective). (180) |

**7.    *Explain how "old-fashioned" and modern discrimination differ.***

| | | |
|---|---|---|
| Prejudice | 7-1. | _____ is a negative attitude toward members of a group. (181) |
| Discrimination | 7-2. | _____ involves behaving differently, usually unfairly, toward the members of a group. (181) |
| diminished | 7-3. | Over the past 40 years, prejudice and discrimination against minority groups have (increased/diminished) in the United States. (181) |
| modern | 7-4. | A new, more subtle form of discrimination has emerged, called (homogeneous/modern/old-fashioned) discrimination. (181) |
| Modern | 7-5. | (Old-fashioned/Modern) discrimination is operating when people endorse equality as an abstract principle but oppose concrete programs intended to promote equality on the grounds that discrimination against minority groups no longer exists. (181) |

**8.    *Describe some of the key determinants of prejudice and explain how they work.***

| | | |
|---|---|---|
| authoritarian | 8-1. | The (authoritarian/authoritative/permissive) personality type is characterized by prejudice toward any group perceived to be different from oneself. (182) |
| conservatives | 8-2. | Right-wing authoritarianism (RWA) is commonly found among political (conservatives/liberals). (182) |
| fundamental | 8-3. | It seems that people are particularly likely to make the (defensive/fundamental/protective) attribution error when evaluating targets of prejudice. (183) |
| more | 8-4. | People are (more/less) likely to recall behavior that confirms their stereotypes than information that is inconsistent with their beliefs. (183) |
| more | 8-5. | The perception of threat to one's ingroup is (more/less) likely to cause hostility between groups than are actual threats to the ingroup. (183) |

| | | |
|---|---|---|
| ingroup | 8-6. | The most common response when collective self-esteem is threatened is to show (ingroup/outgroup) favoritism. (184) |
| derogation | 8-7. | Another way to deal with threats to social identity is to engage in outgroup (attribution/derogation/identification). (184) |

**9.    Describe the operation of several strategies for reducing prejudice.**

| | | |
|---|---|---|
| automatic; controlled | 9-1. | According to Patricia Devine's model of prejudice reduction, people can intentionally inhibit their prejudicial thoughts by shifting from (automatic/ controlled) processing to (automatic/controlled) processing. (184) |
| supports | 9-2. | Research (supports/does not support) the idea that controlled, mindful thinking can reduce stereotyping and prejudice. (184) |
| Superordinate | 9-3. | (Homogeneous/Stereotypic/Superordinate) goals are those that require two or more groups to work together to achieve mutual ends. (185) |
| contact | 9-4. | Research has clearly supported intergroup (competition/contact) as a means of reducing prejudice. (185) |

**10.    Cite the key elements in the persuasion process.**

| | | |
|---|---|---|
| attitudes | 10-1. | Persuasion involves the communication of arguments and information intended to change another person's (attitudes/beliefs/feelings). (185) |
| source; receiver | 10-2. | The (channel/source/receiver) is the person who sends a persuasive communication, and the (channel/source/receiver) is the person to whom the message is sent. (186) |
| channel | 10-3. | The medium through which a message is sent (e.g., mass media, face-to-face) is called the (channel/network/target). (186) |

**11.    Describe several source factors that influence persuasion.**

| | | |
|---|---|---|
| credibility | 11-1. | Persuasion tends to be more successful when the source has high (status/ credibility/standards). (186) |
| enhanced | 11-2. | Trustworthiness is (diminished/enhanced) when people appear to argue against their own interests. (186-187) |
| similar | 11-3. | People tend to respond better to sources that are (similar/dissimilar) in relevant ways. (187) |

**12.    Discuss the evidence on one-sided versus two-sided messages, and the value of arousing fear or positive feelings in persuasion.**

| | | |
|---|---|---|
| Two-sided | 12-1. | (One-sided/Two-sided) arguments are generally more effective. (187) |
| increases | 12-2. | Studies have shown that the arousal of fear often (increases/decreases) persuasion. (187) |

| | |
|---|---|
| is | 12-3.  Generating positive feelings (is/is not) an effective way to persuade people. (187) |

**13.    Describe several receiver factors that influence persuasion.**

| | |
|---|---|
| more | 13-1.  Transient factors, such as forewarning the receiver about a persuasive effort and the receiver's initial position on an issue, seem to be (more/less) influential than the receiver's personality. (188) |
| harder | 13-2.  Receivers are (harder/easier) to persuade when they encounter a position that is incompatible with their existing beliefs. (188) |
| different | 13-3.  People from different cultures respond to (similar/different) themes in persuasive messages. (188) |

**14.    Explain how the two cognitive routes to persuasion operate.**

| | |
|---|---|
| more | 14-1.  According to the elaboration likelihood model, an individual's thoughts about a persuasive message are (more/less) important than the message itself in determining whether attitude change will occur. (188) |
| peripheral | 14-2.  Persuasion usually occurs via the (central/peripheral) route. (188) |
| central | 14-3.  When persuasion occurs via the (central/peripheral) route, the receiver processes the message mindfully, by thinking about the important details of the message. (188-189) |
| central | 14-4.  Attitudes formed via the (central/peripheral) route are longer lasting and more resistant to change. (188) |

**15.    Summarize what Asch discovered about conformity.**

| | |
|---|---|
| social | 15-1.  Conformity occurs when people yield to real or imagined (emotional/private/social) pressure. (190) |
| 25;<br>75 | 15-2.  In Asch's first study, (25/50/75) percent of the participants never caved in to the group, and (25/50/75) percent conformed on at least one trial. (190) |
| increases | 15-3.  From subsequent studies, Asch concluded that as group size increases, conformity (increases/decreases) –up to a point. (190) |
| public;<br>private | 15-4.  Compliance occurs when people yield to social pressure in their (public/private) behavior, even though their (public/private) beliefs have not changed. (191) |

**16.    Discuss the difference between normative and informational influence.**

| | |
|---|---|
| Normative | 16-1.  _____ influence operates when people conform to social norms for fear of negative social consequences. (191) |

Informational

16-2.    _____ influence operates when people look to others for how to behave in ambiguous situations. (191)

**17.    Describe some conformity pressures in everyday life and how people can resist them.**

less

17-1.    The bystander effect is the tendency for individuals to be (more/less) likely to provide help when others are present than when they are alone. (192)

more

17-2.    One suggestion for resisting various conformity pressures is to make an effort to pay (more/less) attention to the social forces operating on you. (192)

match

17-3.    Another suggestion for resisting conformity pressures is if you find yourself in a situation where others are pressuring you, try to identify someone in the group whose views (match/are different from) yours. (192)

**18.    Describe some situational and personality factors involved in obedience to authority.**

compliance

18-1.    Obedience is a form of (attribution/compliance/conformity) that occurs when people follow direct commands, usually from someone in a position of authority. (192)

more

18-2.    Stanley Milgram concluded that obedience to authority was (more/less) common than he or others had anticipated. (193)

authority figure

18-3.    Participants in Milgram's experiment were told that the (authority figure/ teacher) was responsible if anything happened to the learner. (193)

more

18-4.    People who score high on authoritarianism tend to be (more/less) submissive to people in authority. (193)

situation

18-5.    Taken together, the findings for Milgram's experiments suggest that human behavior is determined not so much by the kind of person one is as by the kind of (experiment/mood/situation) one is in. (193)

ethics

18-6.    Critics have questioned the (assumptions/ethics/rationale) of Milgram's procedure. (194)

**19.    Cite an important factor in resisting inappropriate demands of authority figures.**

support

19-1.    A key factor in disobedient behavior seems to be social (comparison/norms/ support). (194)

decrease; increase

19-2.    Especially when disobedience involves risk, aligning oneself with others can (increase/decrease) anxiety and (increase/decrease) safety. (194)

**20.    Describe how culture can affect people's responses to social influence.**

positively

20-1. East Asians view conformity and obedience more (positively/negatively) than either Americans or citizens of some other Western countries. (194)

lower

20-2. Conformity rates tend to be (higher/lower) in individualistic cultures than in collectivist cultures. (194)

consistent

20-3. Beliefs about the desirability of yielding to social influence and conformity behavior are (consistent/inconsistent) with cultural orientations (194)

**21.    Describe two compliance strategies based on the principles of commitment and consistency.**

small;
larger

21-1. The foot-in-the-door technique involves getting people to agree to a (large/small) request to increase the chances that they will agree to a (larger/smaller) request later. (195)

perception

21-2. The best explanation for the effectiveness of the foot-in-the-door technique is based on self-(esteem/help/perception) theory. (196)

lowball

21-3. Getting someone to commit to an attractive proposition before its hidden costs are revealed is called the (lowball/highball) technique. (196)

automobile

21-4. The name for the lowball technique derives from a common practice in (home/automobile/door-to-door) sales. (196)

effective

21-5. Lowballing is generally an (effective/ineffective) compliance strategy. (196)

**22.    Describe several compliance strategies based on the principle of reciprocity.**

reciprocity

22-1. The rule that one should pay back in kind what one receives from others is called the (actualization/payback/reciprocity) principle. (196)

large;
smaller

22-2. The door-in-the-face technique involves making a (large/small) request that is likely to be turned down in order to increase the chances that people will agree to a (larger/smaller) request later. (197)

fair

22-3. The reciprocity norm is meant to promote (fair/unfair) exchanges in social interactions. (197)

minimal;
more

22-4. When people manipulate the reciprocity rule, they usually give something of (maximum/minimal) value in the hopes of getting far (more/less) in return. (197)

**23.    Discuss how the principle of scarcity can increase a person's desire for something.**

hard;
easy

23-1. People have learned that items that are (easy/hard) to get are of better quality than items that are (easy/hard) to get. (197)

more

23-2. When people's choices (of products, services, romantic partners, etc.) are constrained in some way, the often want these items (more/less). (197)

## QUIZ BOXES

*KEY TERMS*

| | |
|---|---|
| **Person perception** | The process of forming impressions of others. |
| **Attributions** | Inferences that people draw about the causes of their own behavior, others' behavior, and events. |
| **Confirmation bias** | The tendency to behave toward others in ways that confirm your expectations about them. |
| **Self-fulfilling prophecy** | Occurs when expectations about a person cause the person to behave in ways that confirm the expectations. |
| **Stereotypes** | Widely held beliefs that people have certain characteristics because of their membership in a particular group. |
| **Fundamental attribution error** | The tendency to explain other people's behavior as the result of personal, rather than situational, factors. |
| **Defensive attribution** | The tendency to blame victims for their misfortune, so that one feels less likely to be victimized in a similar way. |
| **Primacy effect** | Occurs when initial information carries more weight than subsequent information. |
| **Prejudice** | A negative attitude toward members of a group. |
| **Discrimination** | Behaving differently, usually unfairly, toward the members of a group. |
| **Superordinate goals** | Goals that require two or more groups to work together to achieve mutual ends. |
| **Persuasion** | The communication of arguments and information intended to change another person's attitudes. |
| **Attitudes** | Beliefs and feelings about people, objects, and ideas. |
| **Source** | The person who sends a communication. |
| **Receiver** | The person to whom the message is sent. |
| **Message** | The information transmitted by the source. |

| Channel | The medium through which the message is sent. |
|---|---|
| Elaboration likelihood model | Suggests that an individual's thoughts about a persuasive message (rather than the actual message itself) determine whether attitude change will occur. |
| Conformity | Occurs when people yield to real or imagined social pressure. |
| Compliance | Occurs when people yield to social pressure in their public behavior, even though their private beliefs have not changed. |
| Normative influence | Operates when people conform to social norms for fear of negative consequences. |
| Informational influence | Operates when people look to others for how to behave in ambiguous situations. |
| Bystander effect | The tendency for individuals to be less likely to provide help when others are present than when they are alone. |
| Obedience | A form of compliance that occurs when people follow direct commands, usually from someone in a position of authority. |
| Foot-in-the-door technique | Involves getting people to agree to a small request to increase the chances that they will agree to a larger request later. |
| Lowball technique | Involves getting someone to commit to an attractive proposition before its hidden costs are revealed. |
| Reciprocity principle | The rule that one should pay back in kind what one receives from others. |
| Door-in-the-face technique | Involves making a large request that is likely to be turned down in order to increase the chances that people will agree to a smaller request later. |

## KEY PEOPLE

| Solomon Asch | Conducted classic studies of conformity/compliance. |
|---|---|
| Robert Cialdini | Studied social influence tactics used by salespeople and others; wrote the book *Influence: Science and Practice*, which discusses social influence principles in action. |

| Susan Fiske | Discussed the role of snap judgements in person perception. |
|---|---|
| Stanley Milgram | Conducted classic and controversial studies of obedience to authority. |
| Richard Petty and John Cacioppo | Proposed the elaboration likelihood model, which suggests that there are two possible routes for persuasion: the peripheral route and the central route. |
| Muzafer Sherif | Conducted classic study at Robber's Cave State Park in Oklahoma that demonstrated the effects of competition on prejudice. |

# SELF-TEST

## Multiple Choice Items

1.  Which of the following is not one of the key sources of information about other people that we use in the process of person perception?
    a.   appearance
    b.   verbal behavior
    c.   nonverbal messages
    d.   all of the above are key sources

2.  In forming impressions of those who can affect our welfare and happiness, we tend to make _____ judgements.
    a.   snap
    b.   primacy
    c.   systematic
    d.   attributional

3.  Which of the following statements about the attribution process is accurate?
    a.   Our perceptions of others tend to be bias-free.
    b.   We make attributions about everyone we meet.
    c.   The process is sometimes illogical and unsystematic.
    d.   The attributions we make don't have much impact on our everyday social interactions.

4.  Which of the following terms does not belong with the others?
    a.   Pygmalion effect
    b.   self-fulfilling prophecy
    c.   behavioral confirmation
    d.   defensive attribution

5.  The best-known experiments on self-fulfilling prophecy have been conducted in which of the following settings?
    a.   subway stations
    b.   classrooms
    c.   laboratories
    d.   fast-food restaurants

6.  In America, stereotypes are most likely to be based on which of the following?
    a.   gender
    b.   occupation
    c.   height
    d.   athletic ability

7.  Attractive people are most likely to have an advantage in which of the following types of situations?
    a.   social
    b.   academic
    c.   work-related
    d.   sports-related

8.  The fundamental attribution error is the tendency to explain other people's behavior as the result of _____, rather than _____, factors.
    a.   external; fundamental
    b.   fundamental; personal
    c.   personal; situational
    d.   situational; personal

9.  The term "defensive attribution" is synonymous with which of the following?
    a.   modern racism
    b.   blaming the victim
    c.   the self-fulfilling prophecy
    d.   the fundamental attribution error

10. Which of the following is not one of the recurrent themes in the process of person perception?
    a.   consistency
    b.   efficiency
    c.   ambiguity
    d.   selectivity

11. In general, first impressions of other people tend to be particularly potent.  This finding is most closely associated with which of the following effects?
    a.   primacy
    b.   stereotype
    c.   group homogeneity
    d.   self-fulfilling prophecy

12. Which of the following statements about prejudice and discrimination is <u>false</u>?
   a. Prejudice can occur without discrimination.
   b. Discrimination can occur without prejudice.
   c. Over the past 40 years, prejudice and discrimination against minority groups have diminished.
   d. The distinction between blatant and subtle discrimination is a uniquely American phenomenon.

13. Which of the following statements regarding right-wing authoritarianism (RWA) is <u>false</u>?
   a. RWA is characterized by exaggerated deference to those in power.
   b. RWA is commonly found among those who hold politically liberal views.
   c. RWA is associated with strong adherence to values endorsed by authorities.
   d. RWA is correlated with prejudice and discrimination toward minority groups.

14. Which of the following characteristics of a source of a persuasive message is <u>least</u> likely to be effective?
   a. likable                          c. trustworthy
   b. credible                         d. controversial

15. A one-sided argument is most likely to be effective when the audience is
   a. mostly college students          c. uneducated about the issue
   b. just returning from lunch        d. very curious about the message

16. _____ occurs when people yield to social pressure in their public behavior, even though their private beliefs have not changed.
   a. Conformity                       c. Obedience
   b. Compliance                       d. Attribution

17. Employees often follow their boss's instructions even when they believe the instructions don't make sense. This example illustrates the concept of
   a. selective attention              c. normative influence
   b. fundamental attribution          d. informational influence

18. Obedience is generally considered a form of
   a. conformity                       c. reciprocity
   b. compliance                       d. attribution

19. The foot-in-the-door technique involves getting people to agree to a _____ request to increase the chances that they will agree to a _____ request later.
   a. large; larger                    c. small; smaller
   b. large; smaller                   d. small; larger

20. A fast-food restaurant that advertises its "Mammoth Burger" as being available for "a limited time only" is making use of which of the following social influence tactics?
   a. scarcity                         c. the lowball technique
   b. reciprocity                      d. observational learning

## True/False Items

T/F   1. In forming impressions of others, people generally prefer to take their time and consider all information carefully.

T/F   2. Attributions spouses make to explain each other's behavior can affect their marital satisfaction.

T/F     3.  When people are perceived as unique or distinctive, they tend to be seen as having more influence in a group.

T/F     4.  Physically attractive people are generally more intelligent and happier than others.

T/F     5.  The fundamental attribution error involves the tendency to explain other people's behavior as the result of situational, rather than personal, factors.

T/F     6.  In individualistic cultures, it is generally assumed that people are responsible for their actions.

T/F     7.  It is possible for prejudice to occur in the absence of discrimination.

T/F     8.  Prejudice and discrimination against minority groups have diminished in the past 40 years.

T/F     9.  In general, one-sided arguments are more effective than two-sided arguments in persuading others.

T/F     10. Knowing ahead of time about a person's intention to try to persuade you will probably make you less likely to be persuaded.

T/F     11. The terms conformity and compliance are synonymous.

T/F     12. In general, lowballing is not a very effective strategy of social influence.

# ANSWER KEY FOR SELF-TEST ITEMS

*Multiple Choice Items*

| | | |
|---|---|---|
| d | 1. | In addition to actions and situational cues, all of these are important sources of information in our perceptions of others. (172) |
| c | 2. | We want our impressions to be as accurate as possible in these situations, so we tend to take more care in our assessments of others. (173) |
| c | 3. | Snap judgements provide a good example of illogical and unsystematic attributions. The rest of these statements are false. (174) |
| d | 4. | The other three terms are synonymous with the notion that expectations about a person can cause that person to behave in ways that confirm the expectations. (174-175) |
| b | 5. | Many studies have been done examining the effect of teachers' expectations on students' academic performance. The findings generally support the idea of the self-fulfilling prophecy. (175) |
| a | 6. | Although it's possible to form stereotypes based on any of these variables, the most prevalent stereotypes in America are those based on gender, age, and ethnicity. (176) |
| a | 7. | Attractive people seem to have better social skills and they are less socially anxious than others. (176) |
| c | 8. | This is why the fundamental attribution error leads people to leap to conclusions about others' personal qualities. (177) |
| b | 9. | Blaming victims for their misfortunes helps people believe that they won't encounter similar problems. (178) |
| c | 10. | Although there may be an element of ambiguity in person perception, it is not one of the recurrent themes discussed in your textbook. (179-180) |
| a | 11. | The primacy effect occurs when initial information carries more weight than subsequent information. (180) |
| d | 12. | The distinction between blatant and subtle discrimination has been found in European countries, as well as in the United States. (181) |
| b | 13. | Actually, RWA is commonly found among political conservatives as opposed to members of the political left (who are more likely to challenge the status quo). (182) |
| d | 14. | Because all the other characteristics are clearly positive, this should have been a fairly easy choice to make. (186-187) |
| c | 15. | This is one of only a couple of situations in which a one-sided argument will be effective. Another situation that applies is when audience members already favor your view. (187) |
| b | 16. | As opposed to true conformity, in compliance people's private beliefs don't change. So Asch's studies were actually measuring compliance rather than conformity. (191) |
| c | 17. | The principle of normative influence suggests that people will conform to social norms (e.g., following their boss's instructions) for fear of negative social consequences. (191) |

| | | |
|---|---|---|
| b | 18. | Obedience is a form of compliance that occurs when people follow direct commands, usually from someone in a position of authority. (192) |
| d | 19. | Salespeople have long recognized the importance of gaining a little cooperation from potential customers before hitting them with the real sales pitch. (195) |
| a | 20. | Advertisers frequently use scarcity to drive up the demand for their products.  The idea is that if people believe they won't be able to purchase the product after a certain period of time, they will want the product even more. (197) |

### True/False Items

| | | |
|---|---|---|
| False | 1. | Depending on the situation, people may make snap judgements about others. (172-173) |
| True | 2. | This is one way attributions people make about others can impact our everyday social interactions. (174) |
| True | 3. | This phenomenon occurs as a result of categorizing people on the basis of race, gender, age, and so forth. (176) |
| False | 4. | Although attractive people tend to be viewed this way, there is no evidence that they are any different from others when it comes to intelligence, happiness, mental health, or self-esteem. (176) |
| False | 5. | In fact, it's the other way around.  That is, we tend to explain others' behavior in terms of personal, rather than situational, factors. (177) |
| True | 6. | This is because interdependence is valued in individualistic cultures.  In collectivist societies, conformity and obedience to group norms are valued, so it is assumed that one's behavior reflects adherence to group norms. (178) |
| True | 7. | For example, a restaurant owner may be prejudiced against Asian Americans and yet treat them like anyone else because he needs their business. (181) |
| True | 8. | Although this is *technically* true, the bad news is that a more subtle form of prejudice and discrimination has emerged, which has been called "modern discrimination." (181) |
| False | 9. | In general, two-sided arguments tend to be more effective. (187) |
| True | 10. | To some extent forewarning tends to reduce the impact of persuasive arguments. (188) |
| False | 11. | Conformity involves an *actual* change in belief or attitude, whereas compliance is a public change in behavior in the absence of any change in private beliefs. (190-191) |
| False | 12. | Actually, lowballing is a surprisingly effective strategy. (196) |

# Chapter 7
# INTERPERSONAL COMMUNICATION

## PROGRAMMED REVIEW

**1. List and explain the six components of the communication process.**

Interpersonal

1-1. (Bilingual/Interpersonal/Intrapersonal) communication is an interactional process whereby one person sends a message to another. (202)

sender

1-2. The (receiver/sender) is the person who initiates the message. (202)

receiver

1-3. The (receiver/sender) is the person to whom the message is targeted. (202)

message

1-4. The (channel/message/noise) is the content of the communication. (202)

language

1-5. The primary means of sending messages is (facial expressions/gestures/language). (202)

channel

1-6. The (channel/modem/noise) refers to the sensory channel through which the message reaches the receiver. (202)

noise

1-7. Any stimulus that interferes with accurately expressing or understanding a message is termed (context/content/noise). (203)

different

1-8. The cultural context of communication is especially important in the United States because of the varieties of subcultures, many with (similar/different) rules of communication. (203)

**2. List several important differences between face-to-face and computer-mediated communication.**

short

2-1. One guideline for the use of cell phones is to make (long/short) calls. (203)

unobtrusively

2-2. Another guideline for the use of cell phones is to make and receive calls (obtrusively/unobtrusively). (203)

nonverbal

2-3. One of the drawbacks of computer-mediated communication is the lack of (verbal/nonverbal) cues. (204)

**3. Discuss how interpersonal communication is important to adjustment.**

good;
poor

3-1. Research has shown that (good/poor) communication can enhance satisfaction in relationships and that (good/poor) communication ranks high as a cause of break-ups among both gay and straight couples. (204)

**4. List five general principles of nonverbal communication.**

nonverbal

4-1. The transmission of meaning from one person to another through means or symbols other than words is called (symbolic/verbal/nonverbal) communication. (205)

| | | |
|---|---|---|
| channels | 4-2. | Nonverbal communication typically involves simultaneous messages sent through a number of (channels/people/time zones). (206) |
| Few | 4-3. | (Many/Few) nonverbal signals carry universally accepted meanings. (206) |
| feelings | 4-4. | People often communicate their (feelings/intentions/thoughts) without saying a word. (206) |
| nonverbal | 4-5. | Research shows that when someone is instructed to tell a lie, deception is most readily detected through (verbal/nonverbal) signals. (206) |
| different | 4-6. | Nonverbal signals are (similar/different) in different cultures. (206) |

**5.  Define proxemics and discuss personal space.**

| | | |
|---|---|---|
| Proxemics | 5-1. | _____ is the study of people's use of interpersonal space. (206) |
| personal | 5-2. | A zone of space surrounding a person that is felt to "belong" to that person is called (inner/personal/territorial) space. (206) |
| norms | 5-3. | The appropriate distance between people is regulated by social (laws/norms/status). (207) |
| smaller | 5-4. | Women seem to have (larger/smaller) personal-space zones than men do. (207) |
| closer together | 5-5. | People of similar status tend to stand (closer together/farther apart) than people whose status is unequal. (207) |

**6.  Discuss display rules and what can be discerned from facial cues.**

| | | |
|---|---|---|
| six | 6-1. | Paul Ekman and Walter Friesen have identified (six/ten/twenty) distinctive facial expressions that correspond with basic emotions. (207) |
| do | 6-2. | Recent research indicates that individuals (do/do not) accurately recognize emotions in photographs of people from other cultures. (208) |
| display | 6-3. | Norms that govern the appropriate display of emotions are called (display/expression/facial) rules. (208) |
| is | 6-4. | It (is/is not) possible to deliberately deceive others through facial expressions. (208) |
| less | 6-5. | Men typically show (more/less) facial expression than women do. (208) |

**7.  Summarize the characteristics associated with effective eye contact.**

| | | |
|---|---|---|
| gaze | 7-1. | A major channel of nonverbal communication is eye contact, also called mutual (expression/gaze/staring). (208) |
| effective | 7-2. | Among European Americans, people who engage in high levels of eye contact are usually judged to have (effective/ineffective) social skills. (208) |

| | | |
|---|---|---|
| higher | 7-3. | Speakers and interviewers generally receive (higher/lower) ratings of competence when they maintain high rather than low eye contact with their   audience. (208-209) |
| intensity | 7-4. | Gaze can communicate the (intensity/positivity/negativity) of feelings. (209) |
| uncomfortable | 7-5. | A steady gaze causes most people to feel (comfortable/uncomfortable). (209) |
| affects | 7-6. | Culture (affects/does not affect) patterns of eye contact. (209) |
| more | 7-7. | Women tend to gaze at others (more/less) than men do. (209) |

**8.    Describe the roles of body movement, posture, and gestures in communication.**

| | | |
|---|---|---|
| kinesics | 8-1. | The study of communication through body movements is called (kinesics/ physiometry/proxemics). (210) |
| positive | 8-2. | When people lean toward you, it typically indicates a (positive/negative) attitude. (210) |
| more | 8-3. | Generally, a higher-status person will look (more/less) relaxed. (210) |
| spoken words | 8-4. | People use hand gestures to describe and emphasize their (body movement/ posture/spoken words). (210) |

**9.    Summarize the research findings on touching and paralanguage.**

| | | |
|---|---|---|
| higher; lower | 9-1. | In the United States, it's more acceptable for (higher/lower)-status individuals to touch (higher/lower)-status individuals than vice versa. (210) |
| more | 9-2. | Findings from an observational study showed that female-female pairs touched each other significantly (more/less) than male-male pairs. (210) |
| more | 9-3. | In the workplace, touching is (more/less) likely to be perceived as sexual harassment by women than by men. (210) |
| how | 9-4. | Paralanguage refers to (how/when/why) something is said rather than what is said. (210) |
| content | 9-5. | Paralanguage includes all vocal cues other than the (content/intensity/ rhythm) of the verbal message. (210-211) |
| anger | 9-6. | Loud vocalization often indicates (anger/anxiety/uncertainty). (211) |
| rude | 9-7. | Using capital letters throughout an email message is generally considered to be (appropriate/rude/thoughtful). (211) |

**10.    Discuss the difficulty of detecting deception and the nonverbal cues linked to deception.**

| | |
|---|---|
| over | 10-1.    People generally (over/under)-estimate their ability to detect liars. (211) |
| higher | 10-2.    Liars tend to speak in a (higher/lower) pitch. (212) |
| is not | 10-3.    Lying (is/is not) associated with long pauses before speaking. (212) |
| is not | 10-4.    Lying (is/is not) associated with slow talking. (212) |
| nonverbal | 10-5.    Many of the clues that someone is lying "leak" from (verbal/nonverbal) channels. (212) |

**11.    Explain what polygraphs do and cite some problems with their use.**

| | |
|---|---|
| emotion | 11-1.    Although called a "lie detector," the polygraph is really a(n) (attitude/ emotion/truth) detector. (212) |
| physiological | 11-2.    The assumption underlying the use of the polygraph is that when subjects lie, they experience emotions that produce noticeable changes in (social/ physiological/psychological) indicators. (212) |
| is not | 11-3.    The research support for the validity of polygraph testing (is/is not) very impressive. (212) |
| Some people | 11-4.    (Virtually no one/Some people) can lie without experiencing physiological arousal. (212) |
| difficult | 11-5.    The nonverbal behaviors that accompany lying are subtle and (easy/difficult) to spot. (212) |

**12.    Describe the significance of nonverbal messages in interpersonal relationships.**

| | |
|---|---|
| positive; negative | 12-1.    Research findings suggest that people with negative self-concepts will attend to (positive/negative) verbal cues and disregard (positive/negative) nonverbal cues. (213) |
| better than | 12-2.    Some researchers have found that women are (better than/not as good as) men when it comes to "reading" nonverbal cues. (213) |
| does not support | 12-3.    Recent research (supports/does not support) the notion that people in subordinate roles are better at reading the nonverbal behaviors of those in dominant roles than vice versa. (213) |

**13.    List five suggestions for creating a positive interpersonal climate.**

| | |
|---|---|
| empathy | 13-1.    Adopting another's frame of reference so you can understand his or her point of view is called _____. (214) |
| judgemental | 13-2.    You can promote an open interpersonal climate by trying to be (judgemental/ nonjudgemental). (214) |
| honesty | 13-3.    Mutual trust and respect thrive on authenticity and (deceit/honesty). (214) |

| | | |
|---|---|---|
| equal | 13-4. | When you have the higher status, it helps to approach people on (equal/ your own) terms. (214) |
| tentatively | 13-5. | In creating a positive interpersonal climate, it's a good idea to express your opinions (clearly/forcibly/tentatively). (214) |

**14.    Give five steps involved in making small talk.**

| | | |
|---|---|---|
| skills | 14-1. | The art of conversation is based on conversational (skills/tone). (214) |
| nonverbal | 14-2. | One of the principles to consider in making conversation is to use (emotional/nonverbal/social) cues to communicate your interest in the other person. (215) |
| surroundings | 14-3. | One step in making successful small talk is to indicate that you are open to conversation by commenting on your (abilities/problems/surroundings). (215) |
| early | 14-4. | In making successful small talk, it's a good idea to introduce yourself (early/ late) in the conversation. (215) |
| can | 14-5. | In making successful small talk, a good strategy is to select a topic that others (can/cannot) relate to. (215) |
| elaborate on | 14-6. | The best way to keep the conversational ball rolling is to (switch from/ elaborate on) your initial topic. (215) |
| politely | 14-7. | In ending the conversation, it's a good idea to do so (abruptly/gradually/ politely). (215) |

**15.    Cite some ways to reduce the risks of self-disclosure.**

| | | |
|---|---|---|
| disclosure | 15-1. | The act of sharing information about yourself with another person is called _____. (215) |
| critically | 15-2. | Disclosing personal information is (critically/marginally/rarely) important to adjustment. (215) |
| positively | 15-3. | Self-disclosure in romantic relationships correlates (positively/negatively) with relationship satisfaction. (216) |
| gradual | 15-4. | In steering a conversation toward more intimate topics, it's a good idea to use the strategy of (gradual/immediate) self-disclosure. (216) |
| is | 15-5. | Self-disclosure (is/is not) usually reciprocated in depth and topic. (216) |
| nonverbal | 15-6. | When people are uncomfortable with your personal disclosures, they will usually send you a (verbal/nonverbal) message to that effect. (216) |
| less | 15-7. | Because of the relative anonymity of the Internet, self-disclosure in email and chat rooms involves (more/less) risk. (216) |

**16.    Describe the role of self-disclosure in relationship development.**

do not;
do

16-1. Factual self-disclosures (do/do not) lead to feelings of intimacy, but emotional self-disclosures (do/do not). (216)

High

16-2. (High/Low) levels of mutual disclosure occur at the beginning of a relationship. (217)

less

16-3. In established relationships, people are (more/less) likely to reciprocate disclosures. (217)

withdrawing

16-4. When relationships are in distress, one or both individuals may decrease the breadth and depth of their self-disclosures, indicating that they are emotionally (fixated/unstable/withdrawing). (217)

**17. Discuss cultural and gender differences in self-disclosure.**

individualistic

17-1. The notion that personal sharing is essential to close friendships and happy marriages is consistent with a(n) (collectivist/individualistic) culture. (217)

more

17-2. In the United States, it has been found that females generally tend to be (more/less) openly self-disclosing than males. (217)

less

17-3. In other-gender relationships, men who hold traditional gender-role attitudes are (more/less) likely to self-disclose. (217)

personal;
nonpersonal

17-4. In other-gender relationships, women share more (personal/nonpersonal) information, and men share more (personal/nonpersonal) information. (217)

more

17-5. In the beginning of an other-gender relationship, men often disclose (more/less) than women. (217)

**18. Cite four points good listeners need to keep in mind.**

nonverbal

18-1. To be a good listener, you need to communicate your interest in the speaker by using (verbal/nonverbal) cues. (218)

more

18-2. When a speaker has mannerisms the listener finds frustrating (e.g., mumbling, stuttering), the listener is (more/less) likely to interrupt. (218)

active

18-3. To be a good listener, you need to engage in (active/passive) listening. (218)

paraphrase

18-4. To _____ means to state concisely what you believe the speaker said. (218)

nonverbal

18-5. Another key point in being a good listener is to pay attention to the other person's (verbal/nonverbal) signals. (218)

**19. Discuss four responses to communication apprehension.**

talk

19-1. Communication apprehension is defined as the anxiety caused by having to (meet/socialize/talk) with others. (219)

| | | |
|---|---|---|
| avoidance | 19-2. | The most common response to communication apprehension is (aggression/avoidance/breakdown). (219-220) |
| withdrawal | 19-3. | When people unexpectedly find themselves trapped in a communication situation that they can't escape, (disruption/reactance/withdrawal) is likely to occur. (220) |
| Disruption | 19-4. | (Disruption/Engagement/Withdrawal) involves the inability to make fluent oral presentations. (220) |
| overcommuni-cation | 19-5. | People who attempt to dominate social situations by talking nonstop are exhibiting (disruption/overcommunication/withdrawal). (220) |

**20.    Describe five barriers to effective communication.**

| | | |
|---|---|---|
| defensiveness | 20-1. | Perhaps the most basic barrier to effective communication is _____, an excessive concern with protecting oneself from being hurt. (220) |
| feel | 20-2. | The tendency to distort information occurs most often when people are discussing issues they (feel/don't feel) strongly about. (220) |
| negative | 20-3. | Self-preoccupied people tend to arouse (positive/negative) reactions in others. (220) |
| communication | 20-4. | Transactional analysis is a theory of personality and interpersonal relations that emphasizes patterns of (communication/sexual behavior/social behavior). (221) |
| games | 20-5. | According to Eric Berne, _____ are manipulative interactions with predictable outcomes, in which people conceal their real motives. (221) |
| interfere with | 20-6. | Games (facilitate/interfere with) effective communication. (221) |

**21.    Cite some positive outcomes associated with constructive interpersonal conflict.**

| | | |
|---|---|---|
| unavoidable | 21-1. | Conflict is an (avoidable/unavoidable) aspect of interactions. (221) |
| avoid; encourage | 21-2. | Collectivist cultures (such as China and Japan) often (avoid/encourage) conflict, whereas individualistic cultures tend to (avoid/encourage) direct confrontations. (221) |
| negative | 21-3. | The effects of suppressing interpersonal conflict tend to be (positive/ negative). (222) |
| solved | 21-4. | Constructive confrontation may bring problems out into the open where they can be (avoided/ignored/solved). (222) |
| false | 21-5. | A pseudoconflict is a(n) (false/other-gender/severe) conflict. (222) |
| fact | 21-6. | When people disagree about issues of a factual nature, it's termed a (fact/ policy/value)-based conflict. (222) |

policy

21-7. When people disagree about how to handle a particular situation, it's called a (fact/policy/value)-based conflict. (222)

Value

21-8. (Fact/Policy/Value)-based conflicts are a particular problem in intimate relationships. (222)

ego

21-9. The most difficult conflicts to manage are those in which one or both parties view the outcome as a measure of self-worth, in other words (ego/fact/value)-based conflicts. (222-223)

**22. Describe five personal styles of dealing with interpersonal conflict.**

low;
low

22-1. The avoiding/withdrawing style of managing conflict is characterized by (high/low) interest in satisfying one's own concerns and (high/low) interest in satisfying others' concerns. (223)

accommodation

22-2. Those who bring a conflict to a quick end by giving in easily are said to be using (accommodation/avoidance/compromise). (223)

high;
low

22-3. The competing/forcing style of managing conflict is characterized by (high/low) interest in satisfying one's own concerns and (high/low) interest in satisfying others' concerns. (223)

negotiation

22-4. Compromise is a way to resolve conflict by means of (accommodation/competition/negotiation). (224)

high;
high

22-5. The collaborating style of managing conflict is characterized by (high/low) interest in satisfying one's own concerns and (high/low) interest in satisfying others' concerns. (224)

**23. List six tips for coping effectively with interpersonal conflict.**

avoid

23-1. In dealing effectively with interpersonal conflict, it's a good idea to (avoid/use) deceit and manipulation. (224)

specific;
general

23-2. In dealing effectively with interpersonal conflict, it's a good idea to use (general/specific) behaviors to describe another person's annoying habits rather than (general/specific) statements about their personality. (224)

negative

23-3. Certain words are "loaded" in the sense that they tend to trigger (positive/negative) emotional reactions in listeners. (224)

positive

23-4. In dealing effectively with interpersonal conflict, it's a good idea to use a (positive/negative) approach and help the person save face. (224)

recent

23-5. In coping effectively with interpersonal conflict, you should limit your complaints to the other person's (past/predicted/recent) behavior. (224)

feelings

23-6. In dealing effectively with interpersonal conflict, it's a good idea to assume responsibility for your own (complaints/feelings/withdrawal). (224)

**24.    Explain why Deborah Tannen characterizes America as "the argument culture."**

adversarial

24-1.    According to Deborah Tannen, Americans have a tendency to automatically take a(n) (accommodating/adversarial/positive) approach in almost any public situation. (225)

corrosive

24-2.    Deborah Tannen worries that the constant exposure to public arguments is having a(n) (constructive/corrosive/strengthening) effect on Americans' spirits. (225)

**25.    Describe some reasons for increased social contentiousness today.**

adversarial

25-1.    The individualistic culture predisposes Americans to be (accommodating/ adversarial). (225)

opposites

25-2.    Americans (and those in other Western cultures) have a dualistic view of nature and tend to see things in terms of (opposites/similarities). (225)

decline

25-3.    Face-to-face communication is on the (rise/decline), fed by advances in technology. (225)

aggression

25-4.    One contributing factor to social contentiousness is exposure to high levels of physical and verbal (accommodation/aggression/competition), especially in the media. (226)

more

25-5.    People who are exposed to considerable TV violence come to believe that society is (more/less) hostile and dangerous than it actually is. (226)

**26.    Describe what individuals and social institutions can do to reduce the level of public conflict.**

substance; sensationalism

26-1.    Newspapers could encourage reporters to emphasize (sensationalism/ substance) in their reporting and minimize (sensationalism/substance). (226)

Parents

26-2.    (Parents/Professional Athletes/Teachers) have a special role to play in restoring productive public communication by limiting children's exposure to physical and verbal aggression. (226)

**27.    Differentiate assertive communication from submissive and aggressive communication.**

Assertiveness

27-1.    _____ involves acting in your own best interests by expressing your thoughts and feelings directly and honestly. (227)

submissive

27-2.    Consistently giving in to others on points of possible contention is termed (accommodating/assertive/submissive) communication. (227)

Aggressive

27-3.    (Aggressive/Assertive/Submissive) communication focuses on saying and getting what you want, at the expense of others' feelings and rights. (228)

Assertive

27-4.   (Aggressive/Assertive/Submissive) behavior is said to foster high self-esteem, satisfactory interpersonal relationships, and effective conflict management. (228)

**28.     *Describe five steps that lead to more assertive communication.***

clarify

28-1.   The first step in assertiveness training is to (clarify/consider/question) the nature of assertive communication. (228)

nonassertive

28-2.   Once you understand the nature of assertive communication, you should monitor yourself and identify when you are (assertive/nonassertive). (229)

model

28-3.   Once you have identified the situations in which you are nonassertive, think of someone who communicates assertively in those situations and observe that person's behavior closely.  In other words, find someone to _____ yourself after. (229-230)

shaping

28-4.   Most experts recommend that you use (accommodation/punishment/shaping) to increase your assertive communication gradually. (230)

attitude

28-5.   A change in (attitude/setting/relationships) is probably crucial to achieving flexible, assertive, behavior. (231)

## QUIZ BOXES

### KEY TERMS

| | |
|---|---|
| **Interpersonal communication** | An interactional process in which one person sends a message to another. |
| **Noise** | Any stimulus that interferes with accurately expressing or understanding a message. |
| **Context** | The environment in which communication takes place. |
| **Nonverbal communication** | The transmission of meaning from one person to another through means or symbols other than words. |
| **Proxemics** | The study of people's use of interpersonal space. |
| **Personal space** | A zone of space surrounding a person that is felt to "belong" to that person. |
| **Display rules** | Norms that govern the appropriate display of emotions. |
| **Kinesics** | The study of communication through body movements. |
| **Paralanguage** | Includes all vocal cues other than the content of the verbal message itself. |
| **Polygraph** | A device that records fluctuations in physiological arousal as a person answers questions. |
| **Empathy** | Adopting another's frame of reference so you can understand his or her point of view. |
| **Self-disclosure** | The act of sharing information about yourself with another person. |
| **Communication apprehension** | Anxiety caused by having to talk with others. |
| **Games** | Manipulative interactions with predictable outcomes, in which people conceal their real motives. |
| **Interpersonal conflict** | Exists whenever two or more people disagree. |
| **Assertiveness** | Acting in your own best interests by expressing your thoughts and feelings directly and honestly. |

## KEY PEOPLE

| Sharon Anthony Bower and Gordon Bower | Outlined a four-step program intended to help people create successful assertive scripts for themselves; wrote the book *Asserting Yourself: A Practical Guide for Positive Change.* |
|---|---|
| Bella DePaulo | Noted researcher in the area of detecting deception from nonverbal behaviors; summarized evidence on which nonverbal cues are *actually* associated with deception and which are *believed* to be a sign of deception. |
| Paul Ekman and Wallace Friesen | Identified six universal, primary emotions that have distinctive facial expressions: anger, disgust, fear, happiness, sadness, and surprise. |
| Edward T. Hall | Anthropologist who described four interpersonal distance zones that are appropriate for middle-class encounters in American culture. |
| Deborah Tannen | Sociolinguist who characterized contemporary America as the "argument culture;" suggested that an atmosphere of "unrelenting contention" pervades American culture and is fueled by a growing tendency for Americans to automatically take an adversarial approach in almost any public situation. |

## SELF-TEST

*Multiple Choice Items*

1. The primary means of sending messages to another person is through
   a. gestures
   b. language
   c. written memos
   d. facial expressions

2. In nonverbal communication, meaning is transmitted from one person to another
   a. using coded words that have private meanings
   b. with the aid of computers or other forms of technology
   c. without anyone else being aware of it
   d. through means or symbols other than words

3. Which of the following statements regarding nonverbal communication is not true?
   a. Nonverbal communication is multichanneled.
   b. Nonverbal messages may contradict verbal messages.
   c. Nonverbal communication frequently conveys emotions.
   d. Nonverbal messages tend to be less ambiguous than spoken words.

4. Facial expressions are most likely to convey messages dealing with
   a. intimacy
   b. emotions
   c. personality traits
   d. marital satisfaction

5. Which of the following is not one of the six basic emotions associated with distinctive facial expressions identified by Ekman and Friesen?
   a. curiosity
   b. anger
   c. happiness
   d. sadness

6. Norms that govern the appropriate display of emotions are called
   a. proxemics
   b. display rules
   c. nonverbal indicators
   d. attribution features

7. Which of the following aspects of eye contact is generally considered the most meaningful?
   a. its duration
   b. its intensity
   c. the gender of the initiator
   d. the accompanying body language

8. Men are most likely to view touch as a way to
   a. show support
   b. signify affection
   c. assert power
   d. express hostility

9. As an indicator of lying, lack of eye contact is
   a. a fairly reliable index of deceptive intent
   b. not a reliable index of deceptive intent
   c. the best indicator of deceptive intent
   d. more reliable in persons of lower status

10. Which of the following is not monitored by a polygraph?
    a. heart rate
    b. brain waves
    c. perspiration
    d. blood pressure

11. Adopting another's frame of reference to understand his or her point of view is called
    a. empathy
    b. intimacy
    c. sympathy
    d. positive paralanguage

12. Research findings show that self-disclosure in romantic relationships
    a. is positively correlated with relationship satisfaction
    b. is an indication that there may be communication problems
    c. appears to be unrelated to how partners actually feel about each other
    d. may actually be detrimental to the development of feelings of empathy

13. Research findings on gender and self-disclosure indicate that
    a. females consistently disclose more than males
    b. in the beginning of an other-gender relationship, men often disclose more than women
    c. men generally disclose more personal information and feelings than women do
    d. the gender disparity in self-disclosure is consistent across cultures

14. Which of the following is the most common response to communication apprehension?
    a. communication avoidance          c. social phobia
    b. excessive communication          d. an increase in negative self-talk

15. Perhaps the most basic barrier to effective communication is
    a. game playing                     c. self-preoccupation
    b. defensiveness                    d. attribution distortion

16. A pseudoconflict is a(n)
    a. situation in which there is no actual conflict
    b. conflict based on differences in beliefs or values
    c. conflict in which people disagree about issues of a factual nature
    d. interpersonal conflict in which one of the people is an authority figure

17. Which of the following is generally viewed as the most productive approach for dealing with conflict?
    a. avoiding/withdrawing             c. compromising
    b. accommodating                    d. collaborating

18. Which of the following is not good advice for dealing constructively with conflict?
    a. Avoid "loaded" words.
    b. Focus complaints on past behavior.
    c. Assume responsibility for your own feelings.
    d. Make communication open and honest.

19. Research findings suggest that, as a consequence of excessive exposure to media violence,
    a. some children may develop aggressive tendencies
    b. viewers become desensitized to violence and its effects
    c. people come to believe that "television reality" depicts actual reality
    d. All of the above have been found to be consequences of exposure to media violence.

20. Research findings indicate that submissive behavior leads to all but which of the following?
    a. alienation                       c. emotional suppression
    b. self-denial                      d. strained interpersonal relationships

### True/False Items

T/F    1. Women seem to have smaller personal-space zones than do men.

T/F    2. Observers are better at recognizing the emotions in photographs from their own cultural groups than from cultural out-groups.

T/F    3. Men tend to gaze more at others in interactions than women do.

T/F     4.    In terms of body posture, a higher-status person will generally look more relaxed.

T/F     5.    Using capital letters throughout an email message is generally viewed as an indication of friendliness.

T/F     6.    Research indicates that polygraphs are accurate about 90% of the time.

T/F     7.    In trying to create a positive interpersonal climate, it's a good idea to express your opinions tentatively.

T/F     8.    Disclosing personal information about oneself seems to have little to do with psychological adjustment.

T/F     9.    In the United States, it has been found that females tend to be more openly self-disclosing than males.

T/F    10.   Gender differences in self-disclosure appear to be consistent across a variety of cultures.

T/F    11.   Although it can be fairly serious, communication avoidance is not a typical response to communication apprehension.

T/F    12.   Avoidance is one of the best ways of managing serious interpersonal conflicts.

T/F    13.   Excessive exposure to media violence causes viewers to become desensitized to violence and its effects on victims.

T/F    14.   According to your textbook, the terms "aggressive communication" and "assertive communication" are synonymous.

# ANSWER KEY FOR SELF-TEST ITEMS

*Multiple Choice Items*

b      **1.** Although language is the primary means of sending messages, people also communicate to others nonverbally. (202)

d      **2.** Communication at the nonverbal level takes place through a variety of behaviors: interpersonal distance, facial expression, eye contact, body posture and movement, gestures, physical touch, and tone of voice . (205)

d      **3.** Although some popular books on body language imply otherwise, few nonverbal signals carry universally accepted meanings, even within the same culture.  This is why nonverbal signals are most reliable when accompanied by verbal messages. (205-206)

b      **4.** More than anything else, facial expressions convey emotions. (207)

a      **5.** The complete list of the six emotions is: anger, disgust, fear, happiness, sadness, and surprise. (207)

b      **6.** Display rules are social norms that govern when (and whether) it is appropriate to express one's feelings. (208)

a      **7.** A great deal of research has been done on how duration of eye contact is used in communication. (208)

c      **8.** For men, touch is an instrumental behavior used to assert power or show sexual interest. On the other hand, women typically perceive touch to be an expressive behavior signifying affection or support. (210)

b      **9.** Although consistent with popular stereotypes about how liars give themselves away, lack of eye contact is *not* associated with lying. (211)

b      **10.** A polygraph does *not* monitor a person's brain waves. It does, however, monitor key indicators of autonomic arousal, including heart rate, blood pressure, respiration rate, and perspiration. (212)

a      **11.** Learning to feel and communicate empathy is one way to help create a positive interpersonal climate. (214)

a      **12.** More specifically, it may be *equity* in self-disclosure rather than *high* self-disclosure that is the critical factor in helping couples avoid stress. (216)

b      **13.** This is one of the situations in which men seem to be more likely to engage in self-disclosure than women. (217)

a      **14.** If people believe that speaking will make them uncomfortable, they will typically avoid participating. (219-220)

b      **15.** Defensiveness is an excessive concern with protecting oneself from being hurt. (220)

a      **16.** The prefix "pseudo" means "false" or "fake." (222)

d      **17.** Collaborating involves a sincere effort to find a solution that will maximally satisfy both parties. (224)

b       18.   In trying to deal constructively with conflict, it's better to limit complaints to recent behavior and to the present situation.  Bringing up past grievances tends to rekindle old resentments. (224)

d       19.   All of these consequences have been supported by research.  The effect of televised violence is one of the factors that contribute to social contentiousness. (226)

a       20.   Alienation is more likely to occur as a result of *aggressive*, rather than *submissive*, behavior. (228)

### *True/False Items*

True    1.    Also, when talking, women sit or stand closer together than men do. (207)

True    2.    This finding supports the view that the recognition of emotions is culturally specific. (208)

False   3.    Actually, it's the other way around.  The pattern of eye contact is also affected by status. (209)

True    4.    By contrast, a lower-status person will tend to exhibit a more rigid body posture. (210)

False   5.    Using capital letters throughout a message is viewed as shouting and is considered rude behavior. (211)

False   6.    Although polygraph experts may claim that lie detectors are 85%-90% accurate, the research does not support these claims. (212)

True    7.    This lets others know that your beliefs are flexible and subject to revision. (214)

False   8.    Self-disclosure is *critically* important to adjustment.  Among other positive effects, expressing your feelings to someone else can reduce stress. (215)

True    9.    This is generally true, although the disparity seems smaller than once believed. (217)

False   10.   Because these disparities are attributed to socialization, different patterns of self-disclosure are found in other countries. (217)

False   11.   Actually, communication avoidance is the most *common* response to communication apprehension. (219-220)

False   12.   Although avoidance may be useful for minor problems, it is not a good idea to avoid bigger conflicts because this strategy generally just delays the inevitable clash. (223)

True    13.   This is one of several negative consequences of excessive exposure to media violence. (226)

False   14.   Aggressive communication tends to be viewed as maladaptive, whereas assertive communication is much more adaptive than either aggressive communication or submissive communication. (227-228)

# Chapter 8
# FRIENDSHIP AND LOVE

## PROGRAMMED REVIEW

***1. Define close relationships and give some examples.***

a lot of

1-1. People spend (a lot of/very little) time and energy maintaining close relationships. (236)

many

1-2. Close relationships come in (many/one or two) forms. (236)

Not all

1-3. (All/Not all) close relationships are characterized by emotional intimacy. (236)

***2. Describe how members from individualistic cultures and collectivist cultures view love and marriage.***

vary

2-1. Cultures (are similar/vary) in their emphasis on romantic love as a prerequisite for marriage. (236)

economic

2-2. Cultural views of love and marriage are linked both to a culture's values and its (economic/psychological/social) health. (237)

grow;
decline

2-3. A study of couples in India showed that love tended to (decline/grow) over the years in arranged marriages, whereas it tended to (decline/grow) among couples who married for romantic love. (237)

greater

2-4. The expectation that marriage will fill diverse psychological needs places (greater/less) pressure on marital relationships in individualistic societies than on those in collectivistic cultures. (237)

***3. Describe the differences between Internet and face-to-face interactions and how the Internet affects relationship development.***

expanded

3-1. The Internet has dramatically (expanded/reduced) opportunities for people to meet and develop relationships. (237)

positive

3-2. Research to date generally paints a very (positive/negative) picture of the Internet's impact on people's connections with one another. (237)

facilitates

3-3. The relative anonymity of the Internet (facilitates/hinders) the formation of close relationships. (237)

earlier;
more

3-4. Online, where people rely on self-disclosure to develop relationships, similarity of interests and values kicks in (earlier/later) and assumes (more/less) power than it does in face-to-face relationships. (238)

greater

3-5. In terms of self-disclosure, people take (fewer/greater) risks in virtual relationships than they do in face-to-face relationships. (238)

**4.    Discuss the roles of proximity and familiarity in initial attraction.**

Proximity

4-1.    (Exposure/Familiarity/Proximity) refers to geographic, residential, and other forms of spatial closeness. (239)

is not

4-2.    Proximity (is/is not) an issue in cyberspace interactions. (239)

exposure

4-3.    The mere (exposure/familiarity/proximity) effect is defined as an increase in positive feelings toward a novel stimulus (person) based on frequent exposure to it. (240)

like

4-4.    Generally, the more familiar someone is, the more you will (like/dislike) him or her. (240)

**5.    Summarize the findings on physical attractiveness in Initial attraction.**

equally

5-1.    When compared to men, women are (more/less/equally) influenced by physical attractiveness in their behavior. (240)

more

5-2.    In the wording of gay and straight personal advertisements in newspapers, both heterosexual and homosexual men are (more/less) likely to request physically attractive partners than either heterosexual or homosexual women are. (240)

more

5-3.    Research findings indicate that an unattractive body is perceived as being (more/less) of a liability than an unattractive face. (240)

facial

5-4.    Even across different ethnic groups and countries, there seems to be agreement on attractive (bodily/facial) features. (240)

thinness

5-5.    Currently in the United States, there is heightened emphasis on (thinness/ stoutness/the "hourglass" figure) for girls and women. (241)

more

5-6.    In our culture, being physically attractive appears to be (more/less) important for females than for males. (240)

more

5-7.    In his research on newlyweds, David Buss found that men were (more/less) likely than women to emphasize their material resources. (241)

more

5-8.    According to research findings, women are (more/less) likely than men to work at enhancing their appearance by dieting, getting a tan, etc. (240)

matching

5-9.    The (exchange/matching/reciprocity) hypothesis proposes that people of similar levels of physical attractiveness gravitate toward each other. (242)

reproductive

5-10.    Evolutionary social psychologists believe that the research findings on age, status, and physical attractiveness reflect gender differences in inherited (competitive/reproductive/social) strategies. (243)

more

5-11.    Parental investment theory predicts that in comparison to women, men will show (more/less) desire for variety in sexual partners. (243)

| | | |
|---|---|---|
| contradicts | 5-12. | Research evidence (supports/contradicts) the claim made by evolutionary psychologists that culture has little influence on gender differences in mate selection strategies. (243) |

**6.    Discuss the role of reciprocal liking and similarity in getting acquainted.**

| | | |
|---|---|---|
| Reciprocal | 6-1. | _____ liking refers to liking those who show that they like you. (244) |
| is not | 6-2. | By and large, the tactic of "playing hard to get" (is/is not) advisable. (244) |
| off | 6-3. | People are usually turned (on/off) by others who reject them. (244) |
| similar | 6-4. | Research shows that heterosexual married and dating couples tend to be (similar/dissimilar) in characteristics such as age, religion, socioeconomic status, and education. (245) |
| increase | 6-5. | As attitude similarity increases, subjects' ratings of the likability of a stranger (increase/decrease). (245) |
| more | 6-6. | People with similar personality traits are (more/less) likely to be attracted to each other than are those with dissimilar or complementary needs. (245) |

**7.    Describe the personality qualities that people like in others.**

| | | |
|---|---|---|
| more | 7-1. | Personal qualities are (more/less) important than physical characteristics for a future spouse or life partner. (245) |
| attractive appearance | 7-2. | For a sexual partner, both men and women tend to rank (attractive appearance/overall personality) the highest. (245) |

**8.    Give some commonly used relationship maintenance strategies and explain what is meant by "minding" relationships.**

| | | |
|---|---|---|
| maintenance | 8-1. | Relationship (maintenance/monitoring/reciprocity) involves the actions and activities used to sustain the desired quality of a relationship. (246) |
| assurances | 8-2. | When members of a couple stress their commitment to each other they are engaging in the maintenance strategy termed (assurances/positivity/social networking). (246) |
| more | 8-3. | Married couples engage in (more/less) assurances and social networking than do dating partners. (246) |
| high | 8-4. | Developing satisfying and intimate long-term relationships is associated with a (high/low) level of 'minding' and vice versa. (246) |
| low | 8-5. | A lack of interest in your partner's self-disclosures, and generally negative attributions for your partner's behavior are associated with a (high/low) degree of minding. (246) |

**9.** *Define the elements of interdependence theory and explain how rewards, cost, and investments influence relationship satisfaction and commitment.*

Interdepen-dence

9-1.     _____ theory postulates that interpersonal relationships are governed by perceptions of the rewards and costs exchanged in interactions. (247)

reinforcement

9-2.     Interdependence theory is based on B. F. Skinner's principle of (modeling/ reciprocity/reinforcement), which assumes that individuals try to maximize their rewards in life and minimize their costs. (247)

comparison

9-3.     The personal standard of what constitutes an acceptable balance of rewards and costs in a relationship is called the _____ level. (247)

high;
low

9-4.     Consistent with the predictions of exchange theory, research indicates that relationship satisfaction is higher when rewards are perceived to be (high/ low) and costs (high/low). (247)

investments

9-5.     One factor that figures in relationship commitment is (comparisons/ investments/alternatives), or things that people contribute to a relationship that they can't get back if the relationship ends. (247)

similarly

9-6.     Social exchange principles seem to operate (similarly/differently) in heterosexual and homosexual couples. (248)

more

9-7.     Interdependence theory seems to be (more/less) applicable to individualistic cultures than to collectivistic cultures. (248)

communal

9-8.     In (communal/exchange) relationships, rewards are usually given freely without expectation of prompt reciprocation. (248)

**10.** *Summarize the research on what makes a good friend.*

six

10-1.   From a cross-cultural study of informal rules governing friendships, researchers were able to identify (two/six/twelve) such rules. (248-249)

emotional and social

10-2.   The common theme running through these rules seems to be providing (emotional and social/financial) support to friends. (249)

**11.** *Describe some key gender differences in friendships.*

emotionally;
activity

11-1.   In the United States, women's friendships are more often (activity/humor/ emotionally) based, whereas men's tend to be (activity/humor/emotionally) based. (249)

interests;
talking

11-2.   Men's friendships tend to be based on shared (interests/intimacy/talking), while women's friendships more often focus on (activities/talking). (249)

more

11-3.   Women are far (more/less) likely than men to discuss personal problems, feelings, and people. (249)

more

11-4.   The most widely-accepted view is that women's friendships are (more/less) satisfying than men's. (249)

| | |
|---|---|
| inhibits | 11-5. Men are socialized to be "strong and silent," which (encourages/inhibits) self-disclosure. (249) |
| more | 11-6. Several studies have found gender differences in friendships to be (more/less) pronounced in the United States than in India. (250) |

**12. Summarize the research findings on the experience of love in gay and straight couples.**

| | |
|---|---|
| orientation | 12-1. Sexual _____ refers to a person's preference for emotional and sexual relationships with individuals of the same gender, the other gender, or either gender. (250) |
| Heterosexuals | 12-2. _____ seek emotional-sexual relationships with members of the other gender. (250) |
| Homosexuals | 12-3. _____ seek emotional-sexual relationships with members of the same gender. (250) |
| Bisexuals | 12-4. _____ seek emotional-sexual relationships with members of both genders. (250) |
| heterosexism | 12-5. Most studies of romantic love and relationships suffer from _____, or the assumption that all individuals and relationships are heterosexual. (250) |
| more | 12-6. When differences are found in the quality of relationships, they are much (more/less) likely to be rooted in gender than in sexual orientation. (251) |

**13. Discuss some gender differences regarding love.**

| | |
|---|---|
| men | 13-1. Much of the research evidence suggests that (men/women) are the more romantic gender. (251) |
| more; more | 13-2. Men tend to fall in love (more/less) easily than women, while women fall out of love (more/less) easily than men. (251) |
| more | 13-3. Women are (more/less) likely than men to say that they would marry someone they didn't love. (251) |
| more | 13-4. Research supports the view that women are (more/less) selective in choosing a partner than men are. (251) |

**14. Define passion, intimacy, and commitment, and describe Sternberg's eight types of love.**

| | |
|---|---|
| triangular | 14-1. Intimacy, passion, and commitment are the three components of love, according to the (evolutionary/triangular) theory of love. (251) |
| Intimacy | 14-2. _____ refers to warmth, closeness, and sharing in a relationship. (251) |
| is | 14-3. Self-disclosure (is/is not) necessary to achieve and maintain feelings of intimacy in a relationship. (252) |

| | |
|---|---|
| Passion | 14-4.  _____ refers to the intense feelings (both positive and negative) experienced in love relationships, including sexual desire. (252) |
| Commitment | 14-5.  (Commitment/Intimacy/Passion) involves the decision and intent to maintain a relationship in spite of the difficulties and costs that may arise. (252) |
| companionate | 14-6.  According to Sternberg, the combination of intimacy and commitment produces (consummate/fatuous/companionate) love. (252) |
| consummate | 14-7.  When all three components (intimacy, passion, and commitment) are present, Sternberg calls it (companionate/consummate/passionate) love. (252) |
| higher | 14-8.  In one cross-cultural study of American and Chinese heterosexual couples, Americans scored significantly (higher/lower) on the passion scale than did the Chinese. (252) |

**15.    Discuss adult attachment styles, including their correlates and stability.**

| | |
|---|---|
| secure | 15-1.  Most infants develop a(n) (anxious-ambivalent/avoidant/secure) attachment style. (252) |
| secure | 15-2.  Hazan and Shaver found that (anxious-ambivalent/avoidant/secure) adults had the longest relationships and the fewest divorces. (253) |
| avoidant | 15-3.  Those who have difficulty in getting close to others and trusting their partners are called (anxious-ambivalent/avoidant/secure) adults. (253) |
| similar | 15-4.  Cross-cultural studies in Australia and Israel have shown that people are distributed across the three styles with (similar/different) percentages in those countries. (254) |
| negative; positive | 15-5.  According to Bartholomew's model, fearful avoidants have (positive/ negative) self-views, and dismissing avoidants have (positive) self-views. (254) |
| shorter | 15-6.  Studies have found that an avoidant style is associated with (longer/shorter) relationships. (254) |
| more | 15-7.  There is widespread agreement that individuals in the two insecure attachment styles are (more/less) vulnerable to a number of problems and symptoms, including low self-esteem and loneliness. (255) |
| parallel | 15-8.  A number of studies have demonstrated that adult attachment styles (parallel/do not parallel) those in infancy. (256) |
| stable | 15-9.  Research findings suggest that attachment styles tend to be (stable/ unstable). (256) |

**16.    Discuss the course of romantic love over time.**

decline;
increase

16-1. According to Sternberg, passion tends to (increase/decline) over the course of a relationship, while intimacy and commitment tend to (increase/decline). (256)

subside

16-2. Research supports the idea that the intense attraction and arousal one feels for a lover tends to (increase/subside) over time. (256)

fades

16-3. The novelty of a new partner (increases/fades) with increased interactions and knowledge. (256)

does not mean

16-4. Typically, the decline of passion (means/does not mean) the demise of a relationship. (257)

**17.    Explain why relationships fail, and what couples can do to help relationships last.**

50

17-1. If we were to follow seriously dating couples over several years, the proportion that would split up would be about (25/50/75) percent. (257)

commitment

17-2. Research indicates that one of the reasons couples break up is premature (attribution/commitment/passion). (257)

increases

17-3. The likelihood of disagreements (increases/decreases) as couples learn more about each other and become more interdependent. (257)

a more attractive
alternative

17-4. Whether a deteriorating relationship actually ends depends, in great part, on the availability of (financial resources/a more attractive alternative/counseling services). (258)

intimacy and
commitment

17-5. Research has shown that the best predictors of whether a dating couple's relationship would continue were their levels of (intimacy and passion/passion and commitment/intimacy and commitment). (258)

harder

17-6. As relationships continue, it gets (easier/harder) to emphasize the positive qualities in your partner and relationship. (258)

actor-observer

17-7. The tendency to attribute one's own behavior to situational factors and the behavior of others to personal factors is the (actor-observer/mere exposure/reciprocity) effect. (258)

rarely

17-8. Important issues in relationships (often/rarely) disappear on their own. (259)

**18.    Describe various types of loneliness.**

Loneliness

18-1. _____ occurs when a person has fewer interpersonal relationships than desired or when these relationships are not as satisfying as desired. (260)

Emotional

18-2. (Emotional/Social/Transitional) loneliness stems from the absence of an intimate attachment figure. (260)

Social

18-3. (Emotional/Social/Transitional) loneliness results from the lack of a friendship network. (261)

transitional

18-4.   Death, divorce, and relocation can all cause (chronic/transient/transitional) loneliness. (261)

chronic

18-5.   Those who are unable to develop a satisfactory interpersonal network over a period of years are suffering from _____ loneliness. (261)

**19.    *Discuss the prevalence of loneliness.***

contradicts

19-1.   The prevalence of loneliness in specific age groups (is consistent with/ contradicts) stereotypes. (261)

adolescents and young adults

19-2.   The loneliest age group is (children/adolescents and young adults/the elderly). (261)

decreases

19-3.   In general, loneliness (increases/decreases) with age. (261)

lonelier

19-4.   Single, divorced, and widowed adults are (lonelier/less lonely) than their married or cohabiting counterparts. (261)

**20.    *Explain how early experience and current social trends contribute to loneliness.***

social

20-1.   A key problem in the development of loneliness seems to be early negative (academic/emotional/social) behavior that leads to rejection by peers. (262)

insecure

20-2.   One factor that seems to prompt inappropriate social behavior in children is (secure/insecure) attachment styles. (262)

anxious-ambivalent

20-3.   Hazan and Shaver reported that (anxious-ambivalent/avoidant/secure) adults scored the highest on measures of loneliness. (262)

less

20-4.   Because of busy schedules, family members have (more/less) time for face-to-face interactions. (262)

diminish

20-5.   The fact that people watch television so much tends to (enhance/diminish) meaningful family conversation. (262)

**21.    *Describe how shyness, poor social skills, and self-defeating attributions contribute to loneliness.***

physiological

21-1.   Shy people tend to experience (emotional/physiological/social) symptoms of their anxiety, such as a racing pulse or an upset stomach. (263)

situationally

21-2.   Studies have shown that about 60% of shy people indicate that their shyness is (people/setting/situationally) specific. (263)

negatively

21-3.   Studies have found that lonely people evaluate others (positively/negatively). (263)

solitary

21-4.   People who suffer from chronic loneliness tend to spend much of their time in (group/solitary) activities. (263)

| | |
|---|---|
| lower;<br>more | 21-5.   A common finding is that lonely people show (higher/lower) responsiveness to their conversational partners and are (more/less) self-focused. (263) |
| irrational | 21-6.   Lonely people are prone to (rational/irrational) thinking about their social skills. (264) |
| negative | 21-7.   Research has found that lonely people tend to engage in (positive/negative) self-talk that prevents them from pursuing intimacy in a favorable manner. (264) |
| stable;<br>internal | 21-8.   Lonely people tend to attribute their loneliness to (stable/unstable), (internal/external) causes. (264) |

**22.   *Summarize the suggestions for conquering loneliness.***

| | |
|---|---|
| the Internet | 22-1.   One solution for overcoming loneliness is to use (alcohol/the Internet/a dating service). (264) |
| active | 22-2.   Another suggestion for conquering loneliness is to be socially (active/passive). (265) |
| break out of | 22-3.   One strategy for conquering loneliness is to (get into/break out of) the habit of self-defeating attributional style. (265) |
| social | 22-4.   To thwart loneliness, you need to cultivate your (athletic/social/writing) skills. (265) |
| cognitive | 22-5.   Counselors can use (cognitive/psychoanalytic/shock) therapy to help lonely and shy individuals to break the habit of automatic negative thoughts and self-defeating attributions. (265) |

QUIZ BOXES

*KEY TERMS*

| | |
|---|---|
| **Close relationships** | Relationships that are important, interdependent, and long lasting. |
| **Proximity** | Geographic, residential, and other forms of spatial closeness. |
| **Mere exposure effect** | An increase in positive feeling toward a novel stimulus (person) based on frequent exposure to it. |
| **Matching hypothesis** | Proposes that people of similar levels of physical attractiveness gravitate toward each other. |
| **Reciprocal liking** | Liking those who show that they like you. |
| **Relationship maintenance** | The actions and activities used to sustain the desired quality of a relationship. |
| **Interdependence or social exchange theory** | Postulates that interpersonal relationships are governed by perceptions of the rewards and costs exchanged in interactions. |
| **Comparison level** | The personal standard of what constitutes an acceptable balance of rewards and costs in a relationship. |
| **Comparison level for alternatives** | One's estimation of the available outcomes from alternative relationships. |
| **Investments** | Things that people contribute to a relationship that they can't get back if the relationship ends. |
| **Sexual orientation** | A person's preference for emotional and sexual relationships with individuals of the same gender, the other gender, or either gender. |
| **Heterosexism** | The assumption that all individuals and relationships are heterosexual. |
| **Intimacy** | Warmth, closeness, and sharing in a relationship. |
| **Passion** | The intense feelings (both positive and negative) experienced in love relationships, including sexual desire. |

| Commitment | The decision and intent to maintain a relationship in spite of the difficulties and costs that may arise. |
|---|---|
| Attachment styles | Typical ways of interacting in close relationships. |
| Actor-observer effect | The tendency to attribute one's own behavior to situational factors and the behavior of others to personal factors. |
| Loneliness | When a person has fewer interpersonal relationships than desired or when these relationships are not as satisfying as desired. |
| Shyness | Discomfort, inhibition, and excessive caution in interpersonal relations. |

## KEY PEOPLE

| Ellen Berscheid and Elaine Hatfield (Walster) | Conducted a number of studies on romantic relationships. |
|---|---|
| David Buss | Evolutionary social psychologist who suggests that gender similarities and differences in the tactics of attraction are based on reproductive strategies that have been sculpted over thousands of generations by natural selection. |
| Cindy Hazan and Philip Shaver | Suggested that romantic love can be conceptualized as an attachment process, with similarities to the bond between infants and their caregivers. |
| Harold Kelley and John Thibaut | Developed interdependence (social exchange) theory, which postulates that interpersonal relationships are governed by perceptions of the rewards and costs exchanged in interactions. |
| Robert Sternberg | Proposed the triangular theory of love, which posits that all love experiences are based on combinations of three components: intimacy, passion, and commitment. |

# SELF-TEST

*Multiple Choice Items*

1. Love as the basis for marriage is
   a.   a universal phenomenon
   b.   most common in collectivist cultures
   c.   an 18th-century invention of Western culture
   d.   becoming increasingly uncommon across cultures

2. Which of the following statements about online (Internet) versus face-to-face relationships is most accurate?
   a.   Online relationships rarely evolve into face-to-face interactions.
   b.   Proximity is a major influence on initial attraction in online relationships.
   c.   People tend to take greater risks in self-disclosure in face-to-face relationships.
   d.   Research suggests that virtual relationships are just as intimate as face-to-face ones.

3. Which of the following statements about the role of physical attractiveness in relationships is not accurate?
   a.   Good looks play a role in friendships.
   b.   Research shows that attractiveness is an important factor in dating.
   c.   When it comes to actual behavior, women are as influenced by physical attractiveness as men.
   d.   Both genders rate physical attractiveness of a potential mate higher than personal qualities such as kindness and warmth.

4. According to the matching hypothesis,
   a.   people seek potential mates who match their attractiveness ideal
   b.   people of similar levels of physical attractiveness gravitate toward each other
   c.   people tend to gravitate toward those with the same sexual orientation
   d.   physically attractive people have an easier time finding a partner

5. If you want to *have* a friend, *be* a friend.  This statement is most consistent with which of the following concepts?
   a.   proximity                          c.   matching hypothesis
   b.   reciprocity                        d.   mere exposure effect

6. The research on similarity seems to show that married and dating couples
   a.   tend to be similar on most important attributes
   b.   are often far apart on many important attributes
   c.   show no significant relationships on important attributes
   d.   who are too similar soon look for a way out of the relationship

7. Both male and female college students ranked which of the following characteristics as the most important in a sexual partner?
   a.   attractive appearance              c.   sense of humor
   b.   trustworthy                        d.   overall personality

8. Encouraging your partner to disclose his or her thoughts and feelings to you illustrates which of the following relationship maintenance strategies?
   a.   positivity                         c.   openness
   b.   assurances                         d.   social networking

9.  Interdependence theory proposes that
    a.  interpersonal relationships are governed by rewards and costs
    b.  tokens can be exchanged for primary reinforcements
    c.  friendships should be changed occasionally to maintain one's mental health
    d.  interpersonal relationships, once established, tend to be maintained regardless of the cost

10. According to interdependence theory, what constitutes an acceptable balance of rewards and costs in a relationship is
    a.  referred to as mutuality
    b.  determined by Skinner's principle of reinforcement
    c.  based on outcomes one has experienced in past relationships
    d.  determined largely by what one's parents found acceptable

11. Studies indicate that the most important element of friendship is
    a.  generosity                        c.  physical attractiveness
    b.  emotional support                 d.  similar religious attitudes

12. Women's friendships tend to focus on
    a.  talking and emotional intimacy
    b.  the significant men in their lives
    c.  shared interests and doing things together
    d.  global issues as opposed to personal ones

13. Most homosexual women prefer to call themselves
    a.  gays                              c.  bisexuals
    b.  lesbians                          d.  homosexuals

14. Research evidence suggests that
    a.  women are more romantic than men
    b.  men are more romantic than women
    c.  men and women are equally romantic
    d.  there is no relationship between gender and romanticism

15. Which of the following is not one of the components in Robert Sternberg's triangular theory of love?
    a.  passion                          c.  sexuality
    b.  intimacy                         d.  commitment

16. According to Sternberg's triangular theory of love, the combination of intimacy and passion produces
    a.  liking                           c.  romantic love
    b.  infatuation                      d.  companionate love

17. Cindy Hazan and Phillip Shaver suggested that patterns of adult romantic love are related to
    a.  levels of affiliation motive
    b.  psychosexual stages in childhood
    c.  attachment relationships in infancy
    d.  same-gender bonds in adolescence

18. The tendency to attribute one's own behavior to situational factors and others' behavior to personal factors is called
    a.  negative attribution             c.  disruptive social reasoning
    b.  the actor-observer effect        d.  downward social comparison

19.    Lonely people
    a.    have fewer interpersonal relationships than desired
    b.    tend to blame their misery on situational factors
    c.    usually have psychological problems that turn people away
    d.    can be well adjusted if they accept the situation as it is

20.    Which of the following is a personal consequence associated with chronic loneliness?
    a.    hostility                          c.    alcoholism
    b.    depression                         d.    all of the above

## True/False Items

T/F        1.    In virtually all cultures studied, love —especially romantic love —is a prerequisite for marriage.

T/F        2.    Internet relationships tend to be more superficial than face-to-face ones.

T/F        3.    An unattractive body is perceived as being a greater liability than an unattractive face.
T/F        4.    Research indicates that playing "hard to get" is a good way to enhance one's attractiveness.

T/F        5.    The principles of interdependence theory seem to apply to heterosexual relationships, but not to homosexual relationships.

T/F        6.    The fear of homosexuality is stronger in males than in females.

T/F        7.    Research findings indicate that women tend to be more romantic than men.

T/F        8.    Research shows that of several different forms of infant-caregiver attachment, most infants develop a secure attachment.

T/F        9.    The intense attraction and arousal (i.e., passion) one feels for a lover seems destined to fade over time.

T/F        10.    The decline in passion in a relationship inevitably results in the demise of the relationship.

T/F        11.    Loneliness is generally defined as spending time alone.

T/F        12.    In general, women are lonelier than men.

# ANSWER KEY FOR SELF-TEST

*Multiple Choice Items*

c       1.  Arranged marriages remain fairly common in collectivist cultures such as India, Japan, and China. (236)

d       2.  Although there hasn't been a lot of research in this area yet, studies show that virtual relationships are sometimes even *closer* than face-to-face relationships. (238)

d       3.  In fact, *both* genders rate at least some personal qualities higher than physical attractiveness. (241)

b       4.  This hypothesis is supported by findings that both dating and married heterosexual couples tend to be similar in physical attractiveness. (245)

b       5.  As applied to relationships, the reciprocity principle suggests that we tend to like those people who show that they like us. (244)

a       6.  In general the research supports the adage "birds of a feather flock together." (244-245)

a       7.  Personal qualities (e.g., personality, sense of humor) tend to be rated as more important for a future spouse or life partner. (245)

c       8.  In a study of college students, openness (i.e., being open with one's feelings) was the most commonly listed maintenance strategy. (246)

a       9.  The cost-benefits idea is a basic premise of interdependence theory. (247)

b       10. Interdependence theory was based on Skinner's notion that individuals try to maximize their rewards in life and minimize their costs. (247)

a       11. According to several lines of research, the common themes that underlie friendship emphasize the aspect of emotional support. (249)

a       12. Compared to men, women's friendships more often focus on talking --- usually about feelings and relationships. (249)

b       13. Gay can refer to homosexuals of either gender, but most homosexual women prefer to call themselves lesbians. (250)

b       14. Although this finding contradicts the traditional stereotype, the research evidence is fairly consistent on this point. (251)

c       15. Sexual needs constitute just one element of the passion component of love. (251)

c       16. The warmth and closeness of intimacy, plus the intense feelings of passion, yield romantic love. (252)

c       17. Hazan and Shaver suggest that infant attachments and romantic attachments share a number of features, including intense fascination with the other person and distress at separation. (252)

b          18.   This tendency can set up the destructive  habit of chronically blaming the other person for problems in a relationship, and not taking responsibility when one should. (258)

a          19.   In addition to having fewer relationships than desired, the relationships of lonely people are generally not as satisfying as they would like. (260)

d          20.   All of these are personal consequences associated with chronic loneliness. Other possible consequences include low self-esteem, psychosomatic illness, and possibly suicide. (264)

**True/False Items**

False      1.   Love as the basis for marriage is basically an 18th-century invention of Western culture. (236)

False      2.   Interestingly, research to date suggests that virtual relationships are just as intimate as face-to-face ones and are sometimes even closer. (238)

True       3.   Although they are both important factors in perceived attractiveness, people, especially males, tend to place more emphasis on the body build of their partners. (241)

False      4.   People are usually turned off by others who reject them. (244)

False      5.   These principles seem to operate in a similar fashion regardless of a couple's sexual orientation. (248)

True       6.   This fear is often cited as a barrier to intimacy between male friends. (249)

False      7.   Surprisingly, it's the other way around, although women do seem more romantic with regard to *expressions* of love. (251)

True       8.   Although some infants develop anxious-ambivalent attachment and others develop avoidant attachment, the majority of infants tend to develop secure attachment. (252)

True       9.   Regrettably, this seems to be the case.  However, the good news is that both intimacy and commitment seem to increase as time progresses. (256)

False     10.   Some relationships do dissolve when early passion fades; however, many others evolve into different, but deeply satisfying, mixtures of passionate and companionate love. (257)

False     11.   In fact, people can feel lonely even when they are surrounded by others.  Loneliness actually has more to do with individuals being dissatisfied with the number and quality of their relationships. (260)

False     12.   Women are found to be lonelier than men, but only on measures that use words such as "lonely" or "loneliness."  Thus, it is likely that there is no *actual* gender difference but rather a reluctance by men to admit to feeling lonely. (262)

# Chapter 9
# MARRIAGE AND INTIMATE RELATIONSHIPS

## PROGRAMMED REVIEW

**1.** ***Discuss recent trends relating to the acceptance of singlehood and cohabitation, and changing views on the permanence of marriage.***

Marriage

1-1. _____ is defined as the legally and socially sanctioned union of sexually intimate adults. (270)

increasing

1-2. A(n) (increasing/decreasing) proportion of the adult population under age 35 is remaining single (270)

**2.** ***Describe changing views on the permanence of marriage and gender roles.***

cohabitation

2-1. Living together in a sexually intimate relationship without the legal bonds of marriage is called _____ (270)

declining

2-2. Negative attitudes toward cohabitation appear to be (increasing/stable/declining). (270)

lessened

2-3. The social stigma associated with divorce has (increased/lessened). (270)

more; more; more

2-4. Role expectations for husbands and wives are becoming (more/less) varied, (more/less) flexible, and (more/less) ambiguous. (271)

**3.** ***Explain how increased childlessness and the decline of the nuclear family have affected the institution of marriage.***

decreased

3-1. In the past two decades, the percentage of women without children has (increased/decreased) in all age groups. (271)

small minority

3-2. Today, it is estimated that a (small minority/majority/large majority) of American families fit the ideal of a traditional nuclear family—one consisting of a breadwinner father and a homemaker mother. (271)

**4.** ***Discuss several factors influencing the selection of a mate.***

90

4-1. Although alternatives to marriage are more viable than ever, experts project that about (50/75/90) percent of Americans will marry at least once. (272)

is

4-2. Getting married (is/is not) the norm in our society. (272)

social

4-3. Endogamy is the tendency of people to marry within their own (age/economic/social) group. (272)

| homogamy | 4-4. | The tendency to marry others who have similar personal characteristics is called (heterogamy/homogamy/homogeneity). (272) |
|---|---|---|
| is | 4-5. | Homogamy (is/is not) associated with more satisfying marital relations. (272) |
| higher | 4-6. | Women tend to place a (higher/lower) value than men on a potential partner's financial prospects. (273) |
| evolutionary | 4-7. | Most theorists explain gender differences in mate selection preferences in terms of (behavioral/evolutionary/psychoanalytic) concepts. (273) |

**5.    Outline Murstein's stage theory of mate selection.**

| three | 5-1. | Bernard Murstein theorizes that mate selection proceeds through (three/six/ten) stages as couples move toward marriage. (274) |
|---|---|---|
| stimulus | 5-2. | In the first stage of Murstein's model, attraction to members of the other sex depends mainly on their (sexual/social/stimulus) value. (274) |
| values | 5-3. | Progress through the second stage of Murstein's model depends on compatibility in (occupational status/sexual needs/values). (274) |
| intimate | 5-4. | The role to be evaluated in Murstein's third stage is that of (intimate/sexual/social) companion. (274) |

**6.    Summarize evidence on predictors of marital success.**

| is | 6-1. | The marital adjustment of partners (is/is not) correlated with the marital satisfaction of their parents. (274) |
|---|---|---|
| higher | 6-2. | Couples who marry young have (higher/lower) divorce rates. ( 274) |
| higher | 6-3. | Couples who marry at an older age have a (higher/lower) propensity to divorce. (274) |
| greater | 6-4. | Longer periods of courtship are associated with a (greater/lower) probability of marital success. (274) |
| are not | 6-5. | Generally, research has found that partners' specific personality traits (are/are not) predictive of marital success. (275) |
| neuroticism | 6-6. | In terms of the "Big Five" personality traits, there is ample evidence for a negative association between (agreeableness/conscientiousness/neuroticism) and marital satisfaction. (275) |
| positively | 6-7. | Premarital satisfaction is (positively/negatively) correlated with subsequent marital satisfaction. (275) |

**7.    Explain what the family life cycle is.**

| | |
|---|---|
| family life | 7-1. An orderly sequence of developmental stages that families tend to progress through is called the _____ _____ cycle. (275) |
| six | 7-2. Carter and McGoldrick proposed a model of family development that consists of (three/six/ten) stages. (275) |
| risen | 7-3. The percentage of young adults who are postponing marriage until their late twenties or early thirties has (dropped/risen) dramatically. (276) |

**8.     Describe the factors couples weigh in deciding to have children.**

| | |
|---|---|
| increased | 8-1. In recent decades, ambivalence about the prospect of having children has clearly (increased/decreased). (277) |
| costs | 8-2. Couples who choose to remain childless cite the great (costs/joy/distress) associated with raising children. (277) |
| no regret | 8-3. Most parents report (regret/no regret) about their choice to have children. (277) |

**9.     Analyze the dynamics of the transition to parenthood.**

| | |
|---|---|
| more | 9-1. The transition to parenthood tends to have (more/less) impact on mothers than fathers. (277) |
| lower | 9-2. The more children couples have, the (higher/lower) their marital satisfaction tends to be. (277) |
| is not | 9-3. Crisis during the transition to first parenthood (is/is not) universal. (277) |
| realistic | 9-4. The key to making this transition less stressful may be to have (realistic/ unrealistic) expectations about parental responsibilities. (277) |
| higher | 9-5. Divorce rates are (higher/lower) for couples who remain childless. (277-278) |

**10.     Identify common problems that surface as a family's children reach adolescence.**

| | |
|---|---|
| most | 10-1. Parents overwhelmingly rate adolescence as the (most/least) difficult stage of parenting. (278) |
| mothers | 10-2. Conflicts are particularly likely to occur between adolescents (of both sexes) and their (mothers/ fathers). (278) |
| parents | 10-3. In addition to worrying about their adolescent children, middle-aged couples often worry about the care of their (friends/parents/pets). (278) |
| Females | 10-4. (Males/Females) tend to assume most of the responsibility for elderly relatives. (278) |

distress

10-5.   One study found that the number of hours spent caring for an aging parent was correlated with wives' psychological (well-being/distress). (278)

**11.    Discuss the transitions that occur in the later stages of the family life cycle.**

increased

11-1.   The percentage of young adults who live with their parents has (increased/ decreased) in recent decades. (278)

negative

11-2.   Young adults have more (positive/negative) attitudes about returning home than their parents do. (278)

negative

11-3.   Preliminary data suggest that living with one's parents during adulthood has a modest (positive/negative) impact on parent-child relations. (278)

unsuccessful

11-4.   Conflicts are particularly likely when returning children have been (successful/unsuccessful) in moving into autonomous adult roles. (278)

improved

11-5.   Researchers have found that the "empty nest" is associated with (improved/ diminished) well-being for most mothers. (279)

**12.    Discuss how gaps in role expectations may affect marital adjustment.**

negative

12-1.   Gaps between partners in their role expectations appear to have a (positive/negative) effect on couples' marital satisfaction. (280)

wives

12-2.   Studies on American couples indicate that when wives work outside the home, the (husbands/wives) do the bulk of the household chores. (280)

two-thirds

12-3.   Married women perform about (one-third/one-half/two-thirds) of all housework. (280)

more

12-4.   Research shows that women who have nontraditional attitudes about gender roles are (more/less) likely to perceive their share of housework as unfair than women with traditional attitudes. (280-281)

**13.    Summarize how spouses' work affects their marital satisfaction and their children.**

more

13-1.   When pressures increase at work, husbands and wives report (more/fewer) role conflicts. (281)

negative

13-2.   Studies find that spouses' stress at work can have a substantial (positive/ negative) effect on their marital and family interactions. (281)

no consistent

13-3.   Most research finds (consistent/no consistent) differences in the marital adjustment of male-breadwinner versus dual-career couples. (282)

little

13-4.   The vast majority of empirical studies have found (substantial/little) evidence that a mother's working is harmful to her children. (282)

| | |
|---|---|
| have not | 13-5.  Studies generally (have/have not) found a link between mothers' employment status and the quality of infant-mother emotional attachment. (282) |

**14.    Describe how financial issues are related to marital adjustment.**

| | |
|---|---|
| increased; increased | 14-1.  Serious financial worries among couples are associated with (increased/decreased) hostility in husbands and (increased/deceased) depression in wives. (282-283) |
| increases | 14-2.  Evidence consistently demonstrates that the risk of separation and divorce (increases/decreases) as husbands' income declines. (283) |
| decreased | 14-3.  Research has found that perceived financial stress (regardless of a family's actual income) is associated with (increased/decreased) marital satisfaction. (283) |
| more | 14-4.  One study found that in comparison to divorced couples, happy couples engaged in (more/less) joint decision making on finances. (283) |

**15.    Summarize evidence on the relationship between communication quality and marital adjustment.**

| | |
|---|---|
| communication | 15-1.  In a study of couples getting a divorce, (communication/financial/sexual) difficulties were the most frequently cited problem among both husbands and wives. (283) |
| deteriorating | 15-2.  Many partners respond to conflict by withdrawing and refusing to communicate –a pattern associated with (improved/deteriorating) marital satisfaction over time. (283) |
| less | 15-3.  Research indicates that compared to happily married couples, unhappily married spouses are (more/less) likely to recognize that they have been misunderstood. (283) |
| often | 15-4.  Compared to happily married couples, unhappily married spouses (often/seldom) differ in the amount of self-disclosure they prefer in the relationship. (283) |
| normal | 15-5.  John Gottman, a prominent authority on marital communication, asserts that conflict and anger are (normal/abnormal) in marital interactions. (285) |
| stonewalling | 15-6.  According to Gottman, (contempt/defensiveness/stonewalling) involves refusing to listen to one's partner, especially the partner's complaints. (285) |

**16.    Describe the evidence on changing divorce rates.**

| | |
|---|---|
| increased; decreased | 16-1.  Divorce rates (increased/decreased) dramatically between the 1950s and 1980s, although they appear to have (increased/decreased) slightly in recent years. (285) |

| | | |
|---|---|---|
| underestimate | 16-2. | Most people have a tendency to (overestimate/underestimate) the likelihood that they will personally experience a divorce. (286) |
| higher | 16-3. | Divorce rates are (higher/lower) among lower-income couples. (286) |
| early | 16-4. | The vast majority of divorces occur during the (early/middle/later) years of a marriage. (286) |
| more | 16-5. | Many religious denominations are becoming (more/less) tolerant of divorce. (286) |
| diminished | 16-6. | The legal barriers to divorce have (increased/diminished). (286) |

**17.   Discuss how men and women tend to adjust to divorce.**

| | | |
|---|---|---|
| more | 17-1. | Wives' judgments about the likelihood of their marriages ending in divorce tend to be (more/less) accurate than husbands' judgments. (286) |
| wives | 17-2. | Most divorce actions are initiated by (husbands/wives). (288) |
| higher | 17-3. | Research shows that people who are currently divorced suffer a (higher/lower) incidence of both physical and psychological maladies than those who are currently married. (288) |
| stressful | 17-4. | The process of getting divorced is usually (a relief/stressful) for both spouses. (288) |
| more | 17-5. | The economic consequences of divorce are (more/less) severe for women than for men.   (288) |
| | 17-6. | Researchers (find/do not find) consistent gender differences in postdivorce adjustment. (288) |

**18.   Analyze the evidence on the effects of divorce on children.**

| | | |
|---|---|---|
| bleak | 18-1. | Research by Judith Wallerstein and her colleagues has painted a (positive/bleak) picture of how divorce affects youngsters. (288) |
| pessimistic | 18-2. | The results of a long-running study by E. Mavis Hetherington suggest that Wallerstein's conclusions are unduly (optimistic/pessimistic). (289) |
| more | 18-3. | Children have (more/fewer) adjustment problems when their parents have a history of particularly bitter, acrimonious conflict. (289) |
| harmful; beneficial | 18-4. | Overall, the weight of evidence suggests that divorce tends to have (beneficial/harmful) effects on many children, but that divorce can have (beneficial/harmful) effects for children if their parents' relationship is dominated by conflict. (289) |

**19.     Summarize data on the frequency and success of remarriage and its impact on children.**

three-fourths

19-1.    Roughly (one-third/half/three-fourths) of divorced people eventually remarry. (289)

higher

19-2.    Divorce rates are (higher/lower) for second marriages than for first marriages. (289)

less

19-3.    Research suggests that second marriages are slightly (more/less) successful than first marriages. (289)

less;
similar

19-4.    Taken as a whole, the evidence suggests that children in stepfamilies are a little (more/less) well adjusted than children in first marriages and (greater/lower/similar) in adjustment to children in single-parent homes. (289)

**20.     Describe stereotypes of single life and summarize evidence on the adjustment of single people.**

increasing

20-1.    A(n) (increasing/decreasing) proportion of young adults are remaining single. (290)

increase;
increased

20-2.    Much of the growth in the size of the single population is due to the (increase/decrease) in the average age at which people marry and the (increased/decreased) rate of divorce. (291)

more;
less

20-3.    In comparison to married people, single people have sex with (more/fewer) partners, and they have sex (more/less) frequently. (291)

poorer;
less

20-4.    Single people exhibit (better/poorer) mental and physical health than married people, and they rate themselves as (more/less) happy than their married counterparts. (291)

greater

20-5.    The physical health benefits of being married appear to be (greater/lower) for men than women. (291)

easier

20-6.    Research evidence suggests that it's (harder/easier) for women to get along without men than it is for men to get along without women. (291)

higher

20-7.    Married people tend to have (higher/lower) incomes than single people. (291)

**21.     Discuss the prevalence of cohabitation and whether it improves the probability of marital success.**

Cohabitation

21-1.    _____ refers to two people living together in a sexually intimate relationship outside of marriage. (291)

increase

21-2.    Recent years have witnessed a(n) (increase/decrease) in the number of cohabiting couples. (291)

| | |
|---|---|
| short | 21-3.    Cohabiting unions tend to be relatively (long-lasting/short). (291) |
| are not | 21-4.    Increasing rates of cohabitation (are/are not) unique to the United States. (291-292) |
| higher | 21-5.    Cohabitation rates have always been (higher/lower) in the less-educated and lower-income segments of the population. (292) |
| trial | 21-6.    Some theorists see cohabitation as a new stage in the courtship process – a sort of (fake/non-/trial) marriage. (292) |
| increased | 21-7.    Studies have found an association between premarital cohabitation and (increased/decreased) marital discord and divorce rates. (292) |

**22.    Discuss the stability and dynamics of intimate relationships among homosexual couples.**

| | |
|---|---|
| Heterosexuals | 22-1.    _____ are individuals who seek emotional/sexual relationships with members of the other gender. (293) |
| Homosexuals | 22-2.    _____ are individuals who seek emotional/sexual relationships with members of the same gender. (293) |
| 7 | 22-3.    Recent evidence suggests that about (2/7/15) percent of the population could reasonably be characterized as homosexual. (293) |
| more | 22-4.    Attitudes about gay relationships have become (more/less) favorable in recent years. (293) |
| more | 22-5.    The limited data available suggest that gay couples' relationships are (more/less) prone to breakups than heterosexual marriages. (294) |
| commonalities | 22-6.    Recent studies have documented striking (commonalities/differences) between heterosexual and homosexual couples on a number of dimensions. (294) |

**23.    Outline some misconceptions about gay couples.**

| | |
|---|---|
| more | 23-1.    In general, gay couples appear to be (more/less) flexible about role expectations than heterosexuals. (294) |
| exclusive | 23-2.    Lesbian relationships are generally sexually (exclusive/"open"). (295) |
| are | 23-3.    In general, gays (are/are not) very involved in families as sons and daughters, parents and stepparents, etc. (295) |
| heterosexual | 23-4.    The vast majority of children of gay parents grow up to identify themselves as (homosexual/heterosexual). (263) |

**24.    Discuss the incidence and consequences of date rape.**

| | |
|---|---|
| date | 24-1. Forced and unwanted intercourse in the context of dating is referred to as _____ rape. (295) |
| 50 | 24-2. About (20/50/75) percent of all rapes occur in the context of dating. (296) |
| posttraumatic stress | 24-3. Many rape victims suffer from symptoms of (bipolar/posttraumatic stress/ dissociative) disorder. (296) |

**25.    Explain the factors that contribute to date rape.**

| | |
|---|---|
| 50 | 25-1. Alcohol contributes to about (25/50/75) percent of sexually aggressive incidents. (296) |
| increases | 25-2. Alcohol (increases/decreases) women's vulnerability to sexual coercion. (296) |
| indirectly | 25-3. It appears that aggressive pornography (directly/indirectly) induces men to behave aggressively toward women. (296) |
| promotes | 25-4. Society's double standard for sexual behavior generally (promotes/ discourages) sexual aggression. (297) |
| low | 25-5. Men who engage in sexual aggression tend to be (high/low) in empathy. (297) |
| aggressively | 25-6. To reduce the likelihood of being victimized by date rape, a woman should be prepared to act (aggressively/passively) if assertive refusals fail to stop unwanted advances. (297) |

**26.    Discuss the incidence of partner abuse and the characteristics of batterers.**

| | |
|---|---|
| difficult | 26-1. Obtaining accurate estimates of physical abuse is (easy/difficult). (298) |
| 25; 7 | 26-2. Research suggests that about (10/25/50) percent of women and (7/15/25) percent of men have been physically assaulted by an intimate partner at some point in their lives. (298) |
| less | 26-3. Women tend to inflict (more/less) physical damage than men. (298) |
| 25 | 26-4. Women commit about (25/50/75) percent of spousal murders. (298) |
| has not | 26-5. A single profile of men who batter women (has/has not) emerged. (298) |
| elevated | 26-6. High stress is associated with a(n) (elevated/reduced) risk for domestic violence. (298) |
| more | 26-7. Males who were beaten as children or who witnessed their mothers being beaten are (more/less) likely to abuse their wives than other men are. (298) |

**27.    *Discuss why women stay in abusive relationships.***

more

27-1.    Women leave abusive partners (more/less) often than stereotypes suggest. (299)

economic

27-2.    Many women who stay in abusive relationships fear (economic/social) hardship. (299)

homeless

27-3.    Many women who stay in abusive relationships simply have no place to go and fear becoming (homeless/independent/stigmatized). (299)

murder

27-4.    Above all else, many women who stay in abusive relationships fear that if they try to leave, they may precipitate more brutal violence and even (dependence/murder/posttraumatic stress disorder). (299)

## QUIZ BOXES

### *KEY TERMS*

| Marriage | The legally and socially sanctioned union of sexually intimate adults. |
|---|---|
| Cohabitation | Living together in a sexually intimate relationship without the legal bonds of marriage. |
| Endogamy | The tendency of people to marry within their own social group. |
| Homogamy | The tendency of people to marry others who have similar personal characteristics. |
| Family life cycle | An orderly sequence of developmental stages that families tend to progress through. |
| Intimate violence | Aggression toward those who are in close relationship to the aggressor. |
| Date rape | Forced and unwanted intercourse in the context of dating. |

### *KEY PEOPLE*

| John Gottman | Preeminent authority on marital communication; identified four communication patterns that are risk factors for divorce: contempt, criticism, defensiveness, and stonewalling. Eventually added a fifth pattern: belligerence. |
|---|---|
| E. Mavis Hetherington | Conducted a long-running study of children of divorced parents; findings suggested that only about 25% of adult children showed serious psychological problems. |
| Bernard Murstein | Proposed the stimulus-value-role (S-V-R) theory of mate selection, which outlines the three stages through which couples generally proceed as they move toward marriage. |
| Judith Wallerstein | Conducted controversial study that followed a sample of 60 divorced couples and their children since 1971; findings suggested that adult children of divorced parents were still troubled even 25 years after their parents' divorce. |

# SELF-TEST

## Multiple Choice Items

1. Marriage, as a legally and socially sanctioned union, is
   a. gradually losing its popularity and is in danger of disappearing
   b. under assault, but appears to be weathering the storm
   c. being replaced by alternative forms of intimate relationships
   d. as stable an institution today as it was 100 years ago

2. Role expectations for husbands and wives are becoming
   a. less varied and flexible
   b. more specific and stable
   c. less of a concern to married couples
   d. more varied and flexible

3. Which of the following is the main reason most people get married?
   a. the financial security that comes from having dual incomes
   b. to ensure that their children are considered "legitimate" by society
   c. the desire to participate in a socially sanctioned, mutually rewarding, intimate relationship
   d. to avoid the risk of sexually transmitted diseases that is associated with multiple sexual partners

4. Endogamy refers to the tendency of people to marry someone who
   a. has similar personality characteristics
   b. is older
   c. comes from one's own social group
   d. is younger

5. The tendency to marry someone who has personality characteristics similar to one's own is called
   a. endogamy
   b. homogamy
   c. monogamy
   d. homosexuality

6. In assessing a potential mate, women place a higher value than men on all but which of the following?
   a. intelligence
   b. youthfulness
   c. socioeconomic status
   d. financial prospects

7. On reaching Murstein's second stage of mate selection (the "value" stage), couples begin to
   a. explore each other's attitudes about such things as religion, politics, and gender role
   b. focus on the more intimate aspects of a relationship
   c. evaluate the other's physical attractiveness, age, and education
   d. apply the principles of social exchange theory

8. Couples who have high levels of intimacy, closeness, and commitment prior to the birth of the first child
   a. usually exhibit low levels of satisfaction after the child arrives
   b. find the transition to parenthood a difficult experience
   c. may see the newborn as an intruder into their life
   d. maintain a high level of satisfaction after the birth of a child

9. Parents overwhelmingly rate _____ as the most difficult stage of parenting.
   a. infancy
   b. middle childhood
   c. adolescence
   d. early adulthood

10. Conflict between adolescent children and their parents is most likely to involve which of the following issues?
    a.   the adolescent's career plans
    b.   the kinds of clothes the adolescent wears
    c.   whether or not the adolescent plans to attend college
    d.   whether or not the adolescent will engage in sexual relations

11. Research on maternal employment indicates that
    a.   it is not harmful to the children
    b.   it is harmful to the children
    c.   children are not harmed when they are younger but are when they are older
    d.   there is no conclusive evidence about its effect on children

12. According to your textbook, the best way for married couples to avoid troublesome battles over money is probably to
    a.   engage in joint decision making on finances
    b.   avoid discussions related to money
    c.   assign responsibility for financial decisions to one person
    d.   consult on a regular basis with a financial planner

13. After a divorce, children are likely to exhibit all but which of the following?
    a.   aggression                              c.   improved academic performance
    b.   reduced physical health                 d.   precocious sexual behavior

14. Which of the following statements about remarriage is not true?
    a.   Adaption to remarriage can be difficult for children.
    b.   Divorce rates are lower for second than for first marriages.
    c.   Roughly three-quarters of divorced people eventually remarry.
    d.   The average length of time between divorce and remarriage is slightly less than four years.

15. In comparison to married people, single people
    a.   have sex more frequently
    b.   rate themselves as happier
    c.   exhibit poorer physical and mental health
    d.   are more likely to develop posttraumatic stress disorder

16. Which the following statements about cohabitation is true?
    a.   Premarital cohabitation increases the likelihood of subsequent marital success.
    b.   Cohabitants tend to repudiate marriage as a viable alternative for them.
    c.   The majority of cohabitants plan to marry eventually.
    d.   Cohabitants are generally people who shy away from responsibility.

17. The majority of homosexual men and women prefer
    a.   a stable, long-term relationship
    b.   to engage in casual sex with a variety of partners
    c.   to adopt a masculine or feminine role in their relationships
    d.   a heterosexual relationship if the opportunity presents itself

18. Which of the following is considered a "date rape drug"?
    a.   caffeine                                 c.   marijuana
    b.   ecstasy                                  d.   rohypnol

19. Males who engage in sexual aggression are characterized by all but which of the following?
   a. heavy drinkers
   b. relatively impulsive
   c. high in empathy
   d. hostile toward women

20. Which of the following reasons explains why some women in abusive relationships feel that leaving is not a realistic option?
   a. They fear economic hardship.
   b. They simply have no place to go.
   c. They feel guilty and ashamed about their failing relationship.
   d. All of the above.

## True/False Items

T/F    1. Women tend to place a higher value than men on potential partners' socioeconomic status.

T/F    2. In general, studies have found that partners' specific personality traits are not particularly predictive of marital success.

T/F    3. The vast majority of parents rate parenthood as a very positive and satisfying experience.

T/F    4. Today's average married couple has more parents than children.

T/F    5. Marital satisfaction tends to decrease after children leave home.

T/F    6. Studies indicate that wives are still doing the bulk of the household chores, even when they work outside the home.

T/F    7. In general, studies have not found a link between mothers' employment status and the quality of infant-mother emotional attachment.

T/F    8. Divorce rates are higher among people who marry at a relatively young age.

T/F    9. The majority of divorce actions are initiated by the husbands.

T/F    10. Research findings indicate that women have greater problems adjusting to divorce than men do.

T/F    11. Increasing rates of cohabitation are unique to the United States.

T/F    12. In cases of date rape, the more intoxicated perpetrators are, the more aggressive they tend to be.

# ANSWER KEY FOR SELF-TEST ITEMS

*Multiple Choice Items*

| | | |
|---|---|---|
| b | 1. | While shifting social trends are shaking the traditional model of marriage, it does appear that the institution of marriage will weather the storm. (270) |
| d | 2. | The traditional breadwinner and homemaker roles for the husband and wife are being discarded by many couples, as more and more married women enter the workforce. (271) |
| c | 3. | A large variety of motivational factors propel people into marriage, but foremost among them is the desire to participate in a socially sanctioned, mutually rewarding, intimate relationship. (272) |
| c | 4. | Endogamy is promoted by cultural norms and by the way similarity influences interpersonal attraction (see Chapter 8). (272) |
| b | 5. | Among other things, marital partners tend to be similar in age and education, physical attractiveness, and attitudes and values. (272) |
| b | 6. | According to evolutionary theory, women seek male partners who possess or are likely to acquire more material resources that can be invested in children. On the other hand, men look for youth, attractiveness, and other characteristics presumed to be associated with higher fertility. (273) |
| a | 7. | This stage involves the comparison of values and attitudes as a way of assessing compatibility, hence the name "value stage." (274) |
| d | 8. | This finding underscores the notion that crisis during the transition to parenthood is far from universal. (277) |
| c | 9. | Research from the last decade has led to the conclusion that adolescence is not as difficult for youngsters as once believed. However, studies indicate that it is an especially stressful period for adolescents' parents. (278) |
| b | 10. | Conflicts between adolescents and their parents tend to involve everyday matters such as chores and dress. (278) |
| a | 11. | The vast majority of empirical studies have found little evidence that a mother's working is harmful to her children. (282) |
| a | 12. | In comparison to divorced couples, happy couples engage in more joint decision making on expenditures. (283) |
| c | 13. | Not surprisingly, children are likely to show *reduced* academic performance. (289) |
| b | 14. | In fact, divorce rates are *higher* for second than for first marriages. However, this statistic may simply indicate that this group of people see divorce as a reasonable alternative to an unsatisfactory marriage. (289) |
| c | 15. | There are a number of explanations for the health benefits associated with marriage, including the fact that spouses provide emotional and social support that buffers the negative effects of stress, and that they discourage their partners' unhealthy habits. (291) |

| | | |
|---|---|---|
| c | 16. | In fact, about three-quarters of female cohabitants expect to marry their current partner, a finding that's consistent with the view that cohabitation is a new stage in the courtship process –a sort of trial marriage. (292) |
| a | 17. | This finding contradicts the popular misconception that gays only rarely get involved in long-term intimate relationships. (294-295) |
| d | 18. | In addition to gamma hydroxybutyrate (GHB), rohypnol ("roofies") is sometimes used to subdue dates.  Both of these drugs are colorless, odorless, and tasteless, and their effects can be fatal. (296) |
| c | 19. | In fact, these men are likely to be *low* in empathy, the ability to adopt another person's frame of reference so you can understand his or her point of view. (298) |
| d | 20. | In addition, many fear that if they try to leave, they may precipitate more brutal violence and even murder. (299) |

### True/False Items

| | | |
|---|---|---|
| True | 1. | Women also value intelligence, ambition, and financial prospects.  According to evolutionary theory, women seek male partners who possess or are likely to acquire more material resources that can be invested in children. (273) |
| True | 2. | However, there are some traits that show modest correlations with marital adjustment, including such negative predictors of success as perfectionism and insecurity. (275) |
| True | 3. | In spite of the costs involved in raising children, most parents report no regret about their choice. (277) |
| True | 4. | This trend has occurred largely as a result of increased longevity and decreased family size. (278) |
| False | 5. | Middle-aged parents who have launched their children into the adult world report higher marital satisfaction than similar-aged parents who still have children at home. (279) |
| True | 6. | Even when both spouses are employed, many husbands maintain traditional role expectations about housework, child care, and decision making. (280) |
| True | 7. | The vast majority of empirical studies have found little evidence that a mother's working is harmful to her children. (282) |
| True | 8. | This is one of the patterns responsible for the increasing rate of divorce. (286) |
| False | 9. | In fact, wives initiate two-thirds of divorce actions, which may be related to the finding that wives' judgments about the likelihood of their marriages ending in divorce tend to be more accurate than husbands' judgments. (288) |
| False | 10. | Although divorce appears to impose greater stress on women than men, researchers do not find consistent gender differences in postdivorce adjustment. (288) |
| False | 11. | In fact, the cohabitation rates are even higher in many other countries. (291-292) |

True | 12. This is one reason why alcohol contributes to about one-half of sexually aggressive incidents.  Additionally, alcohol increases women's vulnerability to sexual coercion. (296)

# Chapter 10
# GENDER AND BEHAVIOR

## PROGRAMMED REVIEW

**1.** *Explain the nature of gender stereotypes and the connection with instrumentality and expressiveness.*

stereotypes

1-1. Gender (identities/roles/stereotypes) are widely shared beliefs about males' and females' abilities, personality traits, and social behavior. (304)

remained stable

1-2. Gender stereotypes in this country have (changed dramatically/remained stable) since the early 1970s. (305)

instrumentality; expressiveness

1-3. The stereotyped attributes for males generally reflect the quality of _____, an orientation toward action and accomplishment; whereas the stereotypes for females reflect the quality of _____, an orientation toward emotion and relationships. (305)

**2.** *Discuss four important points about gender stereotypes.*

similar

2-1. The stereotypes for African American males and females are more (similar/different) on the dimensions of competence and expressiveness than those for white American males and females. (305)

less

2-2. Since the 1980s, the boundaries between male and female stereotypes have become (more/less) rigid. (305)

androcentrism

2-3. The fact that the traditional male stereotype is more complimentary than the conventional female stereotype is related to _____, or the belief that the male is the norm. (305)

masculine

2-4. Our society is organized in a way that favors (masculine/feminine) characteristics and behavior. (305)

**3.** *Summarize the research findings on gender similarities and differences in verbal, mathematical, and spatial abilities.*

Meta-analysis

3-1. _____-_____ is a technique that combines the statistical results of many studies of the same question, yielding an estimate of the size and consistency of a variable's effects. (306)

have not

3-2. Gender differences (have/have not) been found in overall intelligence. (306)

earlier; larger

3-3. Girls usually start speaking a little (earlier/later), and have (larger/smaller) vocabularies. (306)

Boys

3-4. (Boys/Girls) seem to fare better on verbal analogies. (306)

males

3-5. Meta-analyses of mathematical abilities show small gender differences favoring (males/females). (306-307)

| | | |
|---|---|---|
| males | 3-6. | Gender differences favoring (males/females) are consistently found in the ability to perform mental rotations of a figure in three dimensions. (307) |

**4.    Summarize the research on gender similarities and differences in personality and social behavior.**

| | | |
|---|---|---|
| lower | 4-1. | Research supports the claim that females typically score (higher/lower) than males on tests of self-esteem. (307) |
| increases | 4-2. | The gender difference in self-esteem (increases/decreases) somewhat during adolescence. (307) |
| more | 4-3. | A recent summary of cross-cultural meta-analyses found that males consistently engage in (more/less) physical aggression than females. (308) |
| higher | 4-4. | Females are rated (higher/lower) than males on relational aggression. (308) |
| more | 4-5. | In the sexual domain, a meta-analysis found men to have (more/less) permissive attitudes than women about casual, premarital, and extramarital sex. (308) |
| does not | 4-6. | Research (does/does not) support the idea that females conform more to peer standards. (308) |
| more | 4-7. | A number of studies have found that women express (more/less) emotion than men do. (308-309) |
| do not differ | 4-8. | Recent research findings indicate that males and females (differ/do not differ) in experienced emotions. (309) |
| more | 4-9 | Men talk (more/less) than women. (309) |
| more | 4-10. | Men interrupt women (more/less) than women interrupt men in verbal communication. (309) |
| more | 4-11. | A number of studies have shown women to be (more/less) sensitive to nonverbal cues. (309) |

**5.    Summarize the research on gender and psychological disorders.**

| | | |
|---|---|---|
| minimal | 5-1. | In terms of the overall incidence of mental disorders, (many/minimal) gender differences have been found. (309) |
| more | 5-2. | Anti-social behavior, alcoholism, and other drug-related disorders are (more/ less) prevalent among men than among women. (309) |
| less | 5-3. | Men are (more/less) likely to suffer from depression and anxiety disorders. (309) |
| higher | 5-4. | Women show (higher/lower) rates of eating disorders. (309) |

| | |
|---|---|
| attempt<br>complete | 5-5.    Women (attempt/complete) suicide more often, but men (attempt/complete) suicide more frequently. (309) |

**6.    Summarize the situation regarding overall behavioral similarities and differences between males and females.**

| | |
|---|---|
| great;<br>large | 6-1.    Although the group averages for men and women on a given trait are detectably different, there is (great/little) variability within each gender and (large/minimal) overlap between the two groups. (310) |
| small | 6-2.    Gender accounts for a very (large/small) proportion of the differences between individuals. (310) |
| few;<br>small | 6-3.    Overall, the behavioral differences between males and females are relatively (many/few) in number and (large/small) in size. (310) |

**7.    Give two explanations for why gender differences appear larger than they actually are.**

| | |
|---|---|
| Social role | 7-1.    _____ _____ theory asserts that minor gender differences are exaggerated by the different social roles that males and females occupy. (310) |
| constructionism | 7-2.    Social _____ asserts that individuals construct their own reality based on societal expectations, conditioning, and self-socialization. (310) |

**8.    Summarize evolutionary explanations for gender differences.**

| | |
|---|---|
| natural   selection | 8-1.    Evolutionary psychologists suggest that gender differences in behavior reflect different (natural selection/psychological/social) pressures operating on the genders over the course of human history. (311) |
| are | 8-2.    Gender differences in cognitive abilities, aggression, and sexual behavior (are/are not) found in many cultures. (311) |
| reproductive | 8-3.    Evolutionary psychologists explain the gender gap in aggression in terms of _____ fitness. (311) |
| hunting | 8-4.    Males' superiority on most spatial tasks has been attributed to the adaptive demands of (gathering/hunting/warfare). (311) |

**9.    Review the evidence linking gender differences in cognitive abilities to brain organization.**

| | |
|---|---|
| cerebrum | 9-1.    The largest and most complicated part of the human brain, the (cerebellum/cerebrum/medulla) is responsible for most complex mental activities. (312) |
| more | 9-2.    Males exhibit (more/less) cerebral specialization than females. (312) |

| | |
|---|---|
| corpus callosum | 9-3.  Gender differences have been found in the size of the _____ _____, the band of fibers connecting the two hemispheres of the brain. (312) |
| females | 9-4.  Some studies suggest that (males/females) tend to have a larger corpus callosum. (312) |
| have not | 9-5.  Studies (have/have not) consistently found that males have more specialized brain organization than females. (312) |
| environmental | 9-6.  The biological factors that supposedly cause gender differences in cognitive functioning may actually reflect the influence of (environmental/evolutionary) factors. (312) |

**10.    Review the evidence relating hormones to gender differences.**

| | |
|---|---|
| Hormones | 10-1.  _____ are chemical substances released into the bloodstream by the endocrine glands. (312) |
| prenatal | 10-2.  Hormones play a key role in sexual differentiation during (prenatal/childhood/ adolescent) development. (313) |
| High low | 10-3.  (High/Low) levels of androgen in males and (high/low) levels of androgen in females lead to the differentiation of male and female genital organs. (313) |
| more | 10-4.  Females exposed prenatally to abnormally high levels of androgens exhibit (more/less) male-typical behavior than other females do. (313) |
| testosterone | 10-5.  The hormone (androgen/estrogen/testosterone) plays an important role in sexual desire for both men and women. (313) |

**11.    Define socialization and gender roles, and describe Margaret Mead's findings on the variability of gender roles and their implications.**

| | |
|---|---|
| socialization | 11-1.  The acquisition of the norms and roles expected of people in a particular society is called _____. (313) |
| appropriate | 11-2.  Gender roles are cultural expectations about what is (appropriate/forbidden/ necessary) behavior for each gender. (313) |
| socialization | 11-3.  Margaret Mead's observations suggest that gender roles are acquired through (classical conditioning/heredity/socialization). (314) |

**12.    Explain how reinforcement and punishment, observational learning, and self-socialization operate in gender-role socialization.**

| | |
|---|---|
| operant | 12-1.  In part, gender roles are shaped by the power of rewards and punishment – the key processes in (classical/operant) conditioning. (314) |
| negatively | 12-2.  Parents usually react (positively/negatively) to gender-inappropriate behavior, especially in boys. (314) |

| | |
|---|---|
| models | 12-3. Observational learning occurs when a child's behavior is influenced by observing others, who are called (observees/operants/models). (314) |
| similar | 12-4. According to social learning theory, children are more likely to imitate people who are nurturant, powerful, and (similar/dissimilar) to them. (314) |
| socialization | 12-5. When children are active in their own gender-role socialization, it is referred to as self-(conditioning/referencing/socialization). (314) |
| schemas | 12-6. Gender _____ are cognitive structures that guide the processing of gender-relevant information. (315) |
| concept | 12-7. Self-socialization begins when children link the gender schema for their own gender to their self-(concept/esteem/monitoring). (315) |

**13.    *Describe how parents and peers influence gender-role socialization.***

| | |
|---|---|
| parents, peers, schools, media | 13-1. The four main sources of gender-role socialization are _____, _____, _____, and the _____. (315) |
| different | 13-2. Studies have found that boys and girls are encouraged to play with (similar/different) types of toys. (315) |
| gender stereotypes | 13-3. Household chores tend to be assigned on the basis of (gender stereotypes/personal preference/nontraditional values). (315-316) |
| less | 13-4. African American families seem to place (more/less) emphasis on traditional gender roles than white American families do. (316) |
| different | 13-5. Play among same-gender peers takes (similar/different) forms for boys and girls. (316) |

**14.    *Describe how schools and the media influence gender-role socialization.***

| | |
|---|---|
| more | 14-1. In grade-school reading books, females are (more/less) likely to be shown performing domestic chores. (317) |
| boys | 14-2. Preschool and grade-school teachers tend to pay greater attention to (boys/girls). (317) |
| less | 14-3. Many academic and career counselors tend to guide female students toward (more/less) prestigious careers. (317) |
| less; less | 14-4. An analysis of characters on prime-time television programs showed that, compared to males, females appear (more/less) often, and are (more/less) likely to be employed. (317) |
| more | 14-5. Television commercials are (more/less) stereotyped than TV programs. (317) |

| | |
|---|---|
| women; men | 14-6. Music videos frequently portray (men/women) as sex objects and (men/women) as dominating and aggressive. (317) |
| more | 14-7. Children who watch a lot of television tend to hold (more/less) stereotyped beliefs about gender than children who watch less TV. (318) |

**15.** ***List five elements of the traditional male role and contrast it with the modern male role.***

| | |
|---|---|
| femininity | 15-1. Many psychologists consider anti-(aggression/emotion/femininity) to be the central theme running through the male gender role. (318) |
| beat out | 15-2. A key element of the traditional male role is that to prove their masculinity, men need to (cooperate with/beat out/give in to) other men at work and at sports. (318) |
| aggressively | 15-3. A key element of the traditional male role is that men should (aggressively/passively) defend themselves and those they love against threats. (318) |
| autonomous | 15-4. Another key element of the traditional male role is that men should be self-reliant and not admit to being dependent on others. In other words, they should be (aggressive/autonomous/stoic). (318) |
| heterosexuals | 15-5. According to the traditional male gender role, real men are (heterosexuals/homosexuals/bisexuals). (318) |
| stoic | 15-6. According to the traditional male gender role, men should not share their pain or express their "soft" feelings. In other words, they should be (aggressive/autonomous/stoic). (319) |
| economic | 15-7. According to the modern male role, masculinity is validated by (academic/athletic/economic) achievement. (319) |

**16.** ***Describe three common problems associated with the traditional male role.***

| | |
|---|---|
| unable | 16-1. The majority of men who have internalized the success ethic are (able/unable) to realize their dreams. (319) |
| less | 16-2. Younger men seem (more/less) inclined to embrace the success ethic than older men. (320) |
| hide | 16-3. Males learn early to (express/hide) vulnerable emotions such as love, joy, and sadness. (320) |
| anger | 16-4. One emotion males are allowed to express is (anger/happiness). (320) |
| interfere with | 16-5. Men's obsession with sexual performance can produce anxiety that may (enhance/interfere with) their sexual responsiveness. (320) |

| | |
|---|---|
| intimacy | 16-6.  Another problem is that many men learn to confuse feelings of (anger/lust/ intimacy) and sex. (320) |
| homosexuality | 16-7.  Homophobia is the intense fear and intolerance of _____. (320) |

**17.    List three major expectations of the female role.**

| | |
|---|---|
| married | 17-1.  In the traditional female role, adult status is attained when a woman gets (a job/married/pregnant). (320) |
| children | 17-2.  The imperative of the female role is to have (a good job/a clean home/ children). (320) |
| rising | 17-3.  The percentage of women in the labor force has been steadily (rising/falling) over the last 30 years. (321) |
| heterosexual | 17-4.  The marriage and motherhood mandates fuel women's intense focus on learning how to attract and interest males as prospective mates –in other words, (achievement/heterosexual/task) success. (321) |

**18.    Describe three common problems associated with the female role.**

| | |
|---|---|
| lower | 18-1.  Young women tend to have (higher/lower) aspirations than men with comparable backgrounds and abilities. (323) |
| ability-achievement | 18-2.  The discrepancy between women's abilities and their level of achievement has been termed the _____-_____ gap. (323) |
| 3 | 18-3.  Most women have day-to-day responsibilities in (1/2/3) roles. (323) |
| passive | 18-4.  Many girls are taught that a woman's role in sex is a(n) (active/passive) one. (324) |
| ambivalent | 18-5.  Women are likely to have (ambivalent/negative) feelings about sex instead of the positive feelings common to men. (324) |

**19.    Describe two ways in which women are victimized by sexism.**

| | |
|---|---|
| gender | 19-1.  Sexism is discrimination against people on the basis of their (gender/sexual orientation). (324) |
| lack | 19-2.  Women (have/lack) the same employment opportunities as men. (324) |
| less | 19-3.  Ethnic minority women are (more/less) likely than white women to work in high-status occupations. (324) |
| glass | 19-4.  There appears to be a (glass/job/pay) ceiling that prevents most women and ethnic minorities from advancing beyond middle-management positions. (325) |

harassment

19-5. Aggression toward women in the form of sexual (behavior/bias/harassment) is recognized as a widespread problem that occurs not only on the job but also at home, while walking outside, and in medical and psychotherapy sessions. (325)

**20.    *Explain the basis for traditional gender roles and why they are changing.***

labor

20-1. A key consideration is that gender roles have always constituted a division of (labor/sex roles/territory). (326)

no longer

20-2. Traditional gender roles (still/no longer) make economic sense. (326)

more

20-3. The future is likely to bring (more/less) dramatic shifts in gender roles. (327)

**21.    *Define gender-role identity and discuss two alternatives to traditional gender roles.***

gender-role

21-1. A person's identification with the qualities regarded as masculine or feminine is termed his/her (gender-role/sexual/social) identity. (327)

Androgyny

21-2. _____ refers to coexistence of both masculine and feminine personality traits in a single person. (327)

high;
low

21-3. Males who score (high/low) on masculinity and (high/low) on femininity are said to be gender-typed. (327)

high;
low

21-4. Females who score (high/low) on masculinity and (high/low) on femininity, are said to be cross-gender-typed. (327)

has not

21-5. The weight of the research evidence (has/has not) supported Sandra Bem's hypothesis that androgyny is healthy. (328)

transcendence

21-6. The gender-role _____ perspective suggests that to be fully human, people need to move beyond gender roles as a way of organizing their perceptions of themselves and others. (328)

greater;
more

21-7. The advocates of gender-role transcendence believe that if gender were to be eliminated (or even reduced) as a means of categorizing traits, each individual's unique capabilities and interests would assume (greater/less) importance, and individuals would be (more/less) free to develop their own unique potentials. (328-329)

**22.    *Describe how the different socialization experiences of males and females contribute to communication problems between men and women.***

different

22-1. Deborah Tannen says that males and females are typically socialized in (similar/ different) "cultures." (330)

| | |
|---|---|
| childhood | 22-2.   According to Tannen, gender differences in communication styles develop in (adolescence/childhood/early adulthood) and are fostered by traditional gender stereotypes. (330) |
| dominant | 22-3.   Boys achieve high status in their groups by engaging in (dominant/passive submissive) behavior. (330) |
| verbal | 22-4.   In girls' groups, dominance tends to be gained by (physical/verbal/nonverbal) persuasion. (330) |
| mixed | 22-5.   To date, the findings from research testing Tannen's ideas are (mixed/supportive). (330) |

**23.    Describe expressive and instrumental styles of communication.**

| | |
|---|---|
| instrumental | 23-1.   An (expressive/instrumental) communication style focuses on reaching practical goals and finding solutions to problems. (331) |
| expressive | 23-2.   An (expressive/instrumental) communication style is characterized by being able to express tender emotions easily and being sensitive to the feelings of others. (331) |
| instrumental; expressive | 23-3.   Men are more likely to use an (expressive/instrumental) style of communication and women, an (expressive/instrumental) style. (331) |
| more | 23-4.   In general, women are (more/less) skilled than men in nonverbal communication. (331) |
| women | 23-5.   Regarding verbal communication, (men/women) are better listeners. (331) |

**24.    Describe some common mixed-gender communication problems.**

| | |
|---|---|
| women; men | 24-1.   According to Tannen, (men/women) tend to talk about people, whereas (men/women) tend to talk about things. (331) |
| women; man's | 24-2.   In many mixed-gender conversations, particularly those in public settings, (men/women) often end up playing the listener to the (man's/woman's) "lecture." (332) |
| instrumental | 24-3.   Males' (expressive/instrumental) style of communication tends to be used as the norm against which both women's and men's speech is evaluated. (332) |

## QUIZ BOXES

### KEY TERMS

| | |
|---|---|
| **Gender** | The state of being male or female. |
| **Gender stereotypes** | Widely shared beliefs about males' and females' abilities, personality traits, and social behavior. |
| **Instrumentality** | An orientation toward action and accomplishment. |
| **Expressiveness** | An orientation toward emotion and relationships. |
| **Androcentrism** | The belief that the male is the norm. |
| **Meta-analysis** | A technique that combines the statistical results of many studies of the same question, yielding an estimate of the size and consistency of a variable's effects. |
| **Aggression** | Behavior that is intended to hurt someone, either physically or verbally. |
| **Conformity** | Yielding to real or imagined social pressure. |
| **Social role theory** | Asserts that minor gender differences are exaggerated by the different social roles that males and females occupy. |
| **Social constructionism** | Asserts that individuals construct their own reality based on societal expectations, conditioning, and self-socialization. |
| **Cerebral hemispheres** | The right and left halves of the cerebrum, which is the convoluted outer layer of the brain. |
| **Hormones** | Chemical substances released into the bloodstream by the endocrine glands. |
| **Socialization** | The acquisition of the norms and roles expected of people in a particular society. |
| **Gender roles** | Cultural expectations about what is appropriate behavior for each gender. |
| **Gender schemas** | Cognitive structures that guide the processing of gender-relevant information. |
| **Homophobia** | The intense fear and intolerance of homosexuality. |

| Sexism | Discrimination against people on the basis of their gender. |
|---|---|
| Gender-role identity | A person's identification with the qualities regarded as masculine or feminine. |
| Androgyny | The coexistence of both masculine and feminine personality traits in a single person. |
| Gender-role transcendence perspective | Proposes that to be fully human, people need to move beyond gender roles as a way of organizing their perceptions of themselves and others. |

## KEY PEOPLE

| Sandra Bem | Proposed that androgynous individuals are more flexible and psychologically healthier than those who exhibit conventional gender-typing. |
|---|---|
| Alice Eagly | Proposed social role theory, which asserts that minor gender differences are exaggerated by the different social roles that males and females occupy. |
| Janet Shibley Hyde | Conducted a series of meta-analyses on gender differences in cognitive abilities beginning in the 1980s. |
| Joseph Pleck | Has written extensively on gender-role expectations for males; emphasized the distinction between the traditional male role and the modern male role. |
| Deborah Tannen | Sociolinguist who examined gender differences in communication. Wrote the book *You Just Don't Understand: Women and Men in Conversation.* |

**SELF-TEST**

*Multiple Choice Items*

1.  Widely shared beliefs about males' and females' abilities, personality, and social behavior are called
    a.  sexual prototypes
    b.  gender role differences
    c.  gender misattributions
    d.  gender stereotypes

2.  Androcentrism refers to
    a.  the tendency to fall in love easily
    b.  the belief that women are superior
    c.  the belief that the male is the norm
    d.  the inability to take another's perspective

3.  Which of the following statements regarding gender differences in verbal abilities is accurate?
    a.  Boys have larger vocabularies than girls.
    b.  Girls usually start speaking earlier than boys.
    c.  Girls seem to fare better on verbal analogies.
    d.  Girls are more likely than boys to be stutterers.

4.  Research findings indicate that with respect to aggressive behavior,
    a.  females are slightly more aggressive than males
    b.  males engage in more physical aggression
    c.  males are more aggressive, but only when they are provoked
    d.  males are more aggressive than females, but the difference disappears by about 10 years of age

5.  Regarding gender differences in communication, it has been found that
    a.  women talk more than men
    b.  women tend to speak more tentatively
    c.  men are more sensitive to nonverbal cues
    d.  men tend to interrupt women less than women interrupt men

6.  The overall incidence of mental disorders indicates that
    a.  it is roughly the same for both genders
    b.  they are more likely to occur in women than men
    c.  they are more likely to occur in men than women
    d.  gender differences are unclear because many disorders are unreported

7.  Which of the following disorders is more common in men than in women?
    a.  depression
    b.  eating disorders
    c.  anxiety disorders
    d.  alcoholism

8.  Evolutionary psychologists explain social behaviors such as aggression and mating patterns in terms of different _____ pressures operating on the genders over the course of human history.
    a.  economic
    b.  hormonal
    c.  environmental
    d.  natural selection

9.  The notion that cerebral specialization is linked to gender differences in mental abilities
    a.  is still under debate
    b.  has been rejected by researchers
    c.  has been consistently supported by empirical evidence
    d.  was popular 50 years ago, and has recently resurfaced

10.   Hormones play a role in gender differentiation during
      a.    prenatal development              c.    prepubescent development
      b.    early childhood                    d.    adolescence

11.   Gender-role socialization occurs through
      a.    self-socialization
      b.    observational learning
      c.    reinforcement and punishment
      d.    All of the above play a part in the acquisition of gender roles.

12.   Between the ages of 4 and 6, children tend to separate into
      a.    same-gender groups
      b.    opposite-gender groups
      c.    groups based on their level of socialization
      d.    small groups that are formed on the basis of socioeconomic status

13.   In the modern male role, masculinity is validated by all but which of the following?
      a.    emotional control                  c.    organizational power
      b.    economic achievement               d.    individual physical strength

14.   Men learn to confuse feelings of intimacy and
      a.    sex                                c.    weakness
      b.    power                              d.    femininity

15.   The intense fear and intolerance of homosexuality is
      a.    termed homophobia
      b.    more common in women than in men
      c.    the root cause of anxiety disorders in many men
      d.    virtually nonexistent in Western cultures

16.   Heterosexual success refers to
      a.    the efforts of men to be good husbands and parents
      b.    males' level of sexual activity during late adolescence
      c.    homosexuals' efforts to gain success in a heterosexual world
      d.    women learning how to attract and interest males as prospective mates

17.   An androgynous person is one who
      a.    is said to be gender-typed
      b.    scores above average on measures of both masculinity and femininity
      c.    scores low on measures of both masculinity and femininity
      d.    is said to be gender-role undifferentiated

18.   Sandra Bem suggests that androgynous people are
      a.    less flexible in their behavior
      b.    psychologically healthier than those who are gender-typed
      c.    becoming the norm in modern society
      d.    more likely to engage in homosexual behavior

19. When Deborah Tannen says that males and females are socialized in different "cultures," she means that
   a.   males are influenced by their fathers and females by their mothers
   b.   males learn status and independence, while females learn connection and intimacy
   c.   males tend to have only male friends, whereas females have friends of both genders
   d.   more attention is paid to female children throughout their early childhood

20. Tannen suggests that many frustrations could be avoided if
   a.   men used instrumental communication styles more than they do
   b.   women made greater use of instrumental communication
   c.   men and women were more aware of gender-based differences in communication style
   d.   men and women could learn to relax in their relationships with each other

## True/False Items

T/F     1.   Males generally score higher than females on measures of intelligence.

T/F     2.   Research findings indicate that girls' self-esteem tends to drop dramatically during adolescence.

T/F     3.   Women typically hold lower status in groups than do men.

T/F     4.   Women interrupt men more than men interrupt women.

T/F     5.   Men attempt suicide more often than women, but women complete suicides more frequently than men.

T/F     6.   In general, gender roles in other cultures are similar to those seen in our society.

T/F     7.   Children are basically passive recipients of gender-role socialization.

T/F     8.   Mothers and fathers consistently assign household chores in line with gender stereotypes.

T/F     9.   African-American families seem to place less emphasis on traditional gender-roles than white American families.

T/F     10.  Children who watch a lot of television have been found to hold more stereotyped beliefs about gender than children who watch less TV.

T/F     11.  Younger men seem less inclined to embrace the success ethic than older men.

T/F     12.  In general, young men have lower aspirations than young women with comparable backgrounds and abilities.

T/F     13.  Androgynous people have been found to be psychologically healthier than those who exhibit conventional gender-typing.

T/F     14.  Studies indicate that women are more skilled than men in nonverbal communication.

## ANSWER KEY FOR SELF-TEST

### Multiple Choice Items

| | | |
|---|---|---|
| d | 1. | You may recall from Chapter 6 that stereotypes are widely held beliefs that people possess certain characteristics simply because of their membership in a particular group. In this case, the "groups" are males and females. (304) |
| c | 2. | This belief is based on the idea that our society is organized in a way that favors "masculine" characteristics and modes of behavior. (305) |
| b | 3. | On the whole, gender differences in verbal ability are small; however, there do seem to be a few noteworthy differences that favor females. With the three incorrect alternatives, the findings support the opposite conclusions. (306) |
| b | 4. | Although males generally engage in more physical and public aggression, females are rated higher on *relational* aggression. (308) |
| b | 5. | One explanation attributes women's greater use of tentative and polite language to lower status; another, to gender-specific socialization. (309) |
| a | 6. | There are gender differences in the prevalence of *specific* disorders, but the *overall* incidence of mental disorders is about the same for both genders. (309) |
| d | 7. | Women are more likely than men to suffer from the other three disorders listed. (309) |
| d | 8. | Evolutionary psychologists emphasize the roles of natural selection and reproductive fitness in the development of behavior. (311) |
| a | 9. | Psychologists have a long way to go before they can attribute gender differences in verbal and spatial ability to right brain/left brain specialization. (312) |
| a | 10. | At about 8 to 12 weeks after conception, male and female gonads begin to produce different hormonal secretions that lead to the differentiation in male and female genital organs. (313) |
| d | 11. | Gender socialization takes place through all of these key learning processes. (314-315) |
| a | 12. | This is when peers begin to play an important role in gender-role socialization. (316) |
| d | 13. | Physical strength is more closely associated with the *traditional* male role. (319) |
| a | 14. | This is one of the problems associated with the traditional male role. If a man experiences strong feelings of connectedness, he is likely to interpret them as sexual feelings. (320) |
| a | 15. | Because homosexuality is still largely unaccepted, fear of being labeled homosexual keeps many people, but especially males, adhering to traditional gender roles. (320) |
| d | 16. | Women's focus on heterosexual success is a function of the marriage and motherhood mandates. (321) |
| b | 17. | Androgyny is the coexistence of both masculine and feminine personality traits in a single person. (327) |

| | | |
|---|---|---|
| b | 18. | However, the weight of evidence does not support Bem's hypothesis that androgyny is especially healthy. (328) |
| b | 19. | Tannen likens male-female communications to other "cross-cultural" communications – full of opportunities for misunderstandings to develop. (330) |
| c | 20. | Tannen suggests that if we could see the gender-style differences for what they are, we could eliminate a lot of negative feelings. (332) |

### True/False Items

| | | |
|---|---|---|
| False | 1. | Although some gender differences have been found in specific domains (verbal ability, spatial ability), differences have *not* been found in *overall* intelligence. (306) |
| False | 2. | Researchers have found no support for claims in the popular press that girls' self-esteem drops dramatically during adolescence. (307) |
| True | 3. | This is one of the explanations for the finding that women are more likely than men to conform to group pressure. (308) |
| False | 4. | It's actually the other way around, although the difference is small.  Also, there is evidence indicating that this finding may be a function of differences in status. (309) |
| False | 5. | This is also the other way around.  This is one of the gender differences in the prevalence of specific psychological problems. (309) |
| True | 6. | Although this is *generally* true, it is not *necessarily* the case, as Margaret Mead demonstrated. (314) |
| False | 7. | Actually, children play an active role in the process of socialization.  This is most clearly the case with self-socialization. (314) |
| True | 8. | Girls usually do laundry and dishes, whereas boys mow the lawn and sweep out the garage. (315-316) |
| True | 9. | This is one of several ethnic differences in the influence parents have on their children's gender-role socialization. (316) |
| True | 10. | One explanation for this finding is that television programs and commercials tend to be gender-stereotyped. (318) |
| True | 11. | A significantly smaller proportion of men between the ages of 18 and 37 are work-focused compared to men 38 years and older. (320) |
| False | 12. | Again, it's the other way around.  The discrepancy between women's abilities and their level of achievement has been termed the ability-achievement gap. (323) |
| False | 13. | Sandra Bem proposed this idea, but the empirical evidence does not support it. (328) |
| True | 14. | For example, women are better at reading and sending nonverbal messages. (331) |

# Chapter 11
# DEVELOPMENT IN ADOLESCENCE AND ADULTHOOD

## PROGRAMMED REVIEW

**1.** ***Define and discuss pubescence and secondary sex characteristics.***

is not

1-1. The phenomenon of adolescence (is/is not) universal across cultures. (338)

puberty

1-2. Pubescence refers to the two-year span preceding (adolescence/middle school/puberty) during which the changes leading to physical and sexual maturity take place. (338)

secondary

1-3. Physical features that distinguish one gender from the other but that are not essential for reproduction are termed (primary/secondary/tertiary) sex characteristics. (338)

secondary

1-4. Facial hair in boys and breast growth in girls are examples of (primary/secondary) sex characteristics. (338)

pituitary

1-5. The physical changes associated with the development of secondary sex characteristics are triggered by the (pituitary/thyroid) gland. (338)

**2.** ***Define and discuss puberty and primary sex characteristics.***

adolescence

2-1. Puberty is the stage that marks the beginning of (adolescence/adulthood/pubescence) and during which sexual functions reach maturity. (338)

primary

2-2. The structures necessary for reproduction are called (primary/secondary/gonadal) sex characteristics. (338)

menarche

2-3. The onset of puberty in females is signaled by the first occurrence of menstruation, termed (menarche//pubescence/spermarche). (339)

spermarche

2-4. The first ejaculation in males is called (menarche/pubescence/spermarche). (339)

later

2-5. On the average, puberty arrives two years (earlier/later) in boys than in girls. (339)

earlier;
rapidly

2-6. Today's girls begin puberty (earlier/later), and complete it more (slowly/rapidly) than did their counterparts in earlier generations. (339)

**3.** ***Summarize the findings on early and late maturation in boys and girls.***

early;
late

3-1. Research suggests that girls who mature (early/late) and boys who mature (early/late) seem to feel particularly anxious and self-conscious about their changing bodies. (340)

| | |
|---|---|
| worse;<br>negative | 3-2. Girls who mature early tend to do (better/worse) in school, and have more (positive/negative) body images. (340) |
| more;<br>more | 3-3. Late-maturing boys have been found to feel (more/less) inadequate and (more/less) insecure. (340) |
| on time;<br>early | 3-4. Optimal adjustment for girls is associated with puberty coming (early/on time/ late), whereas optimal adjustment for boys is related to puberty arriving (early/on time/late). (340) |

**4. Describe the cognitive changes that occur during adolescence.**

| | |
|---|---|
| abstractly | 4-1. Compared to those who are younger, adolescents can think (abstractly/ concretely). (340) |
| deductive | 4-2. Adolescents are more skilled than children in the ability to reach logical conclusions when one is given certain information. That is, adolescents have better developed (deductive/inductive/intuitive) reasoning skills. (341) |
| more | 4-3. Research has shown that older adolescents are (more/less) likely than younger adolescents and children to engage in risky behavior (e.g., smoking, drinking). (341) |

**5. Explain Erikson's psychosocial crisis of adolescence and Marcia's four identity statuses.**

| | |
|---|---|
| Identity | 5-1. (Identity/Self-disclosure/Self-esteem) refers to having a relatively clear and stable sense of who one is in the larger society. (342) |
| Freud;<br>eight | 5-2. Building on earlier work by (Bandura/Freud/Skinner), Erik Erikson divided the life span into (four/eight/twelve) stages. (342) |
| identity | 5-3. According to Erik Erikson, the primary challenge of adolescence is achieving (foreclosure/identity/self-esteem). (342) |
| is not | 5-4. For most people, an identity crisis (is/is not) a sudden process. (342) |
| foreclosure | 5-5. According to James Marcia, identity (achievement/foreclosure/moratorium) involves a premature commitment to visions, values, and roles prescribed by one's parents. (343) |
| moratorium | 5-6. Identity (achievement/foreclosure/moratorium) involves delaying commitment for a while to experiment with alternative ideologies. (343) |
| diffusion | 5-7. Identity (achievement/foreclosure/diffusion) is an inability to make identity commitments. (343) |
| achievement | 5-8. Identity (achievement/foreclosure/diffusion) is arriving at a sense of self and direction after some consideration of alternative possibilities. (343) |

| | | |
|---|---|---|
| more;<br>higher | 5-9. | Those individuals who experience identity achievement tend to be (more/less) cognitively flexible, and function at (higher/lower) levels of moral reasoning. (343) |

**6.  Discuss whether adolescence is a period of emotional turmoil and describe recent trends in adolescent suicide.**

| | | |
|---|---|---|
| G. Stanley Hall | 6-1. | (Sigmund Freud/G. Stanley Hall/John Watson), the first psychologist to study adolescence, characterized this stage of development as time of "storm and stress." (343) |
| increase | 6-2. | There is evidence that conflicts with parents (increase/decrease) during (early) adolescence. (343) |
| high | 6-3. | Juvenile delinquents who have a childhood history of behavior problems are at (high/low) risk for adult criminal activity. (344) |
| increased | 6-4. | Suicide among 15- to 24-year-olds has (increased/decreased/remained stable) since 1960. (344) |
| higher | 6-5. | The ratio of attempted to completed suicides among adolescents is (higher/lower) than that for any other age group. (344) |
| attempt;<br>complete | 6-6. | Girls are more likely to (attempt/complete) suicide, and boys are more likely to (attempt/complete) suicide. (344) |

**7.  Summarize the key developmental transitions in early adulthood, including Erikson's views.**

| | | |
|---|---|---|
| social | 7-1. | A person's notion of a developmental schedule that specifies what he or she should have accomplished by certain points in life is called a (biological/psychological/social) clock. (345) |
| intimacy | 7-2. | In Erikson's sixth stage, the psychosocial crisis centers on whether a person can develop the capacity to share (intimacy/resources) with others. (346) |
| pseudointimate | 7-3. | According to Jacob Orlofsky and his colleagues, individuals in the (intimate/preintimate/pseudointimate) status of intimacy are typically involved in a relatively permanent relationship, but it resembles the stereotyped relationship in quality. (346) |
| identity | 7-4. | According to Erikson, the ability to establish and maintain intimate relationships depends on having successfully weathered the (dating/identity/psychosexual) crisis of adolescence. (346) |
| two | 7-5. | On the average, people in their twenties change jobs every (two/five/eight) years. (347) |
| happy | 7-6. | As noted in Chapter 9, the first few years of married life tend to be very (happy/depressing/tumultuous). (347) |

| | | |
|---|---|---|
| majority | 7-7. | The (majority/minority) of married couples plan to have children. (347-348) |
| more | 7-8. | Mothers tend to experience (more/fewer) work-family conflicts than fathers do. (348) |
| more | 7-9. | Compared to married couples, committed homosexual couples are (more/less) likely to have a flexible division of labor. (348) |

**8.    Summarize the key developmental transitions in middle adulthood, including Erikson's views.**

| | | |
|---|---|---|
| generativity | 8-1. | According to Erikson, the challenge of middle adulthood is acquiring (autonomy/generativity/identity), or a concern for the welfare of future generations. (348) |
| generativity | 8-2. | Adults demonstrate (autonomy/generativity/integrity) when they provide unselfish guidance to younger people. (348) |
| aging | 8-3. | Chief among the challenges of middle adulthood is coming to terms with the (aging/death/retirement) process. (348) |
| adolescence | 8-4. | Parents overwhelmingly rate (infancy/early childhood/adolescence) as the most difficult stage of child-rearing. (349) |
| improved | 8-5. | The "empty nest" is associated with (diminished/improved) well-being for most women. (349) |
| stable; changing | 8-6. | At midlife, workers seem to follow one of two patterns: the _____ career pattern, or the _____ careers pattern. (349) |
| is not | 8-7. | Research findings suggest that a midlife crisis (is/is not) typical for most individuals. (349) |

**9.    Summarize the key developmental transitions in late adulthood, including Erikson's views.**

| | | |
|---|---|---|
| ego integrity | 9-1. | In Erik Erikson's last stage (stage eight), the challenge is to achieve (autonomy/ego integrity/identity). (350) |
| decreasing; 62 | 9-2. | Over the years, the average age of retirement has been (increasing/ decreasing), and it is now (55/62/69). (350) |
| variable | 9-3. | Individuals tend to approach retirement with highly (positive/negative/ variable) attitudes. (351) |
| rising | 9-4. | Relationship satisfaction starts (rising/diminishing) later in life. (351) |
| more | 9-5. | Friends seem to play a (more/less) significant role in life satisfaction for older adults than family members do, at least for most white Americans. (351) |

| | |
|---|---|
| larger;<br>more | 9-6. Older men tend to have a (larger/smaller) network of friends than women do, but women's friendships are (more/less) intimate. (351) |
| | **10. Discuss age-related changes in appearance and their psychological significance.** |
| increase | 10-1. The percentage of body weight that is fat tends to (increase/decrease) throughout adulthood. (352) |
| less | 10-2. The net impact of the physical changes associated with aging is that many older people view themselves as (more/less) attractive. (352) |
| more | 10-3. Older women suffer (more/less) than older men as a result of the decline in physical attractiveness. (352) |
| | **11. Describe the sensory, neurological, and endocrine changes that accompany aging.** |
| 50s | 11-1. Noticeable hearing losses do not usually show up until people reach their (40s/50s/60s). (352) |
| farsighted | 11-2. From about age 30 to the mid-60s, most people become increasingly (nearsighted/farsighted). (352) |
| high | 11-3. Drivers over 65 have a (high/low) proportion of car accidents. (352) |
| tasteless | 11-4. Older people often complain that their food is somewhat (bitter/salty/tasteless). (353) |
| Dementia | 11-5. _____ is an abnormal condition marked by multiple cognitive deficits that include memory impairment. (353) |
| Alzheimer's | 11-6. (Alzheimer's/Parkinson's/Senile) disease accounts for about 50-60% of all cases of dementia. (353) |
| do not appear | 11-7. Age-related changes in hormonal functioning (appear/do not appear) to be the chief cause of declining sexual activity in later years. (353) |
| Menopause | 11-8. (Dementia/Menarche/Menopause) is the time when menstruation ceases in women. (354) |
| expectations | 11-9. Women's reactions to menopause vary greatly, depending on their general (health/expectations/weight). (354) |
| do not | 11-10. Males (do/do not) experience reactions similar to those of women during menopause. (354) |
| | **12. Discuss health changes as people age and two things people can do to maintain health.** |

increases

varies

tend

a healthy diet

12-1. The proportion of people with chronic health problems (increases/decreases) with age. (354)

12-2. Nursing home use (is similar/varies) across ethnic groups. (355)

12-3. People who exercise (tend/tend not) to be healthier than those who do not. (355)

12-4. People can also increase the likelihood of maintaining their health by eating (a healthy diet/fewer vegetables/spicy foods). (355)

**13.   Describe age-related changes in intelligence, information processing, and memory.**

is stable

diminishes
somewhat

speed

decrease

decreases

are not

is no

13-1. Current evidence suggests that IQ (is stable, declines gradually) throughout most of adulthood. (355)

13-2. There is evidence that the ability to narrow one's focus of attention (increases/is stable/diminishes somewhat) with increasing age. (356)

13-3. In the cognitive domain, age seems to take its toll on (memory/problem solving/speed) first. (356)

13-4. Overall success on both practical and laboratory problem-solving tasks appears to (increase/remain stable/decrease) as people grow older. (356)

13-5. It seems that the capacity of short-term or working memory (increases/decreases/remains stable) as people age. (356)

13-6. The memory losses associated with aging (are/are not) universal. (357)

13-7. There (is/is no) evidence that the elderly have more numerous or more vivid early memories. (357)

**14.   Summarize evidence on personality change and stability in adulthood.**

stability

contradictory

change

14-1. A number of large-scale longitudinal studies using objective assessments of personality traits provide evidence for long-term (stability/variability) in personality. (358)

14-2. In sum, researchers assessing the stability of personality in adulthood have reached (consistent/contradictory) conclusions. (358)

14-3. Adult personality is characterized by both stability and (abnormality/change/increasing complexity). (358)

**15.   Discuss cultural and individual attitudes about death, including death anxiety.**

| | |
|---|---|
| avoidance | 15-1. The most common strategy for dealing with death in modern Western society is (avoidance/celebration/indirect confrontation). (358) |
| system | 15-2. The collection of rituals and procedures used by a culture to handle death is called a death (celebration/plan/system). (358-359) |
| negative; evasive | 15-3. The death system in modern Western society is (positive/negative) and (confrontational/evasive). (359) |
| less | 15-4. One study found that devout Christians and devout atheists were (more/less) anxious about death than those with ambivalent religious views. (359) |
| declines | 15-5. Death anxiety typically (increases/declines) from early to late adulthood. (359) |

**16.  Describe Kübler-Ross's five stages of dying and research findings about the dying process.**

| | |
|---|---|
| denial | 16-1. The first reaction to being informed of a serious, life-terminating illness is (anger/denial/depression). (359) |
| anger | 16-2. The typical reaction after denial is (acceptance/anger/depression). (359) |
| bargaining | 16-3. In the (acceptance/bargaining/denial) stage, the patient wants more time and asks for favors to postpone death. (359) |
| Depression | 16-4. (Bargaining/Denial/Depression) is a signal that the acceptance process has really begun. (359) |
| acceptance | 15-5. According to Kübler-Ross, the final stage of dying is (acceptance/anger/ bargaining). (359) |
| have not | 16-6. Systematic studies of dying patients (have/have not) consistently found the same progression of emotions that Kübler-Ross described. (359) |

**17.  Describe cultural variations in mourning practices and discuss the grieving process.**

| | |
|---|---|
| bereavement | 17-1. The painful loss of a loved one through death is called (bereavement/ grief/mourning). (359) |
| Considerable | 17-2. (Considerable/Little) variation exists among and within cultures as to how death is acknowledged. (360) |
| encouraged | 17-3. In Asian, African, and Hispanic cultures, the maintenance of emotional ties between the bereaved and their dead loved ones is (encouraged/ discouraged). (360) |
| numbness | 17-4. The initial stage of the grieving process is (numbness/reorganization/ yearning). (360) |

| | |
|---|---|
| yearning | 17-5. During the (numbness/reorganization/yearning) state of the grieving process, survivors try to recover the lost person. (360) |
| does not | 17-6. Research on the process of grieving suggests that grief (does/does not) follow a straightforward path. (360) |
| chronic | 17-7. In the (absent/chronic/normal) pattern of grieving, depression exists before and after the spouse's death. (361) |

**18.  Discuss different types of loss and what helps people cope with bereavement.**

| | |
|---|---|
| child | 18-1. The most difficult type of loss adults must cope with is the death of a (child/parent/spouse). (361) |
| more | 18-2. One study found that women whose husband had died were significantly (more/less) depressed than women who had lost a parent. (361) |
| posttraumatic stress disorder | 18-3. Children and adolescents who have witnessed the death of a schoolmate or teacher in a schoolyard killing are likely to suffer from (bipolar disorder/posttraumatic stress disorder/schizophrenia). (361) |
| overload | 18-4. Bereavement _____ occurs when individuals experience several deaths at the same time or in close succession. (361) |

**19.  Describe Ainsworth's three attachment styles and how caregivers can promote secure attachment in their infants.**

| | |
|---|---|
| eight | 19-1. Most babies tend to develop a strong emotional attachment to a single, familiar caregiver by (two/four/eight) months of age. (363) |
| avoidant | 19-2. Babies with a(n) (avoidant/anxious-ambivalent/secure) attachment style tend to ignore their mothers. (363) |
| anxious-ambivalent | 19-3. Babies with a(n) (avoidant/anxious-ambivalent/secure) attachment style seem to desire contact with the mother, yet they actively resist her when she comes near. (363) |
| secure | 19-4. The majority of infants develop (avoidant/anxious-ambivalent/secure) attachment styles. (363) |
| abused | 19-5. The disorganized/disoriented attachment style appears to be common among (abused/high achieving/well-adjusted) children. (363) |
| secure | 19-6. Ainsworth and her colleagues reported that mothers who were perceptive about the baby's needs, responded to those needs relatively quickly and consistently, and enjoyed physical contact with the baby had babies that showed (avoidant/anxious-ambivalent/secure) attachment. (363) |

**20.  Summarize the research on the effects of day care on infants and children.**

increased

20-1. Research by Jay Belsky suggests that babies under a year who receive nonmaternal care for more than 20 hours per week have a(n) (increased/ decreased) risk of developing insecure attachments to their mothers. (363)

no

20-2. Many studies have found (major/no) differences in attachment between children reared in day care or at home. (363)

quality

20-3. The effects of day care appear to depend on the (cost/quality) of the care provided. (363)

**21.    Discuss Baumrind's parenting styles and their effects on children's development.**

control

21-1. Two major dimensions underlying parental behavior are parental acceptance and parental (attribution/control/integrity). (364)

authoritative

21-2. High acceptance and high control characterize the (authoritative/permissive/ authoritarian) parental style. (364)

Permissive

21-3. (Authoritative/Permissive/Authoritarian) parents make few or no demands of their children. (364)

low;
low

21-4. The neglectful parental style is characterized by (high/low) acceptance and (high/low) control. (364)

authoritative

21-5. The (authoritative/permissive/authoritarian) parenting style is associated with the most positive outcomes. (364)

do not establish

21-6. The data on the association between parenting style and children's traits are correlational and (establish/do not establish) that the parenting style is the cause of the children's traits. (364-365)

**22.    Discuss issues related to the effective parenting of adolescents.**

Authoritative

22-1. (Authoritative/Authoritarian/Permissive) parents are most likely to avoid the turmoil that is sometimes associated with adolescence. (365)

are

22-2. The findings on parenting styles and adjustment in adolescents (are/are not) consistent across a number of ethnic groups. (367)

**23.    List five suggestions for more effective parenting.**

high

23-1. One suggestion for effective parenting is to set (high/low), but reasonable standards for your children. (368)

good

23-2. Parents should stay alert for (good/bad/social) behavior and reward it. (368)

control

23-3. Explaining the purpose of a request to a child tends to encourage self-(control/esteem/monitoring) in the child. (368)

others

consistently

23-4.  Parents should encourage their children to take the perspective of (others/the parents/their pets). (368)

23-5.  Parents should enforce rules (consistently/inconsistently). (368)

**24.   List five suggestions for the effective use of punishment.**

negative

esteem

swift

consistent

should

what not

24-1.  Punishment often has unintended, (positive/negative) side effects. (368)

24-2.  One guideline for the effective use of punishment is that it should not damage the child's self-(control/esteem/perception) (369)

24-3.  To be used effectively, punishment should be (swift/delayed). (369)

24-4.  To be used effectively, punishment should be (consistent/inconsistent). (369)

24-5.  When children are punished, the reason for their punishment (should/should not) be explained. (369)

24-6.  One shortcoming of punishment is that it only tells a child (what/what not) to do. (369)

## QUIZ BOXES

*KEY TERMS*

| Pubescence | The two-year span preceding puberty during which the changes leading to physical and sexual maturity take place. |
|---|---|
| Secondary sex characteristics | Physical features that distinguish one gender from the other but that are not essential for reproduction. |
| Puberty | The stage that marks the beginning of adolescence and during which sexual functions reach maturity. |
| Primary sex characteristics | The structures necessary for reproduction. |
| Menarche | The first occurrence of menstruation. |
| Spermarche | The first ejaculation. |
| Identity | Having a relatively clear and stable sense of who one is in the larger society. |
| Social clock | A person's notion of a developmental schedule that specifies what he or she should have accomplished by certain points in life. |
| Midlife crisis | A turbulent period of doubts and reappraisal of one's life. |
| Neurons | Individual cells that receive, integrate, and transmit information. |
| Dementia | An abnormal condition marked by multiple cognitive deficits that include memory impairment. |
| Menopause | The time when menstruation ceases. |
| Death system | The collection of rituals and procedures used by a culture to handle death. |
| Death anxiety | Fear and apprehension about one's own death. |
| Bereavement | The painful loss of a loved one through death. |
| Mourning | The formal practices of an individual and a community in response to a death. |

| Infant attachment | The emotional bond between infant and mother. |
| --- | --- |

## KEY PEOPLE

| Mary Ainsworth | Described three attachment styles in infants: avoidant, anxious-ambivalent, and securely attached. |
| --- | --- |
| Diana Baumrind | Proposed four parental styles based on the interactions of parental acceptance and parental control: authoritative, authoritarian, permissive, and neglectful. |
| Erik Erikson | Influential psychoanalytic theorist who described eight stages of personality development. Suggested that adolescence was a period of pivotal importance. |
| Elisabeth Kübler-Ross | Described five stages of dying: denial, anger, bargaining, depression, and acceptance. |
| Laurence Steinberg | Conducted research on inter-generational conflicts between adolescents and their parents. Suggested that authoritative parents are most likely to avoid serious conflict. |
| Susan Krauss Whitbourne | Conducted research indicating the existence of adult personality changes on a variety of variables. |

# SELF-TEST

*Multiple Choice Items*

1.  The two-year span preceding puberty is
    a.  called the latency period
    b.  referred to as pubescence
    c.  when growth slows down
    d.  usually considered a time of turmoil

2.  Today's girls begin puberty _____, and complete it more _____ than their counterparts in earlier generations.
    a.  earlier; slowly
    b.  earlier; rapidly
    c.  later; slowly
    d.  later; rapidly

3.  After puberty, boys have an advantage over girls in which of the following areas?
    a.  speed
    b.  strength
    c.  endurance
    d.  all of the above

4.  Optimal adjustment for girls is associated with puberty arriving _____, and optimal adjustment for boys is related to puberty arriving _____.
    a.  early; on time
    b.  early; late
    c.  on time; early
    d.  late; on time

5.  During adolescence, a sense of identity usually develops
    a.  earlier in boys than in girls
    b.  as a result of the first sexual experience
    c.  quickly, during the final stages of puberty
    d.  gradually, following a period of personal questioning

6.  Which of the following statements regarding the notion of adolescence as a time of turmoil is not accurate?
    a.  Conflicts with parents increase during adolescence.
    b.  Adolescence is inherently fraught with chaos and pain.
    c.  Adolescents tend to engage in increased risk behavior (e.g., substance abuse).
    d.  Adolescents experience more volatile emotions and extremes of mood than adults do.

7.  A person's notion of a developmental schedule that specifies what he or she should have accomplished by certain points in life is called a(n)
    a.  social clock
    b.  psychosocial focus
    c.  egocentric timetable
    d.  developmental stopwatch

8.  According to Orlofsky and his colleagues, individuals in which of the following intimacy statuses are capable of forming open and close relationships with both male and female friends and are involved in a committed relationship?
    a.  intimate
    b.  stereotyped
    c.  preintimate
    d.  pseudointimate

9.  Which of the following statements regarding early adulthood is not true?
    a.  Most people get married in their 20s.
    b.  Most married couples are in dual-worker relationships.
    c.  The majority of married couples are now choosing not to have children.
    d.  Marital satisfaction typically declines after the arrival of children.

10. According to Erik Erikson, the challenge in middle adulthood (stage seven) is to acquire generativity, or a concern for
    a.   one's parents
    b.   one's financial status
    c.   work-related accomplishments
    d.   the welfare of future generations

11. Researchers relying on objective measures of emotional stability have found signs of midlife crises in
    a.   most men, but few women
    b.   the majority of men and women
    c.   only a small minority of individuals
    d.   people who are contemplating retirement

12. Although 65 is the age typically associated with retirement, individuals today
    a.   are leaving the workplace earlier
    b.   tend to keep working well into their 70s
    c.   retire at about age 70 and then stay busy with part-time work
    d.   tend to remain actively involved at work until health problems force them to retire

13. Noticeable hearing losses usually begin to show up when people reach their
    a.   30s
    b.   40s
    c.   50s
    d.   60s

14. Dementia
    a.   is part of the normal aging process
    b.   is the main cause of Alzheimer's disease
    c.   is an abnormal condition marked by multiple cognitive deficits
    d.   is a function of the progressive neuronal loss associated with aging

15. Throughout the adult years the IQ
    a.   declines slowly but consistently beginning at about age 45
    b.   is stable throughout most of adulthood, with most declines beginning after age 60
    c.   shows a small but steady increase due to accumulated learning
    d.   shows no predictable pattern of change

16. In the cognitive domain, age seems to take its toll on _____ first.
    a.   speed
    b.   learning
    c.   decision making
    d.   problem solving

17. The memory losses associated with aging are _____ in size and _____ universal.
    a.   large; are
    b.   large; are not
    c.   moderate; are
    d.   moderate; are not

18. Which of the following is the correct order for John Bowlby's four stages of grieving?
    a.   yearning; numbness; reorganization; disorganization and despair
    b.   numbness; reorganization; disorganization and despair; yearning
    c.   numbness; yearning; disorganization and despair; reorganization
    d.   disorganization and despair; reorganization; numbness; yearning

19. According to Diana Baumrind, _____ parenting is most likely to foster social and cognitive competence in children.
    a.   authoritarian
    b.   authoritative
    c.   permissive
    d.   educated

20. Psychologists would say that physical punishment should not be used frequently because it
    a.    can lead to the development of posttraumatic stress disorder
    b.    seldom leads to the suppression of the undesirable behavior
    c.    it is associated with a host of problematic outcomes
    d.    results in overwhelming feelings of guilt in the punisher

**True/False Items**

T/F    1.    Adolescence is a stage of development that is seen in virtually all cultures.

T/F    2.    The capacity to reproduce is attained during pubescence.

T/F    3.    Puberty arrives about two years later in boys than in girls.

T/F    4.    The majority of teenagers who attempt suicide complete the act.

T/F    5.    Girls are more likely to attempt suicide, and boys are more likely to complete suicide.

T/F    6.    The vast majority of married couples plan to have children.

T/F    7.    The "emptying of the nest" is a traumatic event for parents, especially mothers.

T/F    8.    Older men suffer more than older women as a result of the decline in physical attractiveness that comes with aging.

T/F    9.    Research findings support the existence of "male menopause."

T/F    10.   In general, older people have vivid recollections of events in the distant past while being forgetful about recent events.

T/F    11.   Researchers generally agree that personality tends to remain stable throughout adulthood.

T/F    12.   The death system in our culture is negative and evasive.

T/F    13.   Research suggests that babies who receive nonmaternal care for more than 20 hours per week have an increased risk of developing insecure attachments to their mothers.

T/F    14.   To use punishment effectively, parents should use it less often.

# ANSWER KEY FOR SELF-TEST

## Multiple Choice Items

| b | 1. | Pubescence is the two-year span during which the changes leading to physical and sexual maturity take place. (338) |
| --- | --- | --- |
| b | 2. | These generational changes in the timing of puberty have occurred primarily in industrialized nations, although this trend appears to have leveled off in the United States and some other industrialized nations. (339) |
| d | 3. | Before about age 12, boys and girls are similar in these areas, but physical changes that occur during puberty are more marked for boys than girls. (340) |
| c | 4. | Girls who mature early and boys who mature late are most likely to experience social and behavioral problems. (340) |
| d | 5. | According to Erik Erikson, identity emerges out of an "identity crisis" or a period of personal questioning during which individuals reflect on and experiment with various occupational possibilities and value choices. (342) |
| b | 6. | Although adolescence is inherently marked by change and upheaval, it need *not* be fraught with chaos or deep pain. (343) |
| a | 7. | For example, if you feel that you should be married by the time you're 30, that belief creates a marker on your social clock. (345) |
| a | 8. | The intimate status represents the highest quality in terms of a person's relationships with others. (346) |
| c | 9. | Although an increasing number of people are choosing not to have children, the vast majority of married couples still plan to do so. (347-348) |
| d | 10. | Adults demonstrate generativity when they provide unselfish guidance to younger people. (348) |
| c | 11. | Research findings make it clear that the fabled midlife crisis is *not* typical. (350) |
| a | 12. | Over the years, the average age of retirement has been decreasing, and it is now 62. (350) |
| c | 13. | Only about one-third of older adults suffer hearing losses that require corrective treatment. (352) |
| c | 14. | Dementia, which is *not* part of the normal aging process, can be caused by a variety of disorders, such as Alzheimer's disease, Parkinson's disease, and AIDS. (353) |
| b | 15. | About 80% of the individuals in one study showed no declines by age 60, and about two-thirds were still stable through age 81. (355) |
| a | 16. | Studies indicate that one's speed in learning, solving problems and processing information tends to decline with age, probably beginning in middle adulthood. (356) |

| | | |
|---|---|---|
| d | 17. | However, individuals' beliefs about their memory abilities can produce self-fulfilling prophecies. (357) |
| c | 18. | It should be noted, however, that research on the process of grieving suggests that most grief reactions do not follow this straightforward path. (360) |
| b | 19. | In general, authoritative parenting is associated with the most positive outcomes in children. (364) |
| c | 20. | Among these outcomes are reduced quality of parent-child relationships, poorer mental health in childhood and adulthood, and increased delinquency and aggression in childhood. (368) |

**True/False Items**

| | | |
|---|---|---|
| False | 1. | This stage is *not* universal across cultures. In some cultures, young people move almost directly from childhood to adulthood. (338) |
| False | 2. | The capacity to reproduce occurs during puberty, not pubescence. Pubescence is the two-year period that *precedes* puberty. (338) |
| True | 3. | The major reason that adult males are taller than adult females is that males typically experience two additional years of development before the onset of the growth spurt. (339) |
| False | 4. | The ratio of suicide attempts to actual suicide deaths is anywhere from 100:1 to 200:1, which is much higher than that for any other age group. When all age groups are combined, the ratio of suicide attempts to completions is about 8:1. (344) |
| True | 5. | This is because girls tend to use methods that are less lethal (e.g., overdosing on sleeping pills), whereas boys elect methods with a small likelihood of survival (shooting or hanging). (344) |
| True | 6. | This is true even though an increasing number of people are choosing *not* to have children. (347-348) |
| False | 7. | In fact, the "empty nest" is associated with improved mood and well-being for most women. (349) |
| False | 8. | It's the other way around. Because our society dictates that much of a woman's worth is based on her physical appearance, her social status tends to decline along with her attractiveness. (348) |
| False | 9. | Actually, there is no male equivalent to female menopause. (354) |
| False | 10. | This is a popular misconception. In fact, there is no evidence that the elderly have more numerous, or more vivid, early memories. (358) |
| False | 11. | It appears that some personality traits (e.g., emotional stability) tend to remain stable, while others (e.g., masculinity, femininity) tend to change systematically as people grow older. (358) |

True | 12. | However, negativism and avoidance as features of death systems are not universal across cultures. (359)

True | 13. | These findings have raised many eyebrows, and other studies have yielded different results. (363)

True | 14. | The reason for this is that punishment often has unintended, negative side effects, such as reduced quality of parent-child relationships, and increased delinquency and aggression in childhood. (368)

# Chapter 12
# CAREERS AND WORK

## PROGRAMMED REVIEW

**1.    Describe personal and family influences on job choice.**

industrial-
organizational

1-1.    The study of human behavior in the workplace is called _____-_____ psychology. (373)

does

1-2.    Intelligence (does/does not) predict the likelihood of entering particular occupations. (374)

personality

1-3.    Psychologists agree that it is important to choose an occupation that is compatible with your (IQ/parent's wishes/personality). (375)

parents

1-4.    The jobs that appeal to people tend to be like those of their (friends/parents/spouses). (375)

more

1-5.    Compared to European American students, Chinese and Asian students are (more/less) influenced by their parents when it comes to their career aspirations. (375)

**2.    Cite several helpful sources of career information.**

Labor

2-1.    The *Dictionary of Occupational Titles* is published by the United States Department of (Agriculture/Education/Labor) (376)

250

2-2.    The *Occupational Outlook Handbook*, published every two years by the U.S. Bureau of Labor Statistics, provides detailed information for (250/1000/20,000) occupations. (376)

American
Psychological
Association

2-3.    If you're interested in a career in psychology, you can obtain a number of pamphlets or books from the _____ _____ _____. (376)

**3.    List some aspects of potential occupations that are important to know about.**

working conditions

3-1.    When you consider information about potential occupations, you should find out if the work environment is pleasant or unpleasant, and if the job is low key or high pressure.  In other words, you need to know about the (job entry requirements/nature of the work/working conditions). (376)

entry

3-2.    One aspect of a potential occupation that you need to know about is the education and training that are required to break into the occupation.  That is, you need to know about the job (advancement/entry/status) requirements. (376)

advancement     3-3.     When you consider information about potential occupations, you should find out how you move up in this particular field.  In other words, you need to know about the opportunities for (advancement/retirement/status). (376)

educated     3-4.     Experts agree that the future belongs to those who are better (educated/looking/skilled). (376-377)

**4.     Explain the role of occupational interest inventories in career decisions.**

interests     4-1.     Occupational interest inventories measure your (interests/strengths/skills as they relate to various jobs or careers. (377)

do not attempt     4-2.     Occupational interest inventories (attempt/do not attempt) to predict whether you would be successful in various occupations. (377)

satisfaction     4-3.     Occupational interest inventories focus on the likelihood of job (satisfaction/success). (377)

gender     4-4.     Most occupational interest inventories have a lingering (age/gender/ethnic) bias. (377)

**5.     List five important considerations in choosing an occupation.**

multiple     5-1.     Career counselors stress that people have (multiple/relatively few) potentials. (377)

is not     5-2.     It (is/is not) a good idea to choose a career on the basis of salary. (377)

are     5-3.     As you contemplate your career options, it's a good idea to keep in mind that there (are/are no) limits on your career options. (377)

throughout life     5-4.     Career choice is a developmental process that extends (from puberty to one's early 20s/well into one's 40s/throughout life). (378)

may not be     5-5.     Once you invest time, money, and effort in moving along a particular career path, it (is/may not be) easy to change paths. (378)

**6.     Summarize Holland's hexagonal model of career development.**

personality     6-1.     According to Holland, career choice is related to an individual's (attributional/personality/physical) characteristics. (378)

orientations;     6-2.     Holland has identified six personality types called personal (desires/
work               orientations) and six matching (living/social/work) environments. (378)

Realistic     6-3.     (Artistic/Realistic/Social) people describe themselves as good at mechanical tasks and weak in social skills. (378)

| | | |
|---|---|---|
| Artistic | 6-4. | (Artistic/Realistic/Social) people see themselves as imaginative and independent. They tend to be impulsive and creative and are socially aloof. (378) |
| Enterprising | 6-5. | (Artistic/Enterprising/Investigative) people perceive themselves as happy, self-confident, sociable, and popular. They like to use their social skills to lead or persuade others. (378) |
| supports | 6-6. | Holland's hexagonal model has prompted considerable research, and much of it (supports/refutes) his theory. (379) |

**7.    Summarize Super's five-stage model of career development.**

| | | |
|---|---|---|
| retires | 7-1. | Super views occupational development as a process that begins in childhood and ends when one (takes his or her first job/reaches middle age/retires). (379-380) |
| concept | 7-2. | According to Super, decisions about work and career commitments are expressions of people's self-(concept/esteem/perception). (380) |
| childhood | 7-3. | The growth stage of Super's model encompasses (childhood/adolescence/one's early 20s). (380) |
| high school | 7-4. | According to Super, people are expected to narrow their career directions by the end of (childhood/high school/their 20s). (380) |
| establishment | 7-5. | Vacillation in career commitment continues to be common during the first part of the (establishment/growth/maintenance) stage. (380) |
| maintenance | 7-6. | Around their mid-40s, many people cross into the (establishment/growth/maintenance) stage. (381) |
| retirement | 7-7. | In the decline stage, people redirect their energy and attention toward planning for (their children/death/retirement). (381) |
| varied | 7-8. | People approach retirement with highly (positive/negative/varied) attitudes. (381). |
| stronger | 7-9. | A study of adolescents reported that identity status was a (stronger/weaker) predictor of career maturity than was self-esteem. (381) |

**8.    Discuss women's career development.**

| | | |
|---|---|---|
| 60 | 8-1. | It is currently estimated that (30/60/90) percent of women are in the labor force. (381) |
| Most | 8-2. | (Few/Some/Most) women subordinate their career goals to their husbands'. (381) |
| continuous; discontinuous | 8-3. | Men's career paths are usually (continuous/discontinuous), whereas women's tend to be (continuous/discontinuous). (381) |

| | | |
|---|---|---|
| decreasing | 8-4. | The amount of time women are out of the labor force is (increasing/decreasing). (381) |

**9.** **List six work-related trends.**

| | | |
|---|---|---|
| Technology | 9-1. | (The presence of women/Education/Technology) is changing the nature of work. (382) |
| active | 9-2. | Workers must take a more (active/passive) role in shaping their careers. (382) |
| learning | 9-3. | Lifelong (computer use/learning/social development) is a necessity in today's workplace. (382) |
| free agent | 9-4. | According to Daniel Pink, one way to survive in the modern work environment is to become a (free agent/replacement/whistle blower). (383) |
| breaking down | 9-5. | The boundaries between work and home are (increasing/breaking down). (383) |
| professional | 9-6. | The jobs of the next decade will be in the (construction/manufacturing/professional) occupations. (383) |

**10.** **Describe the relationship between education and salary.**

| | | |
|---|---|---|
| lowest | 10-1. | The jobs that exist for individuals with less than a college degree usually offer the (highest/lowest) pay and benefits. (384) |
| higher | 10-2. | The more education one obtains, the (higher/lower) the income one is likely to earn. (384) |
| Computer | 10-3. | _____ literacy is an essential complement to a good basic education. (385) |

**11.** **Summarize important demographic changes that are transforming the workforce.**

| | | |
|---|---|---|
| force | 11-1. | The labor (environment/force/situation) consists of all those who are employed as well as those who are currently unemployed but are looking for work. (385) |
| more | 11-2. | With regard to gender and ethnicity, the workforce is becoming (more/less) diverse. (385) |
| 57 | 11-3. | Figures show that about (33/57/92) percent of women with children under the age of 3 work outside the home. (385) |

do not have

11-4.  Most gay, lesbian, and bi-sexual workers (have/do not have) the same legal protections against employment discrimination as their heterosexual counterparts. (385)

**12.    Cite some problems that women and minorities face in today's workplace.**

segregation

12-1.  The major obstacle to occupational success for women and minority group members is job _____, a process in which jobs are simultaneously typed by gender and race. (386)

white men

12-2.  Women and minorities face discrimination because they are frequently passed over for promotion in favor of (African American men/younger workers/white men). (386)

glass

12-3.  There appears to be a (glass/high/sticky) ceiling, or invisible barrier that prevents most women and ethnic minorities from advancing to the highest levels of occupations. (386)

sticky

12-4.  At the other end of the spectrum, there seems to be a (glass/high/sticky) floor that causes women and minorities to remain in low-paying jobs. (386)

token

12-5.  When there is only one woman or minority person in an office, that person becomes a symbol of all the members of that group, or in other words, a _____. (386)

less

12-6.  Another way the world of work is different for women, ethnic, and gay and lesbian minorities is that they have (more/less) access to same-gender or same-group role models and mentors. (386)

**13.    Describe some challenges presented by workforce diversity to organizations and workers.**

more

13-1.  The (increasingly/decreasingly) diverse workforce presents challenges to both organizations and workers. (387)

resentment

13-2.  Some individuals feel that they are personally paying the price of prejudice in the workplace, and this perception causes (resentment/satisfaction). (387)

reverse

13-3.  Many who advocate abandoning affirmative action programs argue that these programs promote (enhanced/decreased/reverse) discrimination through the use of unfair hiring and promotion practices. (387)

negative

13-4.  Research has demonstrated that attaching an affirmative action label to an employee results in (positive/negative) attributions. (387)

**14.    List some important sources of job stress.**

the workplace

14-1.  Many theorists suspect that (marriage/job status/the workplace) is the primary source of stress in modern society. (387)

| | |
|---|---|
| 48 | 14-2. Current estimates clock the average full-time workweek at (35/48/65) hours. (387) |
| More | 14-3. (More/Fewer) workers are employed in service industries. (388) |
| unpredictable | 14-4. One of the reasons American workers are stressed out is that the economy is (predictable/unpredictable). (388) |
| more | 14-5. The workplace is becoming (more/less) diverse. (388) |
| psychological; decision | 14-6. According to Robert Karasek, the two key factors in occupational stress are the (physical/psychological/social) demands made on a worker and a worker's amount of (decision/environmental/self-) control. (388) |

**15.** *Summarize the effects of job stress on physical and mental health.*

| | |
|---|---|
| increased; increased; higher | 15-1. In the work arena itself, job stress has been linked to a(n) (increased/decreased) number of industrial accidents, (increased/decreased) absenteeism, and (higher/lower) turnover rates. (388) |
| burnout | 15-2. Prolonged stress can lead to _____, characterized by exhaustion, cynicism, and poor job performance. (389) |
| extend | 15-3. The negative effects of occupational stress (extend/do not extend) beyond the workplace. (389) |
| physical | 15-4. Some of the adverse effects of stress on employees' (psychological/physical) health include heart disease, high blood pressure, and ulcers. (389) |

**16.** *Describe actions organizations are taking to reduce job stress.*

| | |
|---|---|
| individual | 16-1. Interventions at the (individual/organizational) level are the most widely used strategy for managing work stress. (389) |
| individual level | 16-2. A workplace wellness program is an example of an intervention at the (individual level/individual-organizational interface). (390) |
| organizational level | 16-3. Interventions at the (individual level/organizational level/individual-organizational interface) are intended to make work environments less stressful. (390) |
| has not | 16-4. According to a national survey of American workers, the workplace (has/has not) been particularly responsive in the area of childcare. (390) |
| more | 16-5. Workers from lower socioeconomic groups typically experience (more/less) work stress than those from higher status groups. (391) |

**17.** *Describe the prevalence and consequences of sexual harassment.*

1980

17-1. Regulations regarding sexual harassment were instituted in (1970/1980/1990). (391)

sexually-oriented

17-2. Sexual harassment occurs when employees are subjected to unwelcome (discrimination/sexually-oriented/sex stereotyping) behavior. (391)

quid pro quo

17-3. The type of sexual harassment in which submission to unwanted sexual advances is a condition of hiring, advancement, or not being fired is called (environmental harassment/quid pro quo/submissive harassment). (391)

hostile environment

17-4. Any type of unwelcome sexual behavior that creates a hostile work environment is termed _____ _____. (391)

power

17-5. Sexual harassment is considered an abuse of (feelings/power/the system) by a person in authority. (391)

more

17-6. Sexual harassment in the workplace is (more/less) widespread than people realize. (391)

increase

17-7. Victims of sexual harassment are likely to experience a(n) (increase/decrease) in alcohol consumption and smoking. (392)

**18.    Cite some ways that organizations and individuals can reduce sexual harassment.**

social situation

18-1. To predict the occurrence of sexual harassment, researchers have developed a two-factor model based on the prospective harasser and the (potential consequences/social situation). (392)

promoting

18-2. Organizations can reduce the incidence of sexual harassment by (promoting/discouraging) norms that are intolerant of it. (392)

protect

18-3. Acknowledging the prevalence and negative impact of sexual harassment, many organizations have taken steps to educate and (promote/protect/punish) their workers. (392)

least

18-4. Among the personal responses to sexual harassment, the most frequently used strategy, avoiding/denial, is also the (most/least) effective one. (392)

infrequently

18-5. In dealing with sexual harassment, confrontation and advocacy seeking are two effective strategies that are (frequently/infrequently) used. (392)

**19.    Describe some causes and effects of unemployment.**

economic

19-1. Unemployment today is caused primarily by dramatic (economic/social) changes. (392)

service

19-2. The shift from a manufacturing to a(n) (agricultural/service/technological) economy has significantly transformed the nature of work. (392)

| | | |
|---|---|---|
| displaced | 19-3. | A major consequence of economic upheaval is _____ workers –individuals who are unemployed because their jobs have disappeared. (393) |
| increases | 19-4. | The rate of attempted and completed suicides (increases/decreases) with unemployment. (393) |
| in middle age | 19-5. | While losing a job at any age is highly stressful, those who are laid off (early in their careers/in middle age/as they near retirement) seem to find the experience most difficult. (393) |
| unfairly | 19-6. | Employees who lose their jobs because of downsizing –instead of poor performance –are likely to believe that they have been treated (fairly/ unfairly). (393) |
| counseling | 19-7. | When a person is out of work for an extended period of time or has little social support, (counseling/medication/self-reflection) may be helpful. (393) |

**20.    Summarize current perspectives on workaholism.**

| | | |
|---|---|---|
| enthusiastic | 20-1. | The (enthusiastic/committed) workaholic works for the pure joy of it. (395) |
| more | 20-2. | Nonenthusiastic workaholics are (more/less) likely to develop burnout. (395) |
| families | 20-3. | Although enthusiastic workaholics really love their work, their devotion to their jobs has a price, one often paid by their (families/employers). (395) |

**21.    Define work-family conflict and discuss the benefits of multiple roles.**

| | | |
|---|---|---|
| dual-earner | 21-1. | One of the biggest changes in the labor force has been the emergence of (computer-controlled/dual-earner/extended family) households. (395) |
| work-family | 21-2. | The feeling of being pulled in multiple directions by competing demands from the job and the family is termed (approach-avoidance/interpersonal/work-family) conflict. (395) |
| wives | 21-3. | In heterosexual dual-earner families, most of the responsibility for child care and housework is borne by (husbands/wives/in-laws). (395-396) |
| more | 21-4. | In gay and lesbian dual-earner households, responsibilities are (more/less) evenly divided. (396) |
| beneficial for | 21-5. | Researchers find that multiple roles are (beneficial for/detrimental to) both men's and women's mental, physical, and relationship health. (396) |

**22.    List several types of leisure activities and summarize the benefits of them.**

| | | |
|---|---|---|
| lags far behind | 22-1. | The paid vacation time of American workers (is greater than/is similar to/lags far behind) that of many European workers. (397) |

| | |
|---|---|
| Leisure | 22-2. _____ refers to unpaid activities people choose to engage in because the activities are personally meaningful. (397) |
| Fewer | 22-3. (More/Fewer) individuals read now than in the past. (397) |
| the Internet | 22-4. A relatively new entry into the world of leisure involves surfing (the Internet/ in the ocean/television channels). (397) |
| is | 22-5. Playing computerized and video games (is/is not) a very popular form of leisure activity. (398) |
| positively; negatively | 22-6. Among adults aged 55 and older, regular participation in a variety of leisure activities is (positively/negatively) correlated with psychological well-being and (positively/negatively) related to depression. (398) |
| watching television | 22-7. One study found that one leisure activity was negatively related to perceived well-being: (playing sports/traveling/watching television). (398) |

**23.     Summarize the guidelines for putting together an effective résumé.**

| | |
|---|---|
| interview | 23-1. The purpose of a résumé is to get you a(n) (good salary/interview/job). (400) |
| should not | 23-2. You (should/should not) use colored paper for your résumé. (400) |
| best | 23-3. You should use the (best/most inexpensive) professional printing service available to print copies of your résumé. (400) |
| short | 23-4. Your résumé should be as (long/short) as possible. (400) |
| is not | 23-5. It (is/is not) a good idea to use complete sentences on your résumé. (400) |
| personal | 23-6. On your résumé, you should avoid giving any (educational/personal/work-related) information that is superfluous to the job. (400) |
| reverse chronological | 23-7. You should list your work experience in (chronological/reverse chronological) order on your résumé. (400) |

**24.     Discuss strategies for targeting companies you would like to work for.**

| | |
|---|---|
| Career Services | 24-1. To learn about the characteristics of different occupations, you should see a reference librarian or visit your (Career Services/Financial Aid/Army Recruiting) office. (401) |
| specific | 24-2. Once you've decided on a work setting, you need to target (a lot of/specific/ various) companies. (401) |
| 80 | 24-3. Experts estimate that up to (20/50/80) percent of all vacancies, especially those above entry level, are never advertised. (402) |

*Business Employment*

24-4.   If you are willing to locate anywhere, a good source for business and professional jobs is the National (*Business Employment/Job Search/Work Finder*) *Weekly*. (402)

least

24-5.   Using Internet job boards is one of the (most/least) effective ways of getting a job. (402)

**25.   Describe several strategies for landing a job interview.**

research

25-1.   One way to increase your chances of being invited for an interview is to persuade the prospective employer that you are interested enough in the company to have done some (research/spying) on the organization. (402)

person in charge of hiring

25-2.   One option is to introduce yourself (by phone or in person) directly to the (company CEO/appropriate vice president/person in charge of hiring) and request an interview. (402)

**26.   List some factors that can influence an interviewer's rating of a job candidate.**

intangible

26-1.   An interviewer will attempt to verify that you have the (tangible/intangible) qualities that will make you a good team player. (402)

are not

26-2.   Interviewers' ratings of job applicants (are/are not) heavily based on job-relevant considerations. (402-403)

higher

26-3.   Researchers have found that more attractive candidates are usually rated (higher/lower) than less attractive ones. (403)

negative

26-4.   Visible tattoos or body piercings can create a (positive/negative) impression at a job interview. (403)

higher

26-5.   Interviewees who emit positive nonverbal cues –leaning forward, smiling, etc. –are rated (higher/lower) than those who do not. (403)

**27.   List the dos and don'ts of interviewing for jobs.**

positive

27-1.   In a job interview, a firm handshake tends to create a (positive/negative) first impression. (361)

is not

27-2.   It (is/is not) a good idea to use humor in a job interview. (361)

is not

27-3.   It (is/is not) a good idea to go into a job interview "cold." (361)

is not

27-4.   It (is/is not) a good idea to discuss salary in an initial interview. (361)

# QUIZ BOXES

## *KEY TERMS*

| Industrial/organizational (I/O) psychology | The study of human behavior in the workplace |
|---|---|
| Occupational interest inventories | Measure your interests as they relate to various jobs or careers. |
| Work | An activity that produces something of value for others. |
| Dual-earner households | Households in which both partners are employed. |
| Underemployment | Settling for a job that does not fully utilize one's skills, abilities, and training. |
| Labor force | Consists of all those who are employed as well as those who are currently unemployed but are looking for work. |
| Glass ceiling | An invisible barrier that prevents most women and ethnic minorities from advancing to the highest levels of occupations. |
| Token | A symbol of all the members of a particular group (e.g., African Americans, Hispanics, women). |
| Sexual harassment | Occurs when employees are subjected to unwelcome sexually oriented behavior. |
| Displaced workers | Individuals who are unemployed because their jobs have disappeared. |
| Work-family conflict | The feeling of being pulled in multiple directions by competing demands from the job and family. |
| Leisure | Unpaid activities people choose to engage in because the activities are personally meaningful. |

## *KEY PEOPLE*

| Nancy Betz | Conducted research on challenges unique to women in the workplace. Suggested that men and women have different patterns of career development. |
|---|---|

| **Richard Nelson Bolles** | Wrote the book *What Color Is Your Parachute? A Practical Manual for Job-Hunters and Career-Changers*, which destroys many of the myths about what does and does not work in seeking jobs. |
|---|---|
| **John Holland** | Proposed the trait measurement and matching model of career development, which describes six personality types (called personal orientations) and their corresponding, ideal work environments. |
| **Robert Karasek** | Proposed a model of occupational stress based on two key factors: *psychological demands* on workers, and amount of *decision control* that workers have. |
| **Donald Super** | Proposed influential, five-stage model of career choice, a developmental model emphasizing the role of self-concept as a factor in career development. |

## SELF-TEST

*Multiple Choice Items*

1.  Psychologists who study human behavior in work settings are called _____ psychologists.
    a.  work                                    c.  behavioral
    b.  developmental                           d.  industrial/organizational

2.  In researching the characteristics of a potential job, you should find out what you can derive in personal satisfaction from the job. That is, you should be concerned with
    a.  working conditions                      c.  intrinsic job satisfaction
    b.  the nature of the work                  d.  opportunities for advancement

3.  Occupational interest inventories
    a.  are focused more on job satisfaction than job success
    b.  are the best measures available to determine your level of job success
    c.  are used by employers to gauge the interest level of prospective employees
    d.  provide you with information about occupations that are related to your college major

4.  Which of the following statements regarding gender bias on occupational interest inventories is accurate?
    a.  There is no evidence of gender bias on these inventories.
    b.  Gender bias existed in the past, but it has been eliminated.
    c.  Gender bias exists, but only for African American women.
    d.  Gender bias has been reduced, but it has not been eliminated.

5.  When making career choices, an important point to keep in mind is:
    a.  any career decision can be easily undone
    b.  your career options are practically limitless
    c.  career choice is a developmental process
    d.  you should be able to find a job that fits you perfectly

6.  According to John Holland's trait measurement and matching model of career development, which of the following personal orientations would be most compatible with a job as a nurse?
    a.  social                                  c.  enterprising
    b.  realistic                               d.  conventional

7.  According to Donald Super, the critical factor that governs career development is one's
    a.  self-concept                            c.  occupational ideal
    b.  need for approval                       d.  drive for heterosexual success

8.  According to Super's developmental model of career choice, which of the following stages involves making a commitment to a specific job, and demonstrating the ability to function effectively in this job?
    a.  growth stage                            c.  establishment stage
    b.  exploration stage                       d.  maintenance stage

9.  The career development of males and females is
    a.  similar because it is against the law to discriminate
    b.  similar in that both appear to be influenced by the same motivational factors
    c.  different, mainly due to genetic predispositions that differ for men and women
    d.  different, in part, because women still subordinate their career goals to those of their husbands

10. The jobs of the next decade are most likely to be in which of the following areas?
    a. service
    b. construction
    c. agriculture
    d. manufacturing

11. Which of the following statements regarding diversity in the workplace is <u>not</u> accurate?
    a. Jobs tend to be typed by gender and race.
    b. Technically, job discrimination on the basis of race and gender is not illegal.
    c. Women and minorities are frequently passed over for promotion in favor of white men.
    d. Employees in female-dominated fields typically earn less than those in male-dominated fields.

12. According to Robert Karasek, occupational stress is most likely to occur under which of the following conditions?
    a. high psychological demands and low decision control
    b. low psychological demands and high decision control
    c. low psychological demands and low decision control
    d. high psychological demands and high decision control

13. Interventions at the _____ are the most widely used strategy for managing work-related stress.
    a. individual level
    b. organizational level
    c. family-organizational interface
    d. individual-organizational interface

14. All but which of the following is a characteristic of the typical female victim of sexual harassment in the workplace?
    a. young
    b. married
    c. is in a nonsenior position
    d. works in a masculine-stereotyped field

15. Which of the following is <u>not</u> one of the results of unemployment discussed in your textbook?
    a. anxiety
    b. depression
    c. loss of self-esteem
    d. All of the above are possible results.

16. Employees who lose their jobs because of downsizing –instead of poor job performance –are likely to believe they have been treated arbitrarily and unfairly –a situation found to be associated with an increase in
    a. anxiety
    b. self-esteem
    c. aggression
    d. job-related stress

17. Research indicates that workaholism may be either constructive or problematic, depending on the
    a. individual's enjoyment of the job
    b. number of hours worked per week
    c. individual's level of performance
    d. opinion of the individual's immediate supervisor

18. Which of the following leisure activities has been found to be negatively related to perceived well-being?
    a. reading
    b. physical exercise
    c. watching television
    d. surfing the Internet

19. The main purpose of a resume is to
    a. get you a job
    b. get you an interview
    c. substitute for an interview
    d. introduce you to the personnel director

20. Which of the following is <u>not</u> good advice for creating the right impression during a job interview?
    a.  Avoid any attempts at humor.
    b.  Go easy on the after-shave lotion or perfume.
    c.  Elevate your perceived worth by criticizing your previous employer.
    d.  Try to anticipate the questions that will be asked and have some answers ready.

## *True/False Items*

T/F      1.   Intelligence is a good predictor of occupational success.

T/F      2.   Socioeconomic status has more influence on career aspirations than does ethnicity.

T/F      3.   If you are undecided about an occupation, it's a good idea to let the results of an occupational interest inventory make the decision for you.

T/F      4.   According to Donald Super's model of career development, the process of occupational development begins in childhood.

T/F      5.   Men and women tend to have different patterns of career development.

T/F      6.   From the worker's point of view, technological advances in the workplace are having both positive and negative effects.

T/F      7.   A contemporary work-related trend is that temporary employment is decreasing.

T/F      8.   The more education a person has, the higher his/her income is.

T/F      9.   Studies have shown that sexual harassment in the workplace rarely occurs in the United States.

T/F    10.   Most of the burdens associated with dual-earner households are borne by wives.

T/F    11.   When compared to European workers, Americans take significantly more paid vacation time.

T/F    12.   Engaging in virtually any leisure activity, including being a "couch potato," is beneficial for one's psychological well-being.

T/F    13.   You should make sure that your resume is very thorough and includes everything you have ever done.

T/F    14.   If possible, you should avoid any discussion of salary in an initial interview.

# ANSWER KEY FOR SELF-TEST

*Multiple Choice Items*

d
1. Among other things, industrial/organizational psychologists study worker motivation and satisfaction, job performance, leadership, personnel selection, and diversity in organizations. (373)

c
2. Intrinsic job satisfaction deals with features of the job, apart from money and formal fringe benefits, from which you can derive personal satisfaction. For example, will the job allow you to have fun, to help people, or to be creative? (376)

a
3. Occupational interest inventories focus more on the likelihood of job *satisfaction* than job *success*. When you take an occupational interest inventory, your scores indicate how similar your interests are to the typical interests of people in various occupations. (377)

d
4. Progress has been made in reducing gender bias in occupational tests, but it has not been eliminated. (377)

c
5. Occupational choice involves not a single decision but a series of decisions. Career choice is a process that continues throughout life. (377-378)

a
6. Social people describe themselves as being understanding and wanting to help others – they are typically found in the helping professions, such as nursing, teaching, and social work. (378)

a
7. According to Super, decisions about work and career commitments reflect people's attempts to express their changing views of themselves (i.e., their self-concept). (380)

c
8. This is the stage during which an individual firmly commits to an occupation. With few exceptions, future job moves will take place *within* this occupational area. (380)

d
9. If a married man wants or needs to move to another job, his wife typically follows him and takes the best job she can find in the new location. Hence, married women usually have less control over their careers than married men do. (381)

a
10. The United States, like many other industrialized nations, is shifting away from a manufacturing or "goods-producing" economy to a service-producing one. (383)

b
11. Job discrimination on the basis of race and gender has been illegal for more than 25 years. (386)

a
12. A job that is very demanding yet doesn't give the worker an opportunity to make his/her own decisions is likely to be stressful. (388)

a
13. Many companies have instituted programs designed to improve individual employees' coping skills (e.g., relaxation training, time management). (389)

b
14. The typical victim is divorced or separated. All of the other characteristics are applicable to the typical victim of sexual harassment. (391)

d
15. All of these are among the psychological problems that can occur as a result of unemployment. (393)

c      16. Violence in the workplace often involves a displaced worker who lashes out in rage and desperation at a supervisor or co-workers. (393)

a      17. The consequences of workaholism depend on whether the individual is an enthusiastic workaholic or a nonenthusiastic workaholic. The enthusiastic workaholic works for the joy of it, and the nonenthusiastic workaholic is driven to work but reports low enjoyment. (395)

c      18. This was found in a 1995 study on the relationship between participation in leisure activities and psychological well-being in adults aged 55 and older. (398)

b      19. The purpose of a resume is *not* to get you a job. Rather, it is to get you an *interview*. (400)

c      20. You should never blame or criticize anyone, especially previous employers, even if you feel that the criticism is justified. (403)


*True/False Items*

False  1. However, intelligence *does* predict the likelihood of entering certain occupations. This is because intelligence is related to the academic success needed for many jobs. (374)

True   2. However, ethnic differences in aspirations are still found. For example, the career decisions of Chinese and Asian American college students are more influenced by their parents compared to European American students. (375)

False  3. Some students naively believe that they should pursue whatever occupation yields the highest score on an occupational interest inventory. That is *not* how the tests are meant to be used. They merely provide information for you to consider. (377)

True   4. Super views occupational development as a process that unfolds gradually across most of the life span. (379-380)

True   5. This difference is due to several factors, one of which is the fact that most women still subordinate their career goals to their husbands' goals. (381)

True   6. On the negative side, computers have reduced the need for workers. On the positive side, technology enables workers to work at home and to communicate with others in distant offices and while traveling. (382)

False  7. As corporations downsize and restructure, they are slashing thousands of permanent jobs and doling out the work to temporary employees, a practice termed "outsourcing." (382-383)

True   8. Although jobs do exist for individuals with less than a college degree, these jobs usually offer the lowest pay and benefits. (384)

False  9. Actually, sexual harassment in the workplace is more common than most people realize. A review of 18 studies indicated that approximately 42% of female workers in the U.S. report having been sexually harassed. (391)

True   10. Although men are taking on more household chores and childcare, most wives still have greater responsibilities in these areas. (395-396)

| False | 11. | The paid vacation time of American workers lags far behind that of many European workers.  Whereas American workers take an average of 16 days of paid annual vacation, workers in most European Union countries get 4 weeks of vacation time by law. (397) |

| False | 12. | One study found that watching television was *negatively* related to perceived well-being. Getting up off the couch is beneficial. (398) |

| False | 13. | It's better to keep it short.  The normal maximum length is two sides of an 8.5" X 11" sheet of paper. (400) |

| True | 14. | The appropriate time for salary negotiation is *after* a firm offer of employment has been extended. (403) |

# Chapter 13
# DEVELOPMENT AND EXPRESSION OF SEXUALITY

## PROGRAMMED REVIEW

**1.** **_List four key aspects of sexual identity._**

identity     1-1. Sexual _____ refers to the complex of personal qualities, self-perceptions, attitudes, values, and preferences that guide one's sexual behavior. (408)

orientation     1-2. Sexual (concept/identity/orientation) refers to one's preference for emotional and sexual relationships with individuals of one gender or the other. (408)

Heterosexuals; bisexuals; homosexuals     1-3. _____ seek emotional-sexual relationships with members of the other gender, _____ with either gender, and _____ with members of the same gender. (408)

physically     1-4. Your body image is how you see yourself (physically/sexually/socially). (408)

double     1-5. An example of a sexual value is the (double/gender/gold) standard, which encourages sexual experimentation in males, but not females. (408)

Erotic     1-6. (Coital/Erotic/Psychosexual) preferences encompass one's attitudes about self-stimulation, oral sex, intercourse, and other sexual activities. (408)

**2.** **_Discuss how hormones influence sexual differentiation and sexual behavior._**

prenatal     2-1. Male and female gonads begin to produce different hormonal secretions during (early adolescent/early childhood/prenatal) development. (408)

androgens; estrogens     2-2. In the male, the testes produce _____, the principal class of male sex hormones, while the female ovaries produce _____, the principal class of female sex hormones. (408)

testosterone     2-3. During prenatal development, the differentiation of the genitals depends primarily on the level of (androgens/estrogens/testosterone) produced. (409)

secondary     2-4. Hormonal changes regulate the maturation of the sexual organs and the development of the (primary/secondary/distinctive) sex characteristics, which are physical features that distinguish the genders but are not directly involved in reproduction. (409)

higher     2-5. High levels of testosterone in female and male subjects correlate with (higher/lower) rates of sexual activity. (409)

greater     2-6. The influence of physiological factors on anatomy is much (greater/less) than their influence on sexual activity. (409)

**3.** **_Discuss how families, peers, schools, and the media shape sexual attitudes and behavior._**

| | | |
|---|---|---|
| want | 3-1. | Most adolescents (want/do not want) their parents to be their primary source of sex information. (409) |
| health care providers | 3-2. | For females, only (health care providers/parents/teachers) are rated higher than peers as a source of sexual health information. (410) |
| support | 3-3. | Surveys show that the vast majority of parents and other adults (support/do not support) sex education programs in the schools. (410) |
| 90 | 3-4. | The results of recent survey of American public, middle, junior, and senior high schools indicated that (50/75/90) percent of schools offered *some* type of sex education. (410) |
| unusual | 3-5. | It is (typical/unusual) to see television characters talking about the consequences of unprotected sex or "using protection." (411) |
| two-thirds | 3-6. | Approximately (one-third/two-thirds/90 percent) of music videos contain sexual imagery. (411) |
| 25 | 3-7. | Among 10- to 17-year-olds, (5/25/50) percent have encountered unwanted pornography on the Internet. (411) |

**4.  Discuss gender differences in sexual socialization and how they affect individuals.**

| | | |
|---|---|---|
| more | 4-1. | According to Letitia Anne Peplau, men have (more/less) interest in sex than women. (411) |
| more | 4-2. | According to Letitia Anne Peplau, the connection between sex and intimacy is (more/less) important for women than for men. (411) |
| more | 4-3. | According to Letitia Anne Peplau, women's sexuality is (more/less) easily shaped by cultural and situational factors. (411) |
| longer | 4-4. | The process of sexual socialization usually takes (longer/less time) for females than for males. (413) |
| negative | 4-5. | Women typically develop (positive/negative) associations about their genitals that males don't experience. (413) |
| less | 4-6. | In terms of sexuality, same-gender couples tend to be (more/less) likely than heterosexual couples to have compatibility problems. (413) |

**5.  Summarize the current thinking on the origins of sexual orientation and attitudes toward homosexuality.**

| | | |
|---|---|---|
| continuum | 5-1. | It is reasonable to view heterosexuality and homosexuality as end points on a (normality scale/continuum/deviance measure). (413) |
| lower | 5-2. | A frequently cited estimate of the number of people who are predominantly homosexual is 10%; however, several recent surveys have all reported (higher/lower) estimates. (413) |

| | | |
|---|---|---|
| Oedipus | 5-3. | Freud believed that homosexuality originated from an unresolved (inferiority/superiority/Oedipus) complex. (414) |
| negative; positive | 5-4. | Learning theorists assert that homosexuality results from early (positive/negative) heterosexual encounters or early (positive/negative) homosexual experiences. (414) |
| no | 5-5. | The most comprehensive study of the causes of sexual orientation found (consistent/moderate/no) support for the leading environmental explanations. (414) |
| is no | 5-6. | There (is/is no) convincing evidence of an association between circulating hormone levels in adults and sexual orientation. (414) |
| different | 5-7. | In terms of explaining male and female homosexuality, it appears that (different/similar) paradigms are applicable. (414) |
| homophobia | 5-8. | The intense fear and intolerance of homosexuals is called _____. (415) |
| Not all | 5-9. | (All/Not all) societies view homosexuality negatively. (416) |

**6. Discuss the identity development and adjustment of lesbians and gay males.**

| | | |
|---|---|---|
| more | 6-1. | People are (more/less) likely to disclose their sexual orientation to close heterosexual friends and siblings than to parents, co-workers, or employers. (416) |
| more | 6-2. | In recent years, high schools and colleges are (more/less) likely to support groups for gay, lesbian, and bisexual students. (417) |
| is not | 6-3. | Homosexuality (is/is not) classified as a psychological disorder. (417) |
| greater | 6-4. | Recent studies suggest that gay males and lesbians are at (greater/less) risk than their straight peers for anxiety, depression, and suicide attempts. (417) |

**7. List some common sexual motives.**

| | | |
|---|---|---|
| power | 7-1. | One of the eight sexual motives described by Hill is enhancing feelings of personal (pride/power/worth). (418) |
| is | 7-2. | Procreating (is/is not) listed among the eight sexual motives described by Hill. (418) |
| more | 7-3. | Generally, women are (more/less) likely than men to associate sex with love. (418) |
| are | 7-4. | Gender differences in the way people view the relationship between sex and love (are/are not) seen among gays. (418) |

**8. Describe four common barriers in communicating about sex.**

| | |
|---|---|
| ignorant | 8-1.   Most Americans are (ignorant/knowledgeable) about sex. (418) |
| response | 8-2.   A common barrier in communicating about sex is one's concern about the partner's (performance/response/sexual history). (418) |
| contradictory | 8-3.   A common barrier in communicating about sex is the fact that attitudes about sex are often (contradictory/deviant/learned). (418) |
| negative | 8-4.   Some people have had (positive/negative) sexual experiences that inhibit their enjoyment of sex. (419) |

**9.   Describe the four phases of the human sexual response cycle.**

| | |
|---|---|
| excitement | 9-1.   During the _____ phase of the human sexual response cycle, the level of arousal escalates rapidly. (420) |
| excitement | 9-2.   Vasocongestion (engorgement of blood vessels) occurs during the (excitement/plateau/orgasm) phase of the human sexual response cycle. (420) |
| does not level | 9-3.   During the plateau phase of sexual response, physiological arousal (levels/does not level) off. (420) |
| Orgasm | 9-4.   _____ occurs when sexual arousal reaches its peak intensity and is discharged in a series of muscular contractions that pulsate through the pelvic area. (421) |
| similar | 9-5.   The subjective experience of orgasm appears to be (similar/different) for men and women. (421) |
| resolution | 9-6.   During the _____ phase, the physiological changes produced by sexual arousal subside. (421) |
| refractory | 9-7.   A (latent/refractory/sedentary) period, during which males are unresponsive to further sexual stimulation, generally follows an orgasm. (421) |

**10.   Discuss gender differences in patterns of orgasm and some reasons for them.**

| | |
|---|---|
| less | 10-1.   During intercourse, women are (more/less) likely than men to reach orgasm. (421) |
| less | 10-2.   In their laboratory, Masters and Johnson found that men took (more/less) time than women to reach orgasm with their partners. (421) |
| clitoris | 10-3.   The most sexually sensitive genital area in most women is the _____. (421) |
| supports | 10-4.   The incidence of orgasm in lesbians (supports/refutes) a socialization-based explanation of gender differences in orgasmic consistency. (422) |
| less | 10-5.   Men are (more/less) likely than women to fake an orgasm. (422) |

**11.     Discuss fantasy as well as kissing and touching as aspects of sexual expression.**

Erogenous

11-1.     _____ zones are areas of the body that are sexually sensitive or responsive. (422)

harmless

11-2.     Most sex therapists view sexual fantasies as (harmful/harmless) ways to enhance sexual excitement and achieve orgasm. (422)

kissing

11-3.     Most two-person sexual activities begin with (fondling/intercourse/kissing). (422)

commonly

11-4.     Heterosexual women (commonly/rarely) complain that their partners are in too much of a hurry. (422-423)

**12.     Discuss the prevalence of self-stimulation and attitudes about it.**

is

12-1.     Sexologists recognize that self-stimulation (is/is not) a normal sexual behavior. (423)

common

12-2.     Self-stimulation is (common/uncommon) in our society. (423)

less

12-3.     Masturbation is (more/less) common among those with less education. (423)

greater

12-4.     Masturbation in marriage is often associated with a (greater/lesser) degree of marital and sexual satisfaction. (423)

**13.     Discuss oral and anal sex as forms of sexual expression.**

cunnilingus

13-1.     Oral stimulation of the female genitals is called (cunnilingus/fellatio/coitus). (423)

fellatio

13-2.     Oral stimulation of the male genitals is called (cunnilingus/fellatio/coitus). (423)

is

13-3.     It (is/is not) possible to contract human immunodeficiency (HIV) through mouth-genital stimulation. (423)

less

13-4.     Anal intercourse is (more/less) popular among heterosexual couples than among homosexual male couples. (424)

**14.     Discuss intercourse and the preferred sexual activities of gay males and lesbians.**

coitus

14-1.     Vaginal intercourse is technically called (coitus/cunnilingus/fellatio). (424)

missionary

14-2.     The most common position used by couples in intercourse is the (missionary/rear-entry/side-by-side) position. (424)

fellatio

14-3.     The most common sexual activity among gay men is (anal intercourse/ fellatio/mutual masturbation). (424)

rarely

14-4. Lesbians (commonly/rarely) use a dildo (an artificial penis) in their sexual activities. (424)

**15.    Describe how the fear of contracting AIDS has influenced sexual attitudes and practices.**

liberal

15-1. American sexual attitudes and behaviors have become more (conservative/liberal) over the last 30 years. (424)

highest

15-2. The teenage birth rate in the United States is one of the (highest/lowest) in the world. (424)

high

15-3. Rates of genital infections among adolescents remain at (high/low) levels. (424)

increased

15-4. The incidence of condom use among high school students (increased/decreased) between 1991 and 2001. (425)

decreased

15-5. The average number of sex partners among high school students (increased/decreased) between 1991 and 2001. (425)

**16.    Summarize attitudes toward and prevalence of early sexual experiences.**

more

16-1. Compared to a generation ago, (more/fewer) believe that sex before marriage is acceptable. (426)

less

16-2. Both men and women are (more/less) approving of sexual activity for women than men. (426)

60

16-3. Recent research indicates that approximately (20/60/90) percent of high school seniors have had sexual intercourse. (426)

similar to

16-4. Adult homosexuals report rates of *heterosexual* premarital intercourse that are (greater than/less than/similar to) those reported by heterosexuals. (426)

don't always

16-5. "Hookups" (almost always/don't always) involve intercourse. (426)

**17.    Summarize the findings on sex patterns in dating couples and married couples.**

is

17-1. Sexual intimacy (is/is not) a positive predictor of relationship stability. (426)

is

17-2. Couples' overall marital satisfaction (is/is not) related to their satisfaction with their sexual relationship. (426)

decrease

17-3. The frequency of sex among married couples tends to (decrease/stay the same/increase) as they get older. (426)

are

17-4. Older people (are/are not) capable of rewarding sexual encounters. (427)

**18.     Compare and contrast sexual behavior in married versus committed homosexual couples.**

decline

18-1.     Among lesbian, gay, and heterosexual couples, there is a general (increase/decline) in the frequency of sexual activity over time. (427)

gay males

18-2.     In the early stages of a relationship, (gay males/lesbians/heterosexuals) engage in sex more frequently than do the other couples. (427)

Lesbians

18-3.     (Gay males/Lesbians/Heterosexuals) have sex less often than other couples. (427)

find

18-4.     Comparative studies (find/do not find) comparable levels of sexual satisfaction in gay, lesbian, and heterosexual couples. (427)

**19.     Summarize the evidence on infidelity in committed relationships.**

extradyadic

19-1.     Infidelity among couples in committed relationships (straight and gay) is termed "_____ sex." (427)

90

19-2.     Approximately (30/60/90) percent of people in our society believe that extramarital sex is "always" or "almost always" wrong. (427)

more

19-3.     According to several recent surveys, men are (more/less) likely than women to have engaged in an extramarital affair. (428)

lower

19-4.     Rates of lesbian extradyadic sex are (higher/lower) than those for married women. (428)

sex;
emotions

19-5.     Men's motivations for infidelity are more closely tied to (emotions/sex) and women's to (emotions/sex). (428)

positively

19-6.     Sexual fidelity is (positively/negatively) correlated with relationship satisfaction for lesbian and heterosexual couples. (429)

**20.     Describe constraints on effective contraception and discuss the merits of hormone-based contraceptives and condoms.**

two-thirds

20-1.     Despite the threat of AIDS, only about (a third/one half/two-thirds) of sexually active females aged 15 to 19 use contraception. (429)

does not increase;
impairs

20-2.     One contributing factor in ineffective contraception is alcohol, which (increases/does not increase) sexual desire, and typically (enhances/impairs) judgment. (429)

ovulation

20-3.     Hormone-based contraceptives contain synthetic hormones that inhibit _____ in women. (430)

does not appear

20-4.     Use of hormone-based contraceptives (appears/does not appear) to increase a woman's overall risk for cancer. (431)

condom

20-5.     A _____ is a sheath worn over the penis during intercourse to collect ejaculated semen. (431)

| | |
|---|---|
| highly effective | 20-6. If used correctly, the condom is (ineffective/moderately effective/highly effective) in preventing pregnancy. (431) |
| more | 20-7. Polyurethane condoms are (more/less) likely to break and to slip off than latex condoms. (431) |
| mifepristone | 20-8. (Mifepristone/Rohypnol/Sexital) is a drug that can induce a miscarriage in the first seven weeks of pregnancy. (431) |

**21.** *Describe the various types of STDs and discuss their prevalence and means of transmission.*

| | |
|---|---|
| 20 | 21-1. There are about (5/10/20) sexually transmitted diseases. (431) |
| under-25 | 21-2. The highest incidence of STDs is seen in the (under-25/25-40/over-40) age group. (431) |
| more | 21-3. AIDS is increasing (more/less) rapidly among women than among men. (431) |
| higher | 21-4. The more sexual partners you have, the (higher/lower) your chances of exposure to a sexually transmitted disease. (432) |
| anal intercourse | 21-5. Engaging in (anal intercourse/oral sex/vaginal intercourse) puts one at a particularly high risk for AIDS. (432) |
| kissing | 21-6. The oral herpes virus (HSV-1) is transmitted primarily through (anal intercourse/vaginal intercourse/kissing). (432) |

**22.** *List some suggestions for safer sexual practices.*

| | |
|---|---|
| abstinence | 22-1. The best way to avoid acquiring sexually transmitted diseases is (abstinence/the use of condoms). (432) |
| may | 22-2. Mouth-genital sex (cannot/may) transmit HIV. (432) |
| anal | 22-3. Because the AIDS virus is easily transmitted through _____ intercourse, it's a good idea to avoid this type of sex. (432) |
| sometimes | 22-4. The symptoms of STDs (always/sometimes/never) disappear as the infection progresses. (434) |

**23.** *List six general suggestions for enhancing sexual relationships.*

| | |
|---|---|
| accurate information | 23-1. The first step in promoting sexual satisfaction is to acquire (accurate information/a sexual partner/an STD). (434) |
| negative; immorality | 23-2. Many sexual problems stem from a (positive/negative) sexual values system that associates sex with (immorality/marriage/recreation). (434) |
| communication | 23-3. Many of the common sexual problems reported by couples are traceable largely to poor (communication/hygiene/performance). (434) |

avoid

23-4.   In enhancing sexual relationships, it's a good idea to (encourage/avoid) goal setting. (435)

fantasies

23-5.   One suggestion for enhancing sexual relationships is to enjoy your sexual (being/communication/fantasies). (435)

to be

23-6.   Another suggestion for enhancing sexual relationships is (to be/not to be) selective about sex. (436)

**24.    Discuss the nature, prevalence, and causes of common sexual dysfunctions.**

dysfunctions

24-1.   Impairments in sexual functioning that cause subjective distress are referred to as sexual _____. (436)

physical

24-2.   Chronic illness, disabilities, and drugs are considered (physical/ psychological/interpersonal) factors that contribute to sexual problems. (436)

more;
easier

24-3.   Acquired erectile difficulties are (more/less) common and (harder/easier) to overcome than lifelong erectile difficulties. (437)

25

24-4.   Experts estimate that about (10/25/50) percent of all cases of erectile dysfunction may be due to side effects of medication. (437)

ejaculation

24-5.   When a man consistently reaches orgasm too quickly, this is termed premature (dysfunction/ejaculation/refraction). (437)

less

24-6.   Orgasmic difficulties are (more/less) common in men than in women. (437)

women

24-7.   Hypoactive sexual desire occurs in both men and women, but it is more common in (men/women). (437)

**25.    Describe the strategies for coping with erectile difficulties, premature ejaculation, orgasmic difficulties, and hypoactive sexual desire.**

therapy

25-1.   Sex (play/talk/therapy) involves the professional treatment of sexual dysfunctions. (438)

80

25-2.   Viagra is about (50/80/95) percent effective for treating erectile difficulties. (438)

Sensate

25-3.   (Erotic/Physical/Sensate) focus is an exercise in which partners take turns pleasuring each other while giving guided verbal feedback and in which certain kinds of stimulation are temporarily forbidden. (439)

manual

25-4.   Both techniques for treating instant ejaculation involve the woman bringing the man to the verge of orgasm through (oral/manual) stimulation. (439)

is

25-5.   Sensate focus (is/is not) an effective technique for treating orgasmic difficulties. (439)

most

25-6.   Therapists find reduced sexual desire the (most/least) challenging sexual problem to treat. (439)

## QUIZ BOXES

### KEY TERMS

| | |
|---|---|
| **Sexual identity** | The complex of personal qualities, self-perceptions, attitudes, values, and preferences that guide one's sexual behavior. |
| **Heterosexuals** | People who seek emotional-sexual relationships with members of the other gender. |
| **Homosexuals** | People who seek emotional-sexual relationships with members of the same gender. |
| **Bisexuals** | People who seek emotional-sexual relationships with members of both genders. |
| **Gonads** | The sex glands. |
| **Androgens** | The principal class of male sex hormones. |
| **Estrogens** | The principal class of female sex hormones. |
| **Homophobia** | The intense fear and intolerance of homosexuals. |
| **Vasocongestion** | Engorgement of blood vessels. |
| **Orgasm** | Occurs when sexual arousal reaches its peak intensity and is discharged in a series of muscular contractions that pulsate through the pelvic area. |
| **Refractory period** | A time following male orgasm during which males are largely unresponsive to further stimulation. |
| **Erogenous zones** | Areas of the body that are sexually sensitive or responsive. |
| **Cunnilingus** | Oral stimulation of the female genitals. |
| **Fellatio** | Oral stimulation of the penis. |
| **Anal intercourse** | Insertion of the penis into a partner's anus and rectum. |
| **Coitus** | Insertion of the penis into the vagina and (typically) pelvic thrusting. |

| Sexually transmitted disease (STD) | A disease or infection that is transmitted primarily through sexual contact. |
|---|---|
| Sexual dysfunctions | Impairments in sexual functioning that cause subjective distress. |
| Erectile difficulties | Occur when a man is persistently unable to achieve or maintain an erection adequate for intercourse. |
| Premature ejaculation | Occurs when sexual relations are impaired because a man consistently reaches orgasm too quickly. |
| Orgasmic difficulties | Occur when people experience sexual arousal but have persistent problems in achieving orgasm. |
| Hypoactive sexual desire | The lack of interest in sexual activity. |
| Sex therapy | The professional treatment of sexual dysfunctions. |
| Sensate focus | An exercise in which partners take turns pleasuring each other while giving guided verbal feedback and in which certain kinds of stimulation are temporarily forbidden. |

## KEY PEOPLE

| Linda Garnets and Douglas Kimmel | Suggested that sexual identity development in gays, lesbians, and bisexuals is complicated and difficult because it takes place in a climate of sexual prejudice. |
|---|---|
| Alfred Kinsey | Devised a seven-point scale used to characterize sexual orientation, which implies that heterosexuality and homosexuality are end points on a continuum. |
| William Masters and Virginia Johnson | Conducted groundbreaking research in the 1960s on the physiology of the human sexual response.  Described four stages of the human sexual response cycle; developed sensate focus for treatment of sexual dysfunction. |
| Letitia Anne Peplau | A major researcher on gender and relationships; suggested four key gender differences in sexuality. |

# SELF-TEST

*Multiple Choice Items*

1.  Research on sexual behavior is
    a.  difficult to do because it is hard to get a representative sample of subjects
    b.  easy to do because people are always willing to talk about their sex lives
    c.  well advanced because it is one of the oldest areas of research in psychology
    d.  in its infancy because the variables are difficult to define

2.  The concept of sexual identity includes
    a.  sexual orientation
    b.  body image
    c.  sexual values and ethics
    d.  all of the above

3.  During prenatal development the sex hormones that are active are
    a.  androgens (in males only)
    b.  estrogens (in females only)
    c.  both androgens and estrogens, in varying amounts
    d.  neither androgens nor estrogens, since they appear at puberty

4.  During prenatal development, the differentiation of the genitals depends primarily on the level of
    _____ produced.
    a.  androgens
    b.  estrogens
    c.  testosterone
    d.  neurotransmitters

5.  For adolescent girls, which of the following is most likely to be seen as associated with sex?
    a.  fun
    b.  love
    c.  social status
    d.  gratification

6.  Sexual prejudice (homophobia) is correlated with which of the following personality types?
    a.  neurotic
    b.  liberal
    c.  conscientious
    d.  authoritarian

7.  One of the ramifications of "rational outness" for homosexuals is that they are likely to
    a.  keep their sexual orientation a well-guarded secret
    b.  disclose their sexual orientation only to close friends and siblings
    c.  engage in sexual relations with those who are unaware of their sexual orientation
    d.  publicly reveal the sexual orientation of their homosexual friends

8.  Homosexuality was initially classified as a psychological disorder by the mental health community. The pioneering research of Evelyn Hooker and others demonstrated that this view was
    a.  a myth
    b.  fairly accurate
    c.  accurate only for gay men
    d.  accurate only for older homosexuals

9.  Negotiating the terms of a sexual relationship
    a.  may not be explicit, but it's there
    b.  occurs if there are problems and a counselor is consulted
    c.  diminishes the intimacy of a sexual relationship and reduces spontaneity
    d.  should be completed before entering a marriage to avoid problems later

10. Greater sexual satisfaction and satisfaction in the relationship come if
    a.  only nonverbal cue are used during sex
    b.  there is open communication about sex
    c.  both partners refrain from expressing themselves during sex
    d.  both partners control their desires so as not to make the other uncomfortable

11.    When a female experiences vaginal lubrication and swelling of the clitoris and vaginal lips, she
    a.    should consult a physician for treatment    c.    is showing external evidence of ovulation
    b.    is likely to be pregnant    d.    is experiencing vasocongestion

12.    The refractory period occurs
    a.    among males after an orgasm
    b.    when a person has strong feelings of guilt and anxiety about sex
    c.    when a person is subjected to unwanted and unwelcome sex
    d.    between the first signs of puberty and actual fertility

13.    Most two-person sexual activities begin with
    a.    oral sex    c.    self-stimulation
    b.    kissing    d.    fondling the genitals

14.    "Coitus" is the technically correct term for
    a.    oral sex    c.    anal intercourse
    b.    self-stimulation    d.    vaginal intercourse

15.    In the early stages of a relationship, _____ engage in sex more frequently than do other couples.
    a.    bisexuals    c.    gay males
    b.    lesbians    d.    married couples

16.    The incidence of infidelity in committed relationships is
    a.    virtually identical for both genders
    b.    somewhat greater for males than females
    c.    somewhat greater for females than males
    d.    unknown because of the difficulty of collecting such data

17.    Which of the following is <u>not</u> considered a hormone-based contraceptive?
    a.    condom    c.    vaginal ring
    b.    the pill    d.    transdermal patch

18.    Which of the following statements regarding sexually transmitted diseases (STDs) is accurate?
    a.    People can be carriers of an STD without being aware of it.
    b.    The more sexual partners you have, the higher the risk of exposure.
    c.    People who know they have an STD often continue to be sexually active.
    d.    All of the above statements are accurate.

19.    In women, hypoactive sexual desire is most often associated with which of the following
    a.    alcohol or drug abuse    c.    chronic medical problems
    b.    relationship difficulties    d.    embarrassment about erectile dysfunction

20.    People use sensate focus when they
    a.    want to avoid pregnancy
    b.    are treating sexual dysfunctions
    c.    want to prolong the pleasure of sex beyond the orgasm
    d.    are not in a situation where sex is appropriate; it is a form of self-stimulation

### True/False Items

T/F    1.    All cultures impose constraints on how people are expected to behave sexually.

| | | |
|---|---|---|
| T/F | 2. | High levels of testosterone in male and female subjects correlate with lower rates of sexual activity. |
| T/F | 3. | Most adolescents want both their parents to be their primary source of sex information. |
| T/F | 4. | "Abstinence only" programs are effective in deterring adolescents from engaging in sex. |
| T/F | 5. | There is no evidence that parents' sexual orientation is linked to that of their children. |
| T/F | 6. | Homosexual individuals tend to disclose their sexual orientation to their parents rather than to friends. |
| T/F | 7. | Disagreements about sex are commonplace for couples. |
| T/F | 8. | During the plateau phase of the sexual response cycle, physiological arousal begins to level off. |
| T/F | 9. | The subjective experience of orgasm is similar in men and women. |
| T/F | 10. | Sexual fantasies are common and normal. |
| T/F | 11. | Self-stimulation remains common among adults even after marriage. |
| T/F | 12. | Both men and women are less approving of sexual activity for women than men. |
| T/F | 13. | Men's motivations for infidelity tend to be tied to sex and women's motivations tend to be tied to emotions. |
| T/F | 14. | Even monogamous partners can develop sexually transmitted diseases (STDs). |
| T/F | 15. | Hypoactive sexual desire (the lack of interest in sexual activity) occurs only in women. |

# ANSWER KEY FOR SELF-TEST

## Multiple Choice Items

| | | |
|---|---|---|
| a | 1. | This is one of the main problems with conducting sex research. Most studies of American sexuality are overrepresented with white, middle-class volunteers. Also, many people are understandably reluctant to discuss their sex lives. (408) |
| d | 2. | Along with erotic preferences, all of these are important elements of one's sexual identity. (408) |
| c | 3. | Both classes of hormones (androgens and estrogens) are present in both genders, but in different proportions. (408) |
| c | 4. | Typically, the level of testosterone is high in males, and low in females. (408-409) |
| b | 5. | Adolescent girls are usually taught to view sex in the context of a loving relationship. On the other hand, boys are encouraged to enjoy sex without emotional involvement. (411) |
| d | 6. | Sexual prejudice is also correlated with conservative religious and political beliefs. (415) |
| b | 7. | The concept of "rational outness" suggests that homosexuals should be as open as possible because it's healthy to be honest, and as closed as necessary to protect against discrimination. (416) |
| a | 8. | Actually, gays and straights do not differ on overall measures of psychological adjustment. (417) |
| a | 9. | Among other things, intimate couples have to negotiate whether, when, and how often they will have sex. (418) |
| b | 10. | Studies show that more extensive disclosure of sexual likes and dislikes positively predicts sexual and relationship satisfaction in committed relationships. (419) |
| d | 11. | Vasocongestion (engorgement of blood vessels) also produces enlargement of the uterus in women. In men, it produces penile erection, swollen testes, and the movement of the scrotum closer to the body. (420) |
| a | 12. | The refractory period is a time following male orgasm during which males are largely unresponsive to further stimulation. (421) |
| b | 13. | Kissing usually starts with the lips but may be extended to almost any area of the partner's body. (422) |
| d | 14. | Coitus involves insertion of the penis into the vagina and (typically) pelvic thrusting. (424) |
| c | 15. | For example, among couples who had been together for 2 years or less, 67% of gay men reported having sex three or more times a week, compared to 45% of married couples, and 33% of lesbian couples. (427) |
| b | 16. | Several recent surveys reported that about 25% of men and about 10% of women had engaged in an extramarital affair at least once. (428) |
| a | 17. | Hormone-based contraceptives contain synthetic forms of estrogen and progesterone (or progesterone only, in the mini-pill), which inhibit ovulation in women. (430) |

| d | 18. | All of these statements about the transmission of STDs are true. (432) |

| b | 19. | This is likely due to the fact that women are more likely than men to "romanticize" sexual desire. (438) |

| b | 20. | Introduced by Masters and Johnson, this treatment for erectile difficulties and other dysfunctions consists of an exercise in which partners take turns pleasuring each other while giving guided verbal feedback and in which certain kinds of stimulation are temporarily forbidden. (439) |

### True/False Items

| True | 1. | People in all cultures are taught that certain expressions of sexuality are "right" while others are "wrong." (408) |

| False | 2. | Actually, it's just the opposite. High levels of testosterone are related to higher levels of sexual activity. (409) |

| True | 3. | Unfortunately, this is not often the case. In a national survey of adolescents and young adults, (ages 13 to 24), only 37% felt that they learned "a lot" of information about relationships and sexual health from their parents. (409) |

| False | 4. | Additionally, these programs do not change teens' attitudes about their sexual intentions. (410) |

| True | 5. | Heterosexual parents are as likely to produce homosexual (or heterosexual) offspring as homosexual parents are. (414) |

| False | 6. | Homosexual individuals tend to disclose their sexual orientation to close heterosexual friends and siblings rather than to parents, co-workers, or employers. (416) |

| True | 7. | This is because people bring differing motives, attitudes, and appetites to sexual liaisons. (418) |

| False | 8. | The name given to the "plateau" phase is misleading, as physiological arousal does not level off. Instead, it continues to build, but at a much slower pace. (420) |

| True | 9. | The subjective experience of orgasm is essentially the same for men and women. (421) |

| True | 10. | According to your textbook, more than 90% of men and women have fantasies during sexual activities with another person. (422) |

| True | 11. | According to one study, 57% of the husbands and 37% of the wives reported engaging in self-stimulation. (423) |

| True | 12. | This fact reflects the continued existence of a sexual double standard for men and women. (426) |

| True | 13. | These gender differences parallel those found in sexual socialization. (428) |

| True | 14. | Basically, no one is immune to sexually transmitted diseases. (421) |

| False | 15. | Although it is more common among women, hypoactive sexual desire occurs in both men and women. (437) |

# Chapter 14
# PSYCHOLOGY AND PHYSICAL HEALTH

## PROGRAMMED REVIEW

***1.*** ***Describe the Type A personality and evidence regarding its most toxic element.***

biopsychosocial

1-1. The (biopsychosocial/evolutionary/sociobiological) model holds that physical illness is caused by a complex interaction of biological, psychological, and sociocultural factors. (444)

Health

1-2. _____ psychology is concerned with how psychosocial factors relate to the promotion and maintenance of health, and with the causation, prevention, and treatment of illness. (444)

coronary

1-3. Coronary heart disease results from a reduction in blood flow through the (aortic/corollary/coronary) arteries, which supply the heart with blood. (445)

Type A

1-4. People with (Type A/Type B/Type C) personality tend to be ambitious, hard-driving perfectionists who are exceedingly time conscious. (446)

Type B

1-5. The relaxed, patient, and easygoing person is likely to have a (Type A/Type B/Type C) personality. (446)

anger and hostility

1-6. In recent years, researchers have found a strong link between personality and coronary risk by focusing on a specific component of the Type A personality: (anger and hostility/competitive orientation/impatience). (446)

angry

1-7. In one study of men and women who had no prior history of heart disease, investigators found an elevated incidence of heart attacks among participants who exhibited a(n) (angry/competitive/extraverted) temperament. (446)

***2.*** ***Discuss possible explanations for the link between hostility and heart disease.***

greater

2-1. Anger-prone individuals appear to exhibit (greater/less) physiological reactivity than those who are lower in hostility. (447-448)

more; more; more; more

2-2. One study found that subjects high in hostility reported (more/fewer) hassles, (more/fewer) negative life events, (more/less) marital conflict, and (more/less) work-related stress than subjects who were lower in hostility. (448)

less

2-3. Hostile individuals tend to have (more/less) social support than others. (448)

higher

2-4. People high in anger and hostility seem to exhibit a (higher/lower) prevalence of poor health habits. (448)

**3.    Summarize evidence relating emotional reactions and depression to heart disease.**

emotions

3-1.    Transient mental stress and the resulting (attributions/emotions/self-talk) that people experience can tax the heart. (448)

trigger

3-2.    Research findings suggest that brief periods of mental stress can (buffer people from/trigger) acute heart disease, such as myocardial ischemia and angina. (448)

increased

3-3.    One study found that the likelihood of ischemia (increased/decreased) when people reported negative emotions, such as tension, frustration, and sadness. (448)

reduce

3-4.    One study showed that stress management training in cardiology patients can (increase/reduce) the likelihood of a second heart attach. (448)

higher

3-5.    Many studies have found (higher/lower) rates of depression among patients suffering from heart disease. (449)

increases

3-6.    Depression (increases/decreases) one's chances of developing heart disease. (449)

**4.    Describe the evidence linking stress and personality to cancer.**

Cancer

4-1.    (Angina/Cancer/Ischemia) refers to malignant cell growth, which may occur in many organ systems in the body. (450)

extremely weak

4-2.    The research linking psychological factors to the onset of cancer is (very strong/moderately strong/extremely weak). (450)

course

4-3.    Although efforts to link psychological factors to the onset of cancer have largely failed, more convincing evidence indicates that stress and personality influence the (course/severity/treatment) of the disease. (450)

**5.    Summarize evidence linking stress to a variety of diseases and immune functioning.**

questionnaires

5-1.    The development of (computer software/polygraphs/questionnaires) to measure life stress has allowed researchers to look for correlations between stress and a variety of diseases. (450)

have

5-2.    Studies (have/have not) found associations between stressful life events and the course of rheumatoid arthritis and the emergence of lower back pain. (450)

defensive

5-3.    The immune response is the body's (defensive/emotional/ psychological) reaction to invasion by bacteria, viral agents, etc. (450-451)

does

5-4.    Research evidence suggests that stress (does/does not) impair immune functioning in humans. (451)

increases

5-5.    Evidence suggests that susceptibility to immune suppression in the face of stress (increases/decreases) as people grow older. (451)

**6.    Evaluate the strength of the relationship between stress and illness.**

correlational

6-1.    Because most of the research evidence is (correlational/experimental), it cannot be demonstrated conclusively that stress causes illness. (451)

modest

6-2.    At present the strength of the relationship between stress and health appears to be (significant/modest/nonexistent). (452)

is not

6-3.    Clearly, stress (is/is not) an irresistible force that produces inevitable effects on health. (452)

**7.    Give some reasons why people develop health-impairing habits.**

one-half

7-1.    A recent analysis of the causes of death in the United States suggests that unhealthy behaviors are responsible for about (one-tenth/one-third/one-half) of all deaths each year. (452)

slowly

7-2.    Many health-impairing habits creep up on people (quickly/slowly). (452)

pleasant

7-3.    Many health-impairing habits involve activities that are quite (pleasant/unpleasant) at the time. (452)

easy

7-4.    It is relatively (easy/difficult) to ignore risks that lie in the distant future. (452-453)

underestimate

7-5.    It appears that people have a tendency to (overestimate/underestimate) the risks associated with their own health-impairing habits. (453)

denial

7-6.    Most people are aware of the dangers related to health-impairing habits but engage in (denial/displacement/regression) when it is time to apply this information to themselves. (453-454)

**8.    Discuss the health effects of smoking and the dynamics of giving up smoking.**

decreased

8-1.    In the United States, the percentage of people who smoke has (increased/decreased) since the mid-1960s. (454)

death

8-2.    Smokers face a greater risk of premature (death/ejaculation) than nonsmokers. (454)

Lung;
heart

8-3.    (Colon/Lung/Skin) cancer and (Parkinson's/heart/liver) disease kill the greatest number of smokers. (454)

reasonably quickly

8-4.    When people give up smoking, their health risks decline (gradually/imperceptibly/reasonably quickly). (454)

| | |
|---|---|
| would | 8-5. Evidence suggests that most smokers (would/would not) like to quit. (454) |
| 25 | 8-6. Research shows that long-term success rates for efforts to quit smoking are in the vicinity of (25/50/75) percent. (455) |
| on their own | 8-7. The vast majority of people who successfully give up smoking do so (on their own/with the help of a counselor/through a formal program). (455) |
| modification | 8-8. The self-(conceptual/modification/monitoring) techniques described in the Application for Chapter 4 can be invaluable in efforts to quit smoking. (455) |
| increase | 8-9. Controlled studies have demonstrated that nicotine substitutes (e.g., gum, skin patches) (increase/have no effect on) long-term rates of quitting smoking. (456) |

**9.   Summarize data on patterns of alcohol use and the short-term risks of drinking.**

| | |
|---|---|
| half | 9-1. Survey data indicate that about (one-fourth/half/two-thirds) of adults in the United States drink. (456) |
| decreased | 9-2. Per capita consumption of alcohol in the United States (increased/decreased) in the 1980s and 1990s. (456) |
| college campuses | 9-3. Drinking is particularly prevalent on (airline flights/college campuses/holidays). (456) |
| encouraged | 9-4. Drinking is a widely (encouraged/discouraged) social ritual in our culture. (457) |
| side | 9-5. Alcohol has a variety of (positive/side) effects, including some that can be very problematic. (457) |
| more | 9-6. Life-threatening overdoses of alcohol are (more/less) common than most people realize. (457) |
| negative | 9-7. In substantial amounts, alcohol has a decidedly (positive/negative) effect on intellectual functioning and perceptual-motor coordination. (457) |
| aggression | 9-8. With their inhibitions released, some drinkers become argumentative and prone to (aggression/depression/suicide). (458) |

**10.   Describe the major long-term health risks and social costs of drinking.**

| | |
|---|---|
| dependence | 10-1. Alcohol (abuse/dependence/use) is a chronic, progressive disorder marked by a growing compulsion to drink and impaired control over drinking that eventually interferes with health and social behavior. (458) |
| increases | 10-2. Heavy drinking (increases/decreases) the risk for heart disease, hypertension, and stroke. (458) |

| | |
|---|---|
| can | 10-3.  Alcoholism (can/cannot) produce psychotic states. (459) |
| social | 10-4.  In addition to the personal risks involved, alcohol abuse also has enormous (psychosexual/sexual/social) costs. (459) |
| higher | 10-5.  Children of alcoholics grow up in environments in which the risk of physical or sexual abuse is (higher/lower) than normal. (459) |

**11.    Discuss the health risks and determinants of obesity.**

| | |
|---|---|
| 20 | 11-1.  One simple, intermediate criterion used to classify people as obese is if their weight exceeds their ideal body weight by (20/50/75) percent. (459) |
| body mass | 11-2.  Many experts prefer to assess obesity in terms of (body mass/largeness/obesity) index, which controls for variations in height. (459) |
| an increase | 11-3.  Recent surveys show (an increase/a decrease/stability) in the incidence of obesity in the United States. (459-460) |
| more | 11-4.  Overweight people are (more/less) vulnerable than others to heart disease, diabetes, hypertension, and respiratory problems. (460) |
| overeat | 11-5.  According to evolutionary theorists, most people in food-replete environments tend to (overeat/under-eat) in relation to their physiological needs. (460) |
| genetic | 11-6.  Chief among the factors contributing to obesity is (genetic/personality/sociocultural) predisposition. (460) |
| decreasing | 11-7.  The increased availability of highly caloric food in America has been paralleled by (increasing/decreasing) physical activity. (461) |
| Set-point | 11-8.  (Set-point/Settling-point) theory proposes that the body monitors fat-cell levels to keep them (and weight) fairly stable. (461) |
| Settling-point | 11-9.  (Set-point/Settling-point) theory proposes that weight tends to drift around the level at which the constellation of factors that determine food consumption and energy expenditure achieve an equilibrium. (461) |

**12.    Outline the key elements in effective weight loss efforts.**

| | |
|---|---|
| beneficial; harmful | 12-1.  Weight loss efforts involving moderate changes in eating and exercise are more (beneficial/harmful) than (beneficial/harmful) to people's health. (461) |
| decrease | 12-2.  Studies have demonstrated that relatively modest weight reductions can (increase/decrease) many of the health risks associated with obesity. (461) |
| essential | 12-3.  Exercise is an (essential/optional) ingredient of an effective weight-loss regimen. (462) |

regain

12-4. Overall, the evidence on weight-loss programs suggests that the vast majority of participants (regain/do not regain) most of the weight that they lose. (462)

**13.    Provide examples of links between nutrition and health and discuss the basis for poor nutrition.**

higher

13-1. In a study of over 42,000 women, it was found that women who reported poorer quality diets had (higher/lower) mortality rates. (462)

increase

13-2. Heavy consumption of foods that elevate serum cholesterol (e.g., eggs, cheeses, butter) appears to (increase/decrease) the risk of cardiovascular disease. (462)

hypertension

13-3. High salt intake is thought to be a contributing factor in the development of (cancer/heart disease/hypertension). (463)

cancer

13-4. High-fat diets have been implicated as possible contributors to some forms of (cancer/schizophrenia/ulcers). (463)

decrease

13-5. Some studies suggest that high-fiber diets may (increase/decrease) one's risk for colon and rectal cancer. (463)

are not

13-6. For the most part, nutritional deficiencies (are/are not) a result of low income. (463)

information

13-7. The first steps toward improved nutrition usually involve changing attitudes and acquiring (a diet plan/information/social support). (463)

**14.    List three general goals intended to foster sound nutrition.**

mono-unsaturated; poly- unsaturated; saturated

14-1. The current thinking is that (saturated/monounsaturated/polyunsaturated) and (saturated/monounsaturated/polyunsaturated) fats are healthy, whereas (saturated/monounsaturated/polyunsaturated) fats should be consumed sparingly. (464)

loaded with

14-2. Many prepackaged foods are (low in/loaded with) salt. (464)

increase

14-3. In improving your nutrition, it's a good idea to (increase/decrease) consumption of polyunsaturated fats, whole-grain carbohydrates, and natural sugars. (464)

**15.    Summarize evidence on the benefits and risks of exercise.**

increased

15-1. Research indicates that regular exercise is associated with (increased/ decreased) longevity. (465)

cardiovascular problems

15-2. An appropriate exercise program can enhance cardiovascular fitness and thereby reduce one's susceptibility to (arthritis/cancer/cardiovascular problems). (465)

decreased

15-3.    Recent studies suggest that physical fitness is associated with a(n) (increased/decreased) risk for colon cancer in men and for breast and reproductive cancer in women. (466)

stress

15-4.    Exercise may serve as a buffer that reduces the potentially damaging physical effects of (insomnia/smoking/stress). (466)

depression

15-5.    Studies have found a consistent association between regular exercise and reduced (depression/motivation/self-esteem). (466)

**16.    List four guidelines for embarking on an effective exercise program.**

enjoyable

16-1.    When devising an effective exercise program, it's a good idea to look for an activity that you will find (enjoyable/monotonous/strenuous). (466)

gradually

16-2.    When embarking on an effective exercise program, you should increase your participation (quickly/gradually). (466)

30

16-3.    A widely cited guideline is that you should plan on exercising vigorously for a minimum of _____ minutes three to five times a week. (467)

reinforce yourself

16-4.    To offset the inconvenience or pain that may be associated with exercise, it's a good idea to (punish yourself/"psych yourself up"/reinforce yourself) for your participation. (467)

**17.    Describe AIDS and summarize evidence on the transmission of the HIV virus.**

immune deficiency

17-1.    AIDS stands for acquired (inter-debilitating/immune deficiency/intoxicant deficit) syndrome. (467)

is not

17-2.    Being infected with the HIV virus (is/is not) equivalent to having AIDS. (467)

increase

17-3.    The worldwide prevalence of AIDS continues to (increase/decrease). (467)

premature

17-4.    The impression among the general public that antiretroviral drugs have transformed AIDS from a fatal disease to a manageable one is (accurate/inaccurate/premature). (468)

bodily

17-5.    The HIV virus is transmitted through person-to-person contact involving the exchange of (bodily/carbonated/salty) fluids. (468)

more

17-6.    In heterosexual relations, male-to-female transmission of AIDS is (more/less) likely than female-to-male transmission. (468)

**18.    Identify some common misconceptions about AIDS and discuss the prevention of AIDS.**

| | |
|---|---|
| unrealistic | 18-1.  A great many people have (realistic/unrealistic) fears that AIDS can be readily transmitted through casual contact (e.g., a handshake, a sneeze) with infected individuals. (468) |
| are not | 18-2.  Blood donors (are/are not) at risk for contracting AIDS. (468) |
| do not disclose | 18-3.  Most bisexual men (disclose/do not disclose) their bisexuality to their female partners. (468) |
| partners; condoms | 18-4.  People can reduce the risk of contracting AIDS by having fewer sexual (fantasies/partners/toys) and by using _____ to control the exchange of semen. (468) |
| less | 18-5.  Recent evidence indicates that new cohorts of young people are (more/less) concerned about the risk of HIV infection than the generation that witnessed the original emergence of AIDS. (468) |

**19.    Summarize evidence on patterns of treatment-seeking behavior.**

| | |
|---|---|
| more | 19-1.  People who are relatively high in anxiety and neuroticism tend to report (more/fewer) symptoms of illness than others do. (469) |
| more | 19-2.  Women are (more/less) likely than men to utilize medical services. (470) |
| delay | 19-3.  The biggest problem in regard to treatment seeking is the tendency of many people to (delay/rush into) the pursuit of needed treatment. (470) |
| bothering | 19-4.  People may delay seeking treatment because they worry about (bothering/ embarrassing/seeing) their physician. (470) |
| plans | 19-5.  People may delay seeking treatment because they are reluctant to disrupt their (plans/families/neighbors). (470) |

**20.    Explain the appeal of the "sick role."**

| | |
|---|---|
| 60 | 20-1.  Up to (20/40/60) percent of patients' visits to their primary care physicians appear to have little medical basis. (470) |
| Fewer | 20-2.  (More/Fewer) demands are placed on sick people. (470) |
| rewarding | 20-3.  The increased attention that comes with the sick role can be (embarrassing/ rewarding). (470) |

**21.    Identify the factors that tend to undermine doctor-patient communication and how to improve it.**

| | |
|---|---|
| communication | 21-1.  Good _____ is a crucial requirement for sound medical decisions, informed choices about treatment, and appropriate follow-through by patients. (470) |

| | |
|---|---|
| overestimate | 21-2. Many health care providers (overestimate/underestimate) their patients' understanding of technical terms. (471) |
| should not | 21-3. In order to improve your communication with health care providers, you (should/should not) be a passive consumer of medical services. (471) |

**22.    Discuss the prevalence of nonadherence to medical advice and its causes.**

| | |
|---|---|
| major | 22-1. Nonadherence to medical advice is a (major/minor/non-) problem in our medical care system. (471) |
| social support | 22-2. One factor that is related to adherence to medical advice is the patient's (personality/social support/socioeconomic status). (471) |
| failure | 22-3. Frequently, noncompliance with medical advice is a (failure/reluctance) to understand the instructions as given. (471) |
| decrease | 22-4. If the regimen prescribed by a physician is unpleasant, compliance will tend to (increase/decrease). (471) |
| increase | 22-5. If a patient has a negative attitude toward a physician, the probability of noncompliance will (increase/decrease). (471) |

**23.    Explain the concepts of drug tolerance, physical and psychological dependence, and overdose.**

| | |
|---|---|
| tolerance | 23-1. Most drugs produce _____ effects, which usually lead people to consume larger and larger doses of a drug to attain the effects they desire. (473) |
| withdrawal | 23-2. Physical dependence exists when a person must continue taking a drug to avoid (psychosomatic/tolerance/withdrawal) illness (which occurs when drug use is terminated). (473) |
| is not | 23-3. Psychological dependence (is/is not) marked by a clear withdrawal reaction. (473) |
| overdose | 23-4. An excessive dose of a drug that can seriously threaten one's life is called a(n) _____. (474) |
| greatest | 23-5. Drugs that are central nervous system depressants —narcotics and sedatives —carry the (greatest/least) risk of overdose. (474) |

**24.    Summarize the main effects and risks of narcotics.**

| | |
|---|---|
| opium | 24-1. Narcotics are drugs derived from _____ that are capable of relieving pain. (474) |
| heroin | 24-2. The most significant narcotics problem in modern, Western society involves the use of (cocaine/heroin/marijuana). (474) |

| | |
|---|---|
| euphoria | 24-3. The main effect of heroin is an overwhelming sense of (euphoria/guilt/paranoia). (474) |
| high | 24-4. Narcotics carry a (high/low) risk for both psychological and physical dependence. (474) |
| is | 24-5. Overdose (is/is not) a real danger with heroin. (474) |

**25.    Summarize the main effects and risks of sedatives.**

| | |
|---|---|
| decrease | 25-1. Sedatives are sleep-inducing drugs that tend to (increase/decrease) central nervous system and behavioral activity. (475) |
| physical and psychological | 25-2. Sedatives have the potential to produce (physical/psychological/physical and psychological) dependence. (475) |
| accidental | 25-3. Sedative users have a high risk of (accidental/brain/leg) injuries because of the drug's effects on motor coordination. (475) |

**26.    Summarize the main effects and risks of stimulant drugs.**

| | |
|---|---|
| Cocaine | 26-1. (Cocaine/Heroin/Marijuana) is an organic substance extracted from the coca shrub. (475) |
| more | 26-2. Smoking crack is (more/less) dangerous than snorting cocaine powder. (475) |
| orally | 26-3. Synthesized in a pharmaceutical laboratory, amphetamines are usually consumed (anally/orally/intravenously). (475) |
| psychological | 26-4. The more common problem with stimulants is (physical/psychological) dependence. (475) |
| paranoia | 26-5. Heavy stimulant use occasionally leads to the onset of a severe psychological disorder called amphetamine or cocaine psychosis, which is dominated by intense (euphoria/lethargy/paranoia). (475) |

**27.    Summarize the main effects and risks of hallucinogens.**

| | |
|---|---|
| perception | 27-1. Hallucinogens intensify and distort (aggression/emotions/perception). (476) |
| is no | 27-2. There (is/is no) potential for physical dependence on hallucinogens. (476) |
| rare | 27-3. Psychological dependence on hallucinogens is (common/rare). (476) |
| flashback | 27-4. A vivid hallucinogenic experience that occurs months after the original drug ingestion is called a(n) (flashback/overdose/tolerance effect). (476) |

**28.    Summarize the main effects and risks of marijuana and ecstasy (MDMA).**

THC

28-1.    (LSD/MDMA/THC) is the active chemical ingredient in cannabis and can be synthesized for research purposes. (476)

are not

28-2.    Overdose and physical dependence (are/are not) serious problems with marijuana use. (476)

has

28-3.    Marijuana (has/does not have) the potential to produce psychological dependence. (476)

little

28-4.    Research evidence suggests that marijuana has (major/little) long-term impact on male smokers' fertility and sexual functioning. (477)

have

28-5.    Recent studies using elaborate and precise assessments of cognitive functioning (have/have not) found an association between chronic, heavy marijuana use and measurable impairments in attention and memory. (477)

1990s

28-6.    MDMA was originally formulated in 1921, but was not widely used in the United States until the (1950s/1970s/1990s). (477)

mescaline

28-7.    Chemically, MDMA is most closely related to (cocaine/marijuana/mescaline). (477)

does not

28-8.    MDMA (does/does not) appear to be addictive. (477)

cognitive

28-9.    Studies of former MDMA users suggest that ecstasy may have subtle, long-term effects on (cognitive/motor/sexual) functioning. (477)

**QUIZ BOXES**

*KEY TERMS*

| Biopsychosocial model | Holds that physical illness is caused by a complex interaction of biological, psychological, and sociocultural factors. |
|---|---|
| Health psychology | Concerned with how psychosocial factors relate to the promotion and maintenance of health, and with the causation, prevention, and treatment of illness. |
| Coronary heart disease | Results from a reduction in blood flow through the coronary arteries, which supply the heart with blood. |
| Atherosclerosis | A gradual narrowing of the coronary arteries. |
| Type A personality | Includes three elements: (1) a strong competitive orientation, (2) impatience and time urgency, and (3) anger and hostility. |
| Type B personality | Marked by relatively relaxed, patient, easygoing, amicable behavior. |
| Cancer | Malignant cell growth, which may occur in many organ systems in the body. |
| Immune response | The body's defensive reaction to invasion by bacteria, viral agents, or other foreign substances. |
| Alcohol dependence (alcoholism) | A chronic, progressive disorder marked by a growing compulsion to drink and impaired control over drinking that eventually interfere with health and social behavior. |
| Body mass index (BMI) | Weight (in kilograms) divided by height (in meters) squared. |
| Set point theory | Proposes that the body monitors fat-cell levels to keep them (and weight) fairly stable. |
| Settling point theory | Proposes that weight tends to drift around the level at which the constellation of factors that determine food consumption and energy expenditure achieve an equilibrium. |
| Nutrition | A collection of processes (mainly food consumption) through which an organism utilizes the materials (nutrients) required for survival and growth. |
| Acquired immune deficiency syndrome (AIDS) | A disorder in which the immune system is gradually weakened and eventually disabled by the human immunodeficiency virus (HIV). |

| Tolerance | A progressive decrease in a person's responsiveness to a drug with continued use. |
|---|---|
| Physical dependence | Exists when a person must continue to take a drug to avoid withdrawal illness (which occurs when drug use is terminated). |
| Psychological dependence | Exists when a person must continue to take a drug to satisfy intense mental and emotional craving for it. |
| Overdose | An excessive dose of a drug that can seriously threaten one's life. |
| Narcotics (or opiates) | Drugs derived from opium that are capable of relieving pain. |
| Sedatives | Sleep-inducing drugs that tend to decrease central nervous system and behavioral activity. |
| Stimulants | Drugs that tend to increase central nervous system and behavioral activity. |
| Hallucinogens | A diverse group of drugs that have powerful effects on mental and emotional functioning, marked most prominently by distortions in sensory and perceptual experience. |
| Cannabis | The hemp plant from which marijuana, hashish, and THC are derived. |

## KEY PEOPLE

| Robin DiMatteo | Suggested a number of reasons why people delay seeking medical treatment. |
|---|---|
| Meyer Friedman and Ray Rosenman | Divided people into two basic types: Type A personality and Type B personality. |
| Janice Kiecolt-Glaser | Conducted studies that related stress to suppressed immune activity in humans. |

# SELF-TEST

*Multiple Choice Items*

1.  The biopsychosocial model holds that physical illness is caused by a complex interaction of all but which of the following factors?
    a.  biological
    b.  sociocultural
    c.  sociological
    d.  psychological

2.  Which of the following characteristics is <u>not</u> associated with the Type A personality?
    a.  patient
    b.  ambitious
    c.  perfectionistic
    d.  achievement-oriented

3.  Recent studies suggest that _____ may be more important for coronary risk than other elements of the Type A personality.
    a.  ambition
    b.  anger and hostility
    c.  strong competitive orientation
    d.  impatience and time urgency

4.  Research consistently indicates that the strength of the relationship between stress and health is
    a.  weak
    b.  modest
    c.  strong
    d.  negligible

5.  People behave in self-destructive ways because
    a.  many health-impairing habits creep up on people slowly
    b.  many health-impairing habits are quite pleasant at the time people engage in them
    c.  the risks associated with health-impairing habits are in the distant future
    d.  All of the above are reasons that people behave in self-destructive ways.

6.  The percentage of people who smoke has _____ since the mid-1960s.
    a.  remained stable
    b.  declined noticeably
    c.  increased slightly
    d.  increased dramatically

7.  About _____ of the adult population in the United States drink alcohol.
    a.  10%
    b.  half
    c.  two-thirds
    d.  90%

8.  That there may be a genetic vulnerability to obesity is supported by the finding that
    a.  some people burn off calories faster than others
    b.  people who lose weight tend to gain back the weight they lost
    c.  adoptees resemble their biological parents more than their adoptive parents
    d.  obese people have more fat cells than other people

9.  The only way to lose weight effectively is to
    a.  change the ratio of energy intake to energy output
    b.  stick to a reputable diet until the desired weight is reached
    c.  stop eating foods with cholesterol
    d.  engage in a vigorous exercise program

10. In order to foster sound nutrition, one should increase consumption of all but which of the following?
    a.  cholesterol
    b.  complex carbohydrates
    c.  foods with fiber
    d.  polyunsaturated fats

11.    A good exercise program should
    a.    impose a little suffering –no pain, no gain!
    b.    include daily workouts involving vigorous exercise
    c.    include some competitive activity for added motivation
    d.    be a physical activity that you find enjoyable

12.    Which of the following statements regarding the treatment of AIDS with antiretroviral drugs is most accurate?
    a.    Virtually all patients have responded favorably to the new drugs.
    b.    The long-term efficacy of the drugs is yet to be determined.
    c.    It is easy for patients to maintain the drug administration regimen.
    d.    Antiretroviral drugs have transformed AIDS from a fatal disease to a manageable one.

13.    The HIV virus can be transmitted
    a.    through the exchange of bodily fluids, especially semen and blood
    b.    by the sharing of needles by intravenous drug users
    c.    through unprotected sexual contact with affected individuals
    d.    through all of the above means

14.    People who are _____ report more symptoms of illness than others.
    a.    unwilling to seek treatment          c.    high in anxiety and low in neuroticism
    b.    genetically predisposed to obesity     d.    high in anxiety and high in neuroticism

15.    Noncompliance with instructions received from physicians
    a.    accounts for the vast majority of serious illnesses in our society
    b.    may be due to the patients' failure to understand the instructions
    c.    is generally caused by lack of confidence in the medical delivery system
    d.    is not a major factor in the medical care system

16.    One factor that is positively related to adherence to medical advice is the patient's
    a.    personality               c.    social support
    b.    family income          d.    medical history

17.    When people need to consume larger and larger doses of a drug to obtain the desired effect, they have developed _____ on/for the drug.
    a.    physical dependence        c.    psychological dependence
    b.    tolerance              d.    all of the above

18.    Technically, cocaine is considered a
    a.    narcotic               c.    stimulant
    b.    sedative              d.    hallucinogen

19.    Which of the following is not considered a hallucinogenic drug?
    a.    LSD                 c.    mescaline
    b.    heroin              d.    psilocybin

20.    Which of the following statements about hallucinogenic drugs is not accurate?
    a.    Psychological dependence is a common problem.
    b.    They have no potential for physical dependence.
    c.    They temporarily impair intellectual functioning.
    d.    Repetitious, frightening flashbacks can be troublesome.

## True/False Items

T/F    1.   Type A personalities tend to have less social support than others.

T/F    2.   There is convincing evidence that stress and personality influence the onset of cancer.

T/F    3.   Research has clearly demonstrated that stress causes a variety of physical illnesses.

T/F    4.   Studies show that if people can give up smoking, their health risks decline reasonably quickly.

T/F    5.   Studies have demonstrated that nicotine substitutes increase long-term rates of quitting smoking in comparison to placebos.

T/F    6.   In the United States, most people's nutritional shortcomings are a result of the inability to afford appropriate foods.

T/F    7.   Recent studies suggest that physical fitness is associated with a decreased risk for some forms of cancer.

T/F    8.   In order to improve fitness, one should exercise on a regular, as opposed to sporadic, basis.

T/F    9.   Being infected with the HIV virus is equivalent to having AIDS.

T/F   10.   The worldwide prevalence of AIDS continues to increase at an alarming rate.

T/F   11.   In heterosexual relations, male-to-female transmission of the HIV virus is more common than female-to-male transmission.

T/F   12.   Although many people tend to delay medical consultations, some people are positively eager to seek medical care.

T/F   13.   Smoking crack is more dangerous than snorting cocaine powder.

T/F   14.   Overdoses on stimulants are relatively infrequent.

# ANSWER KEY FOR SELF-TEST

*Multiple Choice Items*

c     1.    The other three factors form the basis for the biopsychosocial model of physical illness. (444)

a     2.    Actually, time urgency and *impatience* is one of the main elements of the Type A personality. (446)

b     3.    Many studies have found an association between hostility and coronary risk. Your textbook discusses several reasons why anger-prone individuals may be at greater risk for heart disease. (446-447)

b     4.    The correlations typically fall in the .20s and .30s. Basically, stress is one factor among many that influence physical health. (452)

d     5.    These are all reasons why people engage in self-destructive behavior. (452-453)

b     6.    However, about 26% of adult men and 21% of adult women in the United States continue to smoke regularly, and these percentages are even higher among college students. (454)

b     7.    Survey data indicate that about half of adults in the United States drink. (456)

c     8.    This finding is from one influential study dealing with a genetic predisposition for obesity. (460)

a     9.    Specifically, to lose one pound you need to burn up 3500 more calories than you consume. (462)

a     10.   Cholesterol is one of the items mentioned in your textbook that should be avoided, at least in excessive amounts. (464)

d     11.   Engaging in an activity that is enjoyable makes it much easier to follow through and exercise regularly. (466-467)

b     12.   Antiretroviral drugs hold out promise for substantially longer survival of AIDS patients, but the drugs have been rushed into service and their long-term efficacy is unclear. (468)

d     13.   These are all ways that the HIV virus can be transmitted. (468)

d     14.   This is one of the factors involved in the individual interpretation of physical sensations like nausea, stiffness, etc. (469-470)

b     15.   Many providers use too much medical jargon and overestimate their patients' understanding of technical terms. (471)

c     16.   Adherence to medical advice is improved when patients have family, friends, or coworkers who remind them and help them to comply with treatment requirements. (471)

b     17.   Although tolerance builds more rapidly to some drugs than to others, most drugs produce some tolerance effects. (473)

c       18.   Stimulants tend to increase central nervous system activation and behavioral activity. Amphetamines ("speed") are another kind of strong stimulant. (475)

b       19.   Heroin is a narcotic (or opiate). (474-476)

a       20.   Psychological dependence has been reported but appears to be very rare. (476)

### True/False Items

True    1.   This is generally due to their antagonistic ways of relating to others. (448)

False   2.   However, there is evidence that stress and personality can influence the *course* of the disease. (450)

False   3.   The key word here is "causes." Virtually all of the relevant research is correlational, so it cannot demonstrate conclusively that stress *causes* illness. (451)

True    4.   Five years after people stop smoking, their health risk is already noticeably lower than that of people who continue to smoke. (454)

True    5.   However, the increases are modest and the success rates are discouragingly low. (456)

False   6.   Actually, most malnutrition in America is attributable to lack of knowledge about nutrition and lack of effort to ensure good nutrition. (463)

True    7.   Studies suggest that fitness is associated with a decreased risk for colon cancer in men and for breast and reproductive cancer in women. (466)

True    8.   A widely cited rule of thumb is that you should plan on exercising vigorously for a minimum of 30 minutes three to five times a week. (466)

False   9.   AIDS is the final stage of the HIV infection process, typically manifested about 7-10 years after the original infection. (467)

True    10.   This is especially true in certain regions of Africa. (467)

True    11.   Male-to-female transmission is estimated to be about eight times more likely than female-to-male transmission. (468)

True    12.   These are generally people who have learned that potential benefits are to be had in adopting the "sick role." (470)

True    13.   Smoking crack tends to be more dangerous than snorting cocaine powder because smoking leads to a more rapid absorption of the drug into the bloodstream and more concentrated delivery of cocaine to the brain. (475)

False   14.   This used to be true, but in recent years cocaine overdoses have increased sharply as more people experiment with more dangerous modes of ingestion. (476)

# Chapter 15
# PSYCHOLOGICAL DISORDERS

## PROGRAMMED REVIEW

***1.   Describe and evaluate the medical model of abnormal behavior.***

disease

1-1.   The medical model proposes that it is useful to think of abnormal behavior as a(n) (aberration/disease/prescription). (482)

treatment of

1-2.   The rise of the medical model brought improvements in the (attitudes toward/treatment of) those who exhibited abnormal behavior. (482)

norms

1-3.   According to Thomas Szasz, abnormal behavior usually involves a deviation from social _____ rather than an illness. (482)

Diagnosis

1-4.   (Diagnosis/Etiology/Prognosis) involves distinguishing one illness from another. (483)

Etiology

1-5.   (Diagnosis/Etiology/Prognosis) refers to the apparent causation and developmental history of an illness. (483)

prognosis

1-6.   A (diagnosis/etiology/prognosis) is a forecast about the probably course of an illness. (483)

***2.   Explain the most commonly used criteria of abnormality.***

different from

2-1.   As Szasz suggested, people are often said to have a disorder because their behavior is (consistent with/different from) what society considers acceptable. (483)

impaired

2-2.   In many cases, people are judged to have a psychological disorder because their everyday adaptive behavior is (hostile/impaired/strange). (483)

distress

2-3.   Frequently, the diagnosis of a psychological disorder is based on an individual's report of great personal (distress/insight/happiness). (483)

value

2-4.   Diagnoses of psychological disorders involve (normal/snap/value) judgments about what represents normal or abnormal behavior. (483)

do not constitute

2-5.   Normality and abnormality (constitute/do not constitute) an either-or proposition. (484)

***3.   Discuss the history of the DSM system and describe the five axes of DSM-IV.***

1952

3-1.   The first version of the Diagnostic and Statistical Manual of Mental Disorders was published in (1915/1952/1986). (485)

| | |
|---|---|
| DSM-IV | 3-2. The current classification scheme developed by the American Psychiatric Association, which was introduced in 1994, is called the _____. (485) |
| multiaxial; five | 3-3. The publication of the DSM-III in 1980 introduced a new (biological/factorial/ multiaxial) system of classification, which asks for judgments about individuals on (two/five/twelve) separate dimensions, or "axes." (485) |
| I; II | 3-4. The diagnoses of disorders are made on Axes _____ and _____. (485) |
| I | 3-5. Clinicians record most types of disorders on Axis _____. (485) |
| II | 3-6. Long-running personality disorders appear on Axis _____ of the DSM-IV. (485) |

**4.    Summarize data on the prevalence of various psychological disorders.**

| | |
|---|---|
| epidemiology | 4-1. The study of the distribution of mental or physical disorders in a population is called (epidemiology/etiology/clinical psychology). (485) |
| 44 | 4-2. A study of people aged 18-54 suggests that about (22/44/66) percent of the adult population will struggle with some sort of psychological disorder. (485) |
| substance-use | 4-3. The single most common category of disorders is (mood/substance-use/ schizophrenic) disorders. (487) |

**5.    List and describe four types of anxiety disorders.**

| | |
|---|---|
| Anxiety | 5-1. _____ disorders are a class of disorders marked by feelings of excessive apprehension and anxiety. (487) |
| generalized | 5-2. The _____ anxiety disorder is marked by a chronic, high level of anxiety that is not tied to any specific threat. (487-488) |
| phobic | 5-3. A (depressive/panic/phobic) disorder is marked by a persistent and irrational fear of an object or situation that presents no realistic danger. (488) |
| panic | 5-4. A (panic/phobic/schizophrenic) disorder involves recurrent attacks of overwhelming anxiety that usually occur suddenly and unexpectedly. (488) |
| Agoraphobia | 5-5. (Agoraphobia/Arachnophobia/Cynophobia) is a fear of going out to public places. (488) |
| thoughts; actions | 5-6. Obsessions are _____ that repeatedly intrude on one's consciousness, while compulsions are _____ that one feels forced to carry out. (489) |

**6.    Discuss the contribution of biological factors and conditioning to the etiology of anxiety disorders.**

| | |
|---|---|
| weak to moderate | 6-1. Recent studies suggest that there may be a (strong/weak to moderate) genetic predisposition to anxiety disorders. (490) |
| anxiety | 6-2. One influential theory holds that (anxiety/chemical/social) sensitivity may make people vulnerable to anxiety disorders. (490) |
| neurochemical | 6-3. Recent evidence suggests that a link may exist between anxiety disorders and (electrical/neurochemical/pleasure) activity in the brain. (490) |
| classical; operant | 6-4. Many anxiety responses may be acquired through (classical/operant) conditioning and maintained through (classical/operant) conditioning. (490) |
| preparedness | 6-5. The tendency to develop phobias of certain types of objects and situations may be explained by Martin Seligman's concept of (learned helplessness/ modeling/preparedness). (491) |
| inconsistent | 6-6. The evidence in support of the role of preparedness in the acquisition of phobias is (strong/negligible/inconsistent). (491) |

**7.    Explain the contribution of cognitive factors and stress to the etiology of anxiety disorders.**

| | |
|---|---|
| thinking | 7-1. Cognitive theorists maintain that certain styles of (behaving/thinking) make some people particularly vulnerable to anxiety disorders. (491) |
| threat | 7-2. The cognitive view holds that some people are prone to anxiety disorders because they see (hope/monsters/threat) in every corner of their lives. (491) |
| onset | 7-3. There is reason to believe that high stress often helps precipitate the (course/onset/treatment) of anxiety disorders. (491) |

**8.    Describe three types of somatoform disorders.**

| | |
|---|---|
| psychological | 8-1. Somatoform disorders are physical ailments that cannot be fully explained by organic conditions and are largely due to (chemical/psychological) factors. (491) |
| somatization | 8-2. A(n) _____ disorder is marked by a history of diverse physical complaints that appear to be psychological in origin. (492) |
| women; depression | 8-3. Somatization disorders occur mostly in (men/women) and often in conjunction with (depression/schizophrenia) or anxiety disorders. (492) |
| physical | 8-4. Conversion disorders involve a significant loss of (emotional/physical/ psychological) function with no apparent organic cause. (492) |
| physical | 8-5. Hypochondriacs constantly monitor their (physical/psychological) condition, looking for signs of illness. (492) |

**9.**     *Summarize what is known about the causes of somatoform disorders.*

learning

9-1.     Available evidence suggests that somatoform disorders are largely a function of personality and (genetics/learning). (493)

histrionic

9-2.     The prime candidates for developing somatoform disorders appear to be people with (authoritarian/histrionic/multiple) personality characteristics. (493)

catastrophic

9-3.     Recent evidence suggests that people with somatoform disorders tend to draw (catastrophic/medical/psychological) conclusions about minor bodily complaints. (493)

sick

9-4.     One explanation for the development of somatoform disorders is based on the notion that some people grow fond of the role associated with being (depressed/popular/sick). (493)

**10.**     *Describe three types of dissociative disorders.*

identity

10-1.     In dissociative disorders people lose contact with portions of their consciousness or memory, resulting in disruptions in their sense of (belonging/equilibrium/identity). (494)

amnesia

10-2.     Dissociative _____ is a sudden loss of memory for important personal information that is too extensive to be due to normal forgetting. (494)

fugue

10-3.     In dissociative _____, people lose their memory for their sense of personal identity. (494)

identity

10-4.     The formal name for multiple-personality disorder is dissociative _____ disorder. (494)

rare

10-5.     Dissociative identity disorder is relatively (common/rare). (494)

unaware

10-6.     In dissociative identity disorder, the various personalities are often (aware/ unaware) of each other. (494)

**11.**     *Summarize what is known about the causes of dissociative disorders.*

stress

11-1.     Dissociative amnesia and fugue are usually attributed to excessive (alcohol/ neurotransmitter/stress). (495)

creation

11-2.     According to Nicholas Spanos, dissociative identity disorder is a (creation/ function) of modern North American culture. (496)

home life

11-3.     A substantial majority of people with dissociative identity disorder report a history of disturbed (emotions/home life/thinking). (496)

**12.**     *Describe the two major mood disorders and discuss their prevalence.*

| | |
|---|---|
| episodic | 12-1. Mood disorders tend to be (chronic/episodic/life-threatening). (496) |
| depression | 12-2. People with unipolar mood disorders experience emotional extremes at just one end of the mood continuum –(depression/mania). (497) |
| depression; mania | 12-3. People with bipolar mood disorders experience emotional extremes at both ends of the mood continuum, going through periods of both _____ and _____. (497) |
| depressive | 12-4. In major (anxiety/depressive/manic) disorder, people show persistent feelings of sadness and despair and a loss of interest in previous sources of pleasure. (497) |
| months | 12-5. The median duration of depressive episodes is 5 (days/months/years). (498) |
| increasing | 12-6. Evidence suggests that the prevalence of depression is (increasing/decreasing). (498) |
| less | 12-7. Depression is (more/less) common in men than women. (498) |
| manic-depressive | 12-8. Bipolar disorder was formerly know as (generalized anxiety/manic-depressive/obsessive-compulsive) disorder. (498) |
| less | 12-9. Bipolar disorders are much (more/less) common than unipolar depression. (499) |

**13.   *Explain how genetic and neurochemical factors may be related to the development of mood disorders.***

| | |
|---|---|
| concordance | 13-1. A _____ rate indicates the percentage of twin pairs or other pairs of relatives that exhibit the same disorder. (499) |
| are | 13-2. Twin studies, which compare identical and fraternal twins, suggest that genetic factors (are/are not) involved in mood disorders. (499) |
| predisposition | 13-3. Evidence suggests that heredity can create a (barrier/predisposition) to mood disorders. (499) |
| neuro-transmitters | 13-4. Correlations have been found between mood disorders and the levels of (electrical charges/enzymes/neurotransmitters) in the brain. (500) |
| are | 13-5. Drug therapies (are/are not) effective in the treatment of severe mood disorders. (500) |

**14.   *Discuss how cognitive processes may contribute to mood disorders.***

| | |
|---|---|
| helplessness | 14-1. Based largely on animal research, Martin Seligman proposed that depression is caused by learned (emotions/helplessness/sadness). (500) |

pessimistic

high;
low

ruminate

negative

social

unfavorably

a moderately strong

thought

1

common

adaptive

Hallucinations

emotion

14-2.   According to Martin Seligman, people who exhibit a(n) (optimistic/ pessimistic) explanatory style are especially vulnerable to depression. (500)

14-3.   According to hopelessness theory, a pessimistic explanatory style is just one of several or more factors –along with (high/low) stress and (high/low) self-esteem –that may contribute to hopelessness, and thus depression. (500)

14-4.   Susan Nolen-Hoeksema has found that depressed people who (joke/ ruminate/talk) about their problems and setbacks have elevated rates of depression. (500)

14-5.   In sum, cognitive models of depression maintain that (positive/negative) thinking is what leads to depression in many people. (501)

**15.   Explain how interpersonal behavior and stress may contribute to mood disorders.**

15-1.   Some theorists suggest that inadequate (nonverbal/social/writing) skills put people on the road to depressive disorders. (501)

15-2.   Recent evidence indicates that depressed people may gravitate to partners who view them (favorably/unfavorably) and hence reinforce their negative views of themselves. (502)

15-3.   The evidence available today suggests that (a moderately strong/a weak/no) link exists between stress and the onset of mood disorders. (502)

**16.   Describe the prevalence and general symptoms of schizophrenia.**

16-1.   Schizophrenic disorders are a class of disorders marked by disturbances in (mood/sensation/thought) that spill over to affect perceptual, social, and emotional processes. (502)

16-2.   Prevalence estimates suggest that about (1/5/10) percent of the population may suffer from schizophrenic disorders. (502)

16-3.    Delusions are (common/uncommon) among schizophrenics. (503)

16-4.   One of the general symptoms of schizophrenia is a deterioration of (adaptive/excitatory/obsessive) behavior. (503)

16-5.   _____ are sensory perceptions that occur in the absence of a real, external stimulus or that represent gross distortions of perceptual input. (503)

16-6.   A common symptom of schizophrenia is disturbed (emotion/facial patterns/ walking). (503)

**17.   Describe four schizophrenic subtypes.**

Paranoid

17-1. (Disorganized/Paranoid/Undifferentiated) schizophrenics are those who believe that they have enemies who want to harass and oppress them. (503)

motor

17-2. Catatonic schizophrenia is marked primarily by striking (emotional/motor/ social) disturbances. (503)

disorganized

17-3. Aimless babbling and giggling are common in persons suffering from (disorganized/paranoid/undifferentiated) schizophrenia. (504)

undifferentiated

17-4. People who are clearly schizophrenic, but who cannot be placed into any of the other categories are said to have _____ schizophrenia. (504)

**18.    *Distinguish between positive and negative symptoms in schizophrenia.***

do not differ

18-1. The classic schizophrenic subtypes (differ/do not differ) meaningfully in etiology, prognosis, and response to treatment. (504)

negative versus positive

18-2. Nancy Andreasen and others have proposed a new method of typing schizophrenic disorders based on the predominance of (emotional versus unemotional/negative versus positive/treatable versus untreatable) symptoms. (504)

deficits; excesses

18-3. Negative symptoms involve behavioral (deficits/excesses), whereas positive symptoms involve behavioral (deficits/excesses). (504)

greater

18-4. A predominance of positive symptoms is associated with (greater/less) responsiveness to treatment. (504)

disorganization

18-5. In addition to positive and negative symptoms of schizophrenia, some theorists have proposed a third category of symptoms reflecting (classification/disorganization/intensity) of behavior. (504)

**19.    *Identify factors related to the prognosis for schizophrenic patients.***

adolescence or early adulthood

19-1. Schizophrenic disorders usually emerge during (early childhood/ adolescence or early adulthood/middle age). (505)

15-20

19-2. Overall, it appears that about (15-20/30-35/65-70) percent of schizophrenic patients enjoy a full recovery. (505)

later

19-3. A relatively favorable prognosis for schizophrenics can be made if the onset of the disorder occurred at a(n) (earlier/later) age. (505)

low

19-4. A relatively favorable prognosis for schizophrenics can be made if the proportion of negative symptoms is relatively (high/low). (505)

**20.    *Summarize how genetic vulnerability and neurochemical factors may contribute to the etiology of schizophrenia.***

vulnerability

20-1.   Several converging lines of evidence indicate that people inherit a genetically transmitted (barrier/vulnerability) to schizophrenia. (505)

dopamine

20-2.   Excess (dopamine/serotonin/electrical) activity in the brain has been implicated as a likely cause of schizophrenia. (505)

**21.   Discuss the evidence relating schizophrenia to structural abnormalities in the brain and neurodevelopmental insults to the brain.**

neurological

21-1.   Cognitive deficits associated with schizophrenia suggest that the disorder may be caused by (emotional/neurological/physical) defects. (505)

ventricles

21-2.   Advances in brain-imaging technology have yielded findings that suggest an association between enlarged brain (cells/capacity/ventricles) and chronic schizophrenic disturbance. (506)

maturational

21-3.   The neurodevelopmental hypothesis suggests that schizophrenia is caused in part by various disruptions in the normal (chemical/electrical/maturational) processes of the brain before or at birth. (506)

influenza

21-4.   Several studies have found a link between exposure to (alcohol/caffeine/influenza) during pregnancy and increased prevalence of schizophrenia. (506)

more

21-5.   Research suggests that minor physical abnormalities that would be consistent with prenatal neurological damage are (more/less) common among people with schizophrenia than in other people. (507)

**22.   Summarize how expressed emotion and stress may contribute to schizophrenia.**

course

22-1.   Studies show that a family's expressed emotion is a good predictor of the (course/onset/type) of schizophrenia. (508)

triggering

22-2.   Many theories of schizophrenia assume that stress plays a role in (stopping/ treating/triggering) schizophrenic disorders. (508)

vulnerable

22-3.   High stress may serve to precipitate a schizophrenic disorder in someone who is (depressed/older/vulnerable). (508)

**23.   Explain the reasoning underlying the insanity defense, and discuss how often it is used.**

Insanity

23-1.   (Abnormality/Insanity/Psychotic) is a legal status indicating that a person cannot be held responsible for his or her actions because of mental illness. (508)

| | |
|---|---|
| would not | 23-2. Most people with diagnosed psychological disorders (would/would not) qualify as insane. (508) |
| schizophrenic | 23-3. The people most likely to qualify as insane are those troubled by severe (anxiety/mood/schizophrenic) disturbances. (508) |
| less; less | 23-4. The insanity defense is actually used (more/less) frequently and (more/less) successfully than widely believed. (508) |

**24.     Discuss the legal grounds for involuntary commitment.**

| | |
|---|---|
| involuntary | 24-1. In (voluntary/involuntary/psychiatric) commitment, people are hospitalized in psychiatric facilities against their will. (508-509) |
| the courts | 24-2. The final decisions regarding long-term involuntary commitment are made by (psychologists/psychiatrists/the courts). (509) |
| themselves or others | 24-3. Most involuntary commitments occur because people appear to be dangerous to (themselves/others/themselves or others). (509) |

**25.     Describe the symptoms and medical complications of anorexia nervosa and bulimia nervosa.**

| | |
|---|---|
| Anorexia | 25-1. (Anorexia/Bulimia) nervosa involves intense fear of gaining weight, disturbed body image, refusal to maintain normal weight, and dangerous measures to lose weight. (510) |
| amenorrhea | 25-2. Among the medical problems associated with anorexia nervosa is _____, a loss of menstrual cycles in women. (510) |
| Bulimia | 25-3. (Anorexia/Bulimia) nervosa involves habitually engaging in out-of-control overeating followed by unhealthy compensatory efforts, such as self-induced vomiting, fasting, abuse of laxatives and diuretics, and excessive exercise. (510) |
| less | 25-4. Bulimia is a (more/less) life-threatening condition than anorexia. (510) |

**26.     Discuss the history, prevalence, and gender distribution of eating disorders.**

| | |
|---|---|
| 20th | 26-1. Anorexia nervosa did not become a common affliction until the middle of the _____ century. (510) |
| Western | 26-2. Both anorexia and bulimia are a product of modern (Asian/Russian/Western) culture. (510) |
| large | 26-3. There is a (small/moderate/large) gender gap in the likelihood of developing eating disorders. (510) |

| | |
|---|---|
| young | 26-4. Eating disorders mostly afflict (young/middle-age/older) women. (511) |
| | **27.** **Explain how genetic factors, personality, and culture may contribute to eating disorders.** |
| vulnerability | 27-1. Some people may inherit a genetic (barrier/vulnerability/aversion) to eating disorders. (511) |
| are | 27-2. Most of the personality traits associated with anorexia nervosa and bulimia nervosa (are/are not) influenced by genetics. (511) |
| thin | 27-3. In Western society, young women are socialized to believe that they must be attractive, and to be attractive they must be (shapely/stocky/thin). (511) |
| | **28.** **Explain how family dynamics and disturbed thinking may contribute to eating disorders.** |
| family | 28-1. Many theorists emphasize how (family/group/relationship) dynamics can contribute to the development of anorexia nervosa and bulimia nervosa in young women. (512) |
| thinking | 28-2. Cognitive theorists emphasize the role of disturbed (emotions/sexuality/thinking) in the etiology of eating disorders. (513) |
| better | 28-3. The prognosis for recovery is somewhat (better/worse) for bulimia nervosa than for anorexia nervosa. (513) |

**QUIZ BOXES**

*KEY TERMS*

| Medical model | Proposes that it is useful to think of abnormal behavior as a disease. |
|---|---|
| Diagnosis | Involves distinguishing one illness from another. |
| Etiology | The apparent causation and developmental history of an illness. |
| Prognosis | A forecast about the probable course of an illness. |
| Epidemiology | The study of the distribution of mental or physical disorders in a population. |
| Prevalence | The percentage of a population that exhibits a disorder during a specified time period. |
| Anxiety disorders | A class of disorders characterized by feelings of excessive apprehension and anxiety. |
| Generalized anxiety disorder | Disorder marked by a chronic, high level of anxiety that is not tied to any specific threat. |
| Phobic disorder | Disorder marked by a persistent and irrational fear of an object or situation that presents no realistic danger. |
| Panic disorder | Disorder characterized by recurrent attacks of overwhelming anxiety that usually occur suddenly and unexpectedly. |
| Agoraphobia | A fear of going out to public places. |
| Obsessive-compulsive disorder (OCD) | Disorder marked by persistent, uncontrollable intrusions of unwanted thoughts (obsessions) and urges to engage in senseless rituals (compulsions). |
| Neurotransmitters | Chemicals that carry signals from one neuron to another. |
| Somatoform disorders | A class of disorders characterized by physical ailments that cannot be fully explained by organic conditions and are largely due to psychological factors. |
| Somatization disorder | Disorder marked by a history of diverse physical complaints that appear to be psychological in origin. |

| Conversion disorder | Disorder characterized by a significant loss of physical function with no apparent organic basis, usually in a single organ system. |
| --- | --- |
| Hypochondriasis (more widely known as hypochondria) | Disorder marked by excessive preoccupation with health concerns and incessant worry about developing physical illnesses. |
| Dissociative disorders | A class of disorders in which people lose contact with portions of their consciousness or memory, resulting in disruptions in their sense of identity. |
| Dissociative amnesia | Disorder characterized by a sudden loss of memory for important personal information that is too extensive to be due to normal forgetting. |
| Dissociative fugue | Disorder in which people lose their memory for their sense of personal identity. |
| Dissociative identity disorder (DID) | Disorder that involves the coexistence in one person of two or more largely complete, and usually very different, personalities. |
| Mood disorders | A class of disorders marked by emotional disturbances that may spill over to disrupt physical, perceptual, social, and thought processes. |
| Major depressive disorder | Disorder that occurs when people show persistent feelings of sadness and despair and a loss of interest in previous sources of pleasure. |
| Bipolar disorder (formerly known as manic-depressive disorder) | Disorder marked by the experience of both depressed and manic periods. |
| Concordance rate | Measure that indicates the percentage of twin pairs or other pairs of relatives that exhibit the same disorder. |
| Schizophrenic disorders | A class of disorders marked by disturbances in thought that spill over to affect perceptual, social, and emotional processes. |
| Delusions | False beliefs that are maintained even though they clearly are out of touch with reality. |
| Hallucinations | Sensory perceptions that occur in the absence of a real external stimulus or that represent gross distortions of perceptual input. |

| Paranoid schizophrenia | Type of schizophrenia dominated by delusions of persecution, along with delusions of grandeur. |
|---|---|
| Catatonic schizophrenia | Type of schizophrenia marked by striking motor disturbances, ranging from muscular rigidity to random motor activity. |
| Disorganized schizophrenia | Type of schizophrenia marked by a particularly severe deterioration of adaptive behavior. |
| Undifferentiated schizophrenia | Type of schizophrenia marked by idiosyncratic mixtures of schizophrenic symptoms. |
| Insanity | A legal status indicating that a person cannot be held responsible for his or her actions because of mental illness. |
| Involuntary commitment | Situation in which people are hospitalized in psychiatric facilities against their will. |
| Eating disorders | Severe disturbances in eating behavior characterized by preoccupation with weight and unhealthy efforts to control weight. |
| Anorexia Nervosa | Disorder that involves intense fear of gaining weight, disturbed body image, refusal to maintain normal weight, and dangerous measures to lose weight. |
| Bulimia Nervosa | Disorder that involves habitually engaging in out-of-control overeating followed by unhealthy compensatory efforts, such as self-induced vomiting, fasting, abuse of laxatives and diuretics, and excessive exercising. |

## KEY PEOPLE

| Nancy Andreasen | Suggested that schizophrenic disorders can be divided into two categories, based on positive versus negative symptoms. |
|---|---|
| Susan Nolen-Hoeksema | Found that people who ruminate about their problems and setbacks have elevated rates of depression and tend to remain depressed longer than those who do not ruminate. |
| David Rosenhan | Conducted classic study of pseudopatients admitted to mental hospitals; findings illustrate the difficulty in distinguishing normality from abnormality. |

| **Martin Seligman** | Proposed the concept of preparedness, which asserts that people may be biologically prepared to acquire certain fears; suggested that learned helplessness may cause depression. |
| --- | --- |
| **Thomas Szasz** | Criticized the medical model of abnormality; suggested that abnormal behavior involves a deviation from social norms rather than an illness. |

# SELF-TEST

*Multiple Choice Items*

1.  Prior to the eighteenth century, most conceptions of abnormal behavior were based on
    a.  the medical model
    b.  superstition
    c.  DSM-I
    d.  Greek mythology

2.  Thomas Szasz has criticized the medical model because he believes that abnormal behavior
    a.  involves deviation from social norms rather than an illness
    b.  does not really exist since it is the society that is abnormal
    c.  has a psychological rather than a physical cause
    d.  has a physical cause and is therefore a physical illness

3.  When David Rosenhan studied accuracy of diagnosis, he found that
    a.  even mental health professionals had difficulty distinguishing normality from abnormality
    b.  mental health professionals were able consistently to distinguish normal from abnormal
    c.  any normal person could recognize abnormal behavior
    d.  abnormality can be easily diagnosed by consulting the DSM

4.  The current version of the DSM was introduced in
    a.  1952
    b.  1974
    c.  1994
    d.  1998

5.  The current DSM uses a system of classification that asks for judgements about individuals on five separate dimensions. This approach is termed a _____ system.
    a.  multiaxial
    b.  dimensional
    c.  statistical
    d.  multi-tasking

6.  The study of the distribution of mental or physical disorders in a population is called
    a.  etiology
    b.  epidemiology
    c.  psychopathology
    d.  biopsychology

7.  Which of the following is a common complication of panic disorders?
    a.  acrophobia
    b.  agoraphobia
    c.  bipolar disorder
    d.  schizophrenia

8.  Obsessions are
    a.  thoughts that repeatedly intrude into consciousness
    b.  actions that one feels forced to carry out
    c.  both thoughts and actions that cause subjective distress
    d.  stereotyped rituals that temporarily relieve anxiety

9.  The typical age of onset for obsessive-compulsive disorder is
    a.  early childhood
    b.  early adolescence
    c.  early adulthood
    d.  middle adulthood

10. Physical ailments that have no organic basis but are due to psychological factors are called _____ disorders.
    a.  anxiety
    b.  somatoform
    c.  dissociative
    d.  schizophrenic

11. A person suffering from a loss of hearing with no organic basis probably has which of the following disorders?
  a. hypochondriasis
  b. conversion disorder
  c. somatization disorder
  d. obsessive-compulsive disorder

12. Dissociative amnesia and fugue are usually attributed to
  a. excessive stress
  b. classical conditioning
  c. structural abnormalities in the brain
  d. patterns of negative thinking

13. According to your textbook, Abraham Lincoln, Ernest Hemingway, and Kurt Cobain all suffered from
  a. schizophrenia
  b. severe mood disorders
  c. obsessive-compulsive disorder
  d. dissociative identity disorder

14. Bipolar mood disorders were formerly known as
  a. schizophrenia
  b. depressive disorders
  c. manic-depressive disorders
  d. multiple-personality disorders

15. The idea that learned helplessness may contribute to depressive disorders is most consistent with which of the following theoretical approaches?
  a. cognitive
  b. interpersonal
  c. neurochemical
  d. evolutionary

16. A person whose behavior is marked by striking motor disturbances, ranging from muscular rigidity to random motor activity, is most likely suffering from the _____ type of schizophrenia.
  a. paranoid
  b. catatonic
  c. disorganized
  d. undifferentiated

17. Schizophrenic disorders usually emerge during
  a. early childhood
  b. adolescence or early adulthood
  c. a midlife crisis
  d. late adulthood

18. Which of the following is not one of the conditions under which a person can be involuntarily committed to a psychiatric facility?
  a. The person is potentially violent.
  b. The person is potentially suicidal.
  c. The person is in need of treatment.
  d. The person is diagnosed as schizophrenic.

19. Eating disorders mostly affect
  a. young men
  b. young women
  c. middle-aged men
  d. middle-aged women

20. Which of the following statement concerning bulimia nervosa is not accurate?
  a. Bulimia nervosa shares many features with anorexia nervosa.
  b. Anorexia nervosa is more prevalent in Western societies than is bulimia nervosa.
  c. People with bulimia are more prone to cooperate with treatment than are anorexics.
  d. People suffering from bulimia nervosa typically maintain a reasonably normal body weight.

## True/False Items

T/F    1. The rise of the medical model brought improvements in the treatment of people who exhibited abnormal behavior.

T/F    2. Everyone displays some maladaptive behavior and acts in deviant ways once in a while.

T/F    3.    Panic disorder is more common in males than in females.

T/F    4.    People with phobias can generally recall or identify a traumatic experience that led to their phobia.

T/F    5.    Dissociatve identity disorder is also known as schizophrenia.

T/F    6.    The prevalence of major depressive disorder is much higher in women than it is in men.

T/F    7.    Bipolar disorders are seen more often in women than in men.

T/F    8.    Cognitive theorists suggest that depression develops through the process of classical conditioning.

T/F    9.    Some theorists suggest that inadequate social skills put people on the road to depressive disorders.

T/F    10.    Visual hallucinations are the most common form of perceptual distortion associated with schizophrenia.

T/F    11.    The emergence of schizophrenia may be either sudden or gradual.

T/F    12.    Many theories of schizophrenia assume that stress plays a role in triggering schizophrenic disorders.

T/F    13.    The insanity defense is actually used less frequently and less successfully than widely believed.

T/F    14.    Eating disorders originated in developing countries, where access to adequate food is often precarious.

## ANSWER KEY FOR SELF-TEST

### Multiple Choice Items

b       1.      People who behaved strangely were thought to be possessed by demons, to be witches in league with the devil, or to be victims of God's punishment. (482)

a       2.      Szasz contends that these deviations are "problems in living" rather than medical problems. (482)

a       3.      Rosenhan's findings support the idea that people with psychological disorders do not behave in bizarre ways that are very different from the behavior of normal people. (484)

c       4.      The current edition, DSM-IV, was introduced in 1994. The first version of the DSM was unveiled in 1952. (485)

a       5.      The multiaxial system was introduced in 1980 in DSM-III. (485)

b       6.      These studies have yielded estimates indicating that one-third to 44% of the population may have some sort of psychological disorder. (485)

b       7.      Agoraphobia, the fear of going out to public places, frequently occurs in individuals with panic disorder when their concern about exhibiting panic in public escalates to the point where they are afraid to leave home. (488-489)

a       8.      Obsessions are commonly linked with compulsions (actions that one feels forced to carry out) in the obsessive-compulsive disorder. (489)

c       9.      Most cases of obsessive-compulsive disorder emerge before the age of 35. (490)

b       10.     Somatoform disorders are physical illnesses that appear largely psychological in origin. (491)

b       11.     Conversion disorder is characterized by a significant loss of physical function or by other physical symptoms (with no apparent organic basis), usually in a single organ system. (492)

a       12.     However, little is known about why this extreme reaction to stress occurs in a tiny minority of people, but not in the vast majority who are subjected to similar stress. (495)

b       13.     Although mood disorders can be terribly debilitating, people with mood disorders may still achieve greatness, because such disorders tend to be episodic in nature. (496)

c       14.     This is because bipolar disorder is marked by the experience of both manic and depressed states. (498)

a       15.     Seligman originally considered learned helplessness to be a product of conditioning but eventually revised his theory, giving it a cognitive slant. (500)

b       16.     The catatonic subtype is not particularly common, and its prevalence seems to be declining. (503)

b       17.     Schizophrenic disorders rarely emerge after the age of 45. (504-505) d          18.  Most involuntary commitments occur because people appear to be dangerous to themselves or others. (509)

b          19.  About 90-95% of individuals with eating disorders are females, with a typical age of onset of 14-18 for anorexia and 15-21 for bulimia. (510-511)

b          20.  Studies of young women suggest that about twice as many develop bulimia nervosa as compared to anorexia nervosa. (511)

### *True/False Items*

True       1.  As victims of an illness, they were viewed with more sympathy and less hatred and fear. (482)

True       2.  This illustrates how difficult it is to draw a line that clearly separates normality from abnormality.  Basically, normality and abnormality exist on a continuum. (484)

False      3.  About two-thirds of those who suffer from panic disorder are female. (489)

False      4.  In fact, many people with phobias cannot recall or identify a traumatic conditioning experience that led to their phobia.  This is one of several problems with conditioning models of phobias. (491)

False      5.  This is a common misconception, perpetuated by the popular media. (494)

True       6.  The prevalence of depression is about twice as high in women as it is in men. (498)

False      7.  Bipolar disorders are seen equally often in men and women. (499)

False      8.  Actually, cognitive models of depression (e.g., Seligman's hopelessness theory) maintain that hopelessness, and a pessimistic explanatory style of thinking, are what make people feel depressed. (500)

True       9.  According to this notion, depression-prone people lack the social finesse needed to acquire important kinds of reinforcers, such as good friends and top jobs.  This lack of reinforcers could understandably lead to negative emotions and depression. (501)

False      10. Actually, auditory hallucinations (e.g., hearing voices) are the most common form of perceptual distortion in schizophrenia. (503)

True       11. A person's likelihood of recovery seems to be greater when the onset is sudden rather than gradual. (505)

True       12. According to this notion, various biological and psychological factors influence individuals' vulnerability to schizophrenia; high stress may then precipitate the disorder. (508)

True       13. One study found that the general public estimates that the insanity defense is used in 37% of felony cases, when in fact it is used in less than 1%.  Another study of over 60,000 indictments in Baltimore found that only 190 defendants (0.31%) pleaded insanity, and of these, only 8 were successful. (508)

False | 14. In fact, eating disorders are a product of modern, affluent, Western culture, and they have only recently started showing up in developing nations. (510)

# Chapter 16
# PSYCHOTHERAPY

**1.** *Identify the three major categories of therapy.*

Insight

1-1. _____ therapy is "talk therapy" in the tradition of Freud's psychoanalysis. (518)

solutions

1-2. The goal of insight therapies is to pursue increased insight regarding the nature of the client's difficulties and to sort through possible (causes/explanations/solutions). (518)

Behavior

1-3. (Behavior/Biomedical/Insight) therapies are based on the principles of learning and conditioning. (518)

behaviors

1-4. Behavior therapists work on changing a client's overt (behaviors/emotions/thought processes). (518)

Biomedical

1-5. _____ approaches to therapy involve interventions into a person's physiological functioning. (518)

**2.** *Discuss why people do or do not seek psychotherapy.*

clients

2-1. In the therapeutic triad (therapists, treatments, clients), the greatest diversity of all is seen among the _____. (518)

15

2-2. About (15/30/60) percent of the U.S. population uses mental health services in a given year. (518)

anxiety

2-3. The two most common presenting problems are excessive (anxiety/drinking/use of defense mechanisms) and depression. (518-519)

less

2-4. Men are (more/less) likely to receive therapy than are women. (519)

stigma

2-5. According to the U.S. Surgeon General's report on mental health, the biggest roadblock to seeking therapy is the (cost/stigma/time) associated with treatment. (519)

**3.** *Describe the various types of mental health professionals involved in the provision of therapy.*

full-fledged disorders; everyday problems

3-1. In theory, clinical psychologists are trained to treat (everyday problems/full-fledged disorders), whereas the training of counseling psychologists emphasizes the treatment of (everyday problems/full-fledged disorders). (520)

| | |
|---|---|
| more;<br>more | 3-2. In comparison to psychologists, psychiatrists devote (more/less) time to relatively severe disorders, and are (more/less) likely to use psychoanalytic methods. (521) |
| drug | 3-3. In providing therapy, psychiatrists increasingly emphasize (behavioral/drug/group) therapies. (521) |
| master's | 3-4. Psychiatric social workers and counselors typically have a (doctoral/master's) degree. (521) |

**4.    *Explain the logic of psychoanalysis and describe the techniques used to probe the unconscious.***

| | |
|---|---|
| unconscious;<br>free | 4-1. Psychoanalysis is an insight therapy that emphasizes the recovery of (conscious/unconscious) conflicts, motives, and defenses through techniques such as (free/loose/sexual) association, dream analysis, and transference. (522) |
| unconscious | 4-2. Freud believed that neurotic problems are caused by (parental/social/unconscious) conflicts left over from early childhood. (522) |
| censorship | 4-3. In free association, clients spontaneously express their thoughts and feelings exactly as they occur, with as little (censorship/explanation/rumination) as possible. (522) |
| symbolic | 4-4. In dream analysis, the therapist interprets the (actual/symbolic) meaning of the client's dreams. (523) |
| dreams | 4-5. For Freud, (dreams/neurotic behaviors/sexual urges) were the "royal road to the unconscious." (523) |

**5.    *Discuss interpretation, resistance, and transference in psychoanalysis.***

| | |
|---|---|
| Interpretation | 5-1. _____ involves the therapist's attempt to explain the inner significance of the client's thoughts, feelings, memories, and behaviors. (523) |
| Resistance | 5-2. _____ involves largely unconscious defensive maneuvers intended to hinder the progress of therapy. (524) |
| unconscious | 5-3. Clients often try to resist therapeutic efforts because they don't want to face up to the painful conflicts that are buried in their (preconscious/unconscious/backyard). (524) |
| therapist | 5-4. In transference, the client transfers conflicting feelings about important people onto his or her (siblings/parents/therapist). (524) |
| is not | 5-5. Psychoanalysis as done by Freud (is/is not) widely practiced today. (524) |
| psycho-dynamic | 5-6. Descendants of Freud's original approach to psychoanalysis are collectively known as (analytic/behavioral/psychodynamic) approaches to therapy. (524) |

**6.    Explain the logic of client-centered therapy.**

Carl Rogers;
humanistic

6-1.    Devised by (Carl Jung/Carl Rogers/John Watson), client-centered therapy is based on the (behavioral/humanistic/psychoanalytic) perspective. (524)

incongruence

6-2.    Rogers maintained that most personal distress is due to the (correlation/incongruence) between a person's self-concept and reality. (524)

respect

6-3.    Client-centered therapists encourage clients to (discard/question/respect) their own feelings and values. (525)

**7.    Describe therapeutic climate and process in client-centered therapy.**

unconditional;
empathy

7-1.    To create an atmosphere of emotional support, Rogers believed that therapists must provide genuineness, (conditional/unconditional) positive regard, and (empathy/instructions). (525)

clarification

7-2.    The key task of the therapist in client-centered therapy is (clarification/resistance/transference). (525)

personality

7-3.    Client-centered therapy resembles psychoanalysis in that both seek to achieve a major reconstruction of a client's (personality/sexual orientation/value system). (525-526)

**8.    Discuss the logic, goals, and techniques of cognitive therapy.**

thoughts;
maladaptive

8-1.    Cognitive therapy is a treatment that emphasizes recognizing and changing negative (desires/karma/thoughts) and (adaptive/maladaptive) beliefs. (526)

depression

8-2.    Cognitive therapy was originally devised as a treatment for (depression/neuroticism/schizophrenia). (526)

reality

8-3.    In cognitive therapy, clients are trained to subject their automatic negative thoughts to (psychological/reality) testing. (526)

are

8-4.    Unlike client-centered therapists, cognitive therapists (are/are not) actively involved in determining the pace and direction of treatment. (526)

behavior

8-5.    Cognitive therapy is a creative blend of "talk therapy" and (behavior/drug/shock) therapy. (527)

**9.    Describe how group therapy is generally conducted.**

Group

9-1.    _____ is the simultaneous treatment of several or more clients in a group. (527)

encounter

9-2.    The ideas underlying Carl Rogers's client-centered therapy spawned the much-publicized (encounter/social) group movement. (527)

| | |
|---|---|
| 5-10 | 9-3.  A therapy group typically consists of about (2-4/5-10/15-20) participants. (527) |
| cohesiveness | 9-4.  In group therapy the therapist often stays in the background and tries to promote group (conflict/cohesiveness/transference). (527) |
| more | 9-5.  The therapist and clients are on (more/less) equal footing in group therapy than in individual therapy. (527) |
| therapists | 9-6.  In group therapy, participants essentially function as (challengers/parents/therapists) for one another. (527) |

**10.    Identify some advantages of group therapy.**

| | |
|---|---|
| is not | 10-1.  In group therapy, participants often come to realize that their misery (is/is not) unique. (528) |
| social | 10-2.  Group therapy provides participants an opportunity to work on their (social/therapeutic/thinking) skills in a safe environment. (528) |
| peer | 10-3.  In (peer/psychodynamic/humanistic) self-help groups, people who have a problem in common get together regularly to help one another out. (528) |

**11.    Summarize evidence on the efficacy of insight therapies.**

| | |
|---|---|
| allegiance | 11-1.  The fact that researchers comparing different therapies tend to obtain results that favor the therapeutic approach they champion is termed the (allegiance/attribution/confirmation) effect. (528) |
| is | 11-2.  Many studies indicate that insight therapy (is/is not) superior to no treatment or to placebo treatment. (529) |
| had | 11-3.  In one widely discussed study that focused on patients' self-reports, the vast majority of the respondents subjectively felt that they (had/had not) derived benefit from their therapy. (529) |
| common | 11-4.  Some theorists argue that (common/sexual/social) factors account for virtually all of the progress that clients make in therapy. (529) |

**12.    Summarize both sides of the recovered memories controversy.**

| | |
|---|---|
| therapy | 12-1.  The subject of the controversy is the spate of prominent reports involving the recovery of repressed memories of sexual abuse and other childhood trauma through (drug treatment/shock treatment/therapy) –often using methods that some critics characterize as questionable. (529) |
| therapists | 12-2.  Many accused parents have argued that their children's recollections are false memories created inadvertently by well-intentioned (friends/siblings/therapists) through the power of suggestion. (530) |

| | |
|---|---|
| false | 12-3. Child abuse usually takes place behind closed doors, and in the absence of corroborative evidence, there isn't any way to reliably distinguish genuine recovered memories from those that are (accurate, but unrecovered/false). (530) |
| sharply divided | 12-4. Psychologists are (in agreement/sharply divided) on the issue of recovered memories. (530) |
| hypnotized | 12-5. Studies have shown that subtle suggestions made to (hypnotized/medicated) subjects can be converted into "memories" of things they never saw. (530-531) |
| can | 12-6. It seems pretty clear that therapists (can/cannot) unknowingly create false memories in their patients. (532) |
| don't have | 12-7. At this point, we (have/don't have) adequate data to estimate the proportion of recovered memories of abuse that are authentic versus those that are the product of suggestion. (532) |

**13.    Summarize the general approach and principles of behavior therapies.**

| | |
|---|---|
| learning | 13-1. Behavior therapies involve the application of the principles of (learning/psychoanalysis/sociology) to direct efforts to change clients' maladaptive behavior. (532) |
| learning | 13-2. Behavioral therapists assume that behavior is a product of (evolution/heredity/learning). (532) |
| unlearned | 13-3. Behavior therapists assume that what has been learned can be (modeled/transferred/unlearned). (533) |
| modification | 13-4. Both behavior therapy and self-(modification/monitoring/perception) use the same principles of learning to alter behavior directly. (533) |

**14.    Describe the three steps in systematic desensitization and the logic underlying the treatment.**

| | |
|---|---|
| counter-conditioning | 14-1. Systematic desensitization is a behavior therapy used to reduce clients' anxiety responses through (counterconditioning/insight/medication). (533) |
| classical | 14-2. Systematic desensitization is a treatment that assumes that most anxiety responses are acquired through (classical/operant) conditioning. (533) |
| hierarchy | 14-3. The first step in systematic desensitization is for the therapist to help the client build an anxiety (bridge/hierarchy/repertoire). (533) |
| relaxation | 14-4. In systematic desensitization the client must learn to engage in deep and thorough (relaxation/sleep/thought) on command from the therapist. (533) |
| hierarchy | 14-5. In the final step, the client tries to work through the (hierarchy/transference), learning to remain relaxed while imagining each stimulus. (533) |

| | |
|---|---|
| incompatible | 14-6. According to Wolpe, the principle at work in systematic desensitization is that anxiety and relaxation are (complementary/incompatible/unconscious) responses. (534) |
| has | 14-7. Systematic desensitization's effectiveness in eliminating specific anxieties (has/has not) been well documented. (534) |

**15.    Describe the use of aversion therapy and social skills training.**

| | |
|---|---|
| undesirable | 15-1. Aversion therapy is a behavior therapy in which an aversive stimulus is paired with a stimulus that elicits a(n) (desirable/undesirable) response. (534) |
| is not | 15-2. Typically, aversion therapy (is/is not) the only element in a treatment program. (535) |
| learning | 15-3. According to behavior therapists, people acquire their social skills through (genetics/learning/practice). (535) |
| modeling | 15-4. Behavior therapists make use of (classical conditioning/systematic desensitization/modeling) by encouraging clients to watch socially skilled friends and colleagues. (536) |
| role-playing | 15-5. In behavioral rehearsal, the client practices social techniques in structured (confrontational/desensitized/role-playing) exercises. (536) |

**16.    Summarize evidence on the efficacy of behavior therapies.**

| | |
|---|---|
| ample | 16-1. There is (ample/very little) evidence regarding the effectiveness of behavior therapy. (536) |
| small | 16-2. In direct comparisons of the effectiveness of behavior therapy to that of insight therapy, the differences are usually (small/large/nonexistent). (536) |
| are not | 16-3. Behavior therapies (are/are not) well suited to the treatment of such problems as vague feelings of discontent. (536) |

**17.    Describe the principal drug therapies used in the treatment of psychological disorders and summarize evidence regarding their efficacy.**

| | |
|---|---|
| Biomedical | 17-1. (Biomedical/Evolutionary/Psychodynamic) therapies are physiological interventions intended to reduce symptoms associated with psychological disorders. (536) |
| Valium Xanax | 17-2. The most popular antianxiety drugs go by the trade names of _____ and _____. (537) |
| almost immediately | 17-3. Antianxiety drugs exert their effects on tension and nervousness (almost immediately/gradually). (537) |

| | |
|---|---|
| schizophrenia | 17-4. Antipsychotic drugs are used primarily in the treatment of (depression/ neurosis/schizophrenia). (537) |
| tardive dyskinesia | 17-5. One of the major side effects of antipsychotic drugs is a severe and lasting neurological problem called _____ _____, which is marked by chronic tremors and involuntary spastic movements. (538) |
| atypical | 17-6. Psychiatrists are currently enthusiastic about a new class of antipsychotic agents, called (atypical/typical) antipsychotic drugs. (538) |
| mood | 17-7. Antidepressant drugs gradually elevate a person's (mood/thinking). (538) |
| gradually | 17-8. Like antipsychotic drugs, antidepressants exert their effects (almost immediately/gradually). (538) |
| serotonin | 17-9. Today, psychiatrists are likely to prescribe a new class of antidepressants, called selective serotonin reuptake inhibitors (SSRIs), which slow the reuptake process at _____ synapses. (538) |
| suicide | 17-10. A major concern in recent years has been evidence from a number of studies that SSRIs may increase the risk for (cancer/diabetes/suicide). (538) |
| bipolar mood | 17-11. Lithium is a chemical used to control mood swings in patients with (bipolar mood/obsessive-compulsive/schizophrenic) disorders. (539) |
| severe | 17-12. What is especially impressive about the use of drug therapies is that they can be effective with (mild/severe/imagined) disorders that otherwise defy therapeutic endeavors. (539) |

**18.    Discuss some of the problems associated with drug therapies and their overall value.**

| | |
|---|---|
| superficial | 18-1. Some critics argue that drug therapies often produce (artificial/severe/ superficial) curative effects. (539) |
| over-prescribed over-medicated | 18-2. Critics also charge that many drugs are (over-prescribed/under-prescribed) and many patients (over-medicated/under-medicated). (539) |
| worse | 18-3. Some critics charge that the side effects of therapeutic drugs are (better/ worse) than the illnesses the drugs are supposed to cure. (539) |
| brief | 18-4. Industry-financed drug trials often tend to be too (brief/objective/superficial) to detect the long-term risks associated with new drugs. (539) |

**19.    Describe ECT and discuss its efficacy and risks.**

| | |
|---|---|
| cortical | 19-1. Electroconvulsive therapy is a biomedical treatment in which electric shock is used to produce a(n) (cortical/epileptic/muscular) seizure accompanied by convulsions. (540) |
| is not | 19-2. ECT (is/is not) a rare form of therapy. (540) |

| depression | 19-3. | Although ECT was once considered appropriate for a wide range of disorders, in recent decades it has primarily been recommended for the treatment of (anxiety disorders/depression/schizophrenia). (541) |

| does | 19-4. | Overall, there (does/does not) seem to be enough favorable evidence to justify conservative use of ECT. (541) |

| high | 19-5. | Relapse rates after ECT tend to be (high/low). (541) |

| memory | 19-6. | Even ECT proponents acknowledge that loss of (hearing/memory/vision) and other cognitive deficits are common short-term side effects of ECT. (541) |

| is no | 19-7. | There (is/is no) objective evidence that ECT causes structural damage in the brain. (541) |

| anecdotal | 19-8. | The evidence that ECT-induced cognitive deficits are often significant and sometimes permanent is largely (anecdotal/correlational/experimental). (541) |

**20.     Discuss how managed health care has affected the provision of therapy.**

| lower | 20-1. | Under managed health care, consumers generally pay (higher/lower) prices for their care. (542) |

| may not | 20-2. | Under managed health care, consumers (may/may not) obtain whatever treatments they believe necessary. (542) |

| long-term | 20-3. | Under managed health care, (short-term/long-term) therapy is becoming a thing of the past unless patients can pay for it out of their own pockets. (542) |

| confidentiality | 20-4. | The extensive utilization review procedures required by managed care have raised concerns about providers' autonomy and clients' (confidentiality/diagnoses/recovery). (542) |

**21.     Discuss the merits of blending approaches to therapy.**

| treatment team | 21-1. | Multiple approaches to therapy are particularly likely when a (counselor/psychiatrist/treatment team) provides therapy. (542) |

| is | 21-2. | Studies suggest that there (is/is no) merit in combining approaches to treatment. (542) |

| eclectic | 21-3. | In recent surveys of psychologists' theoretical orientations, researchers have found that the greatest proportion of respondents describe themselves as (behavioral/eclectic/psychodynamic) in approach. (542) |

**22.     Explain why therapy is underutilized by ethnic minorities.**

| reluctant | 22-1. | In times of psychological distress, some cultural groups are (encouraged/reluctant) to turn to formal, professional sources of assistance. (543) |

are not

22-2.    Most hospitals and mental health agencies (are/are not) adequately staffed with therapists who speak the languages used by minority groups in their service areas. (544)

are not

22-3.    The vast majority of therapists (are/are not) familiar with the cultural backgrounds and unique characteristics of various ethnic groups. (544)

more

22-4.    Studies show that ethnic minorities are (more/no more) likely to go to mental health facilities that are staffed by a higher proportion of people who share their ethnic background. (544)

**23.    Discuss when and where to seek therapy.**

problems

23-1.    You should begin to think seriously about therapy when your life is seriously disrupted by your (friends/family/problems). (545)

are not

23-2.    Most therapists (are/are not) in private practice. (545)

**24.    Evaluate the potential importance of a therapist's gender and professional background.**

have not

24-1.    Researchers (have/have not) found reliable associations between therapists' professional background and therapeutic efficacy. (545)

drugs

24-2.    Some critics argue that many psychiatrists are too quick to use (drugs/ insight therapy/self-modification) to solve problems. (546)

inhibit

24-3.    Feeling uncomfortable with a therapist of one gender or the other could (enhance/inhibit) the therapeutic process. (546)

sliding

24-4.    Many community mental health centers and social service agencies use a _____ scale, so that clients are charged according to how much they can afford to pay. (547)

**25.    Summarize the evidence on whether therapists' theoretical approach influences their effectiveness.**

cognitive;
systematic
desensitization

25-1.    Martin Seligman suggests that panic disorders respond best to (cognitive/ insight) therapy, and that specific phobias are most amenable to treatment with (drugs/systematic desensitization). (547)

skills

25-2.    Effectiveness in therapy appears to depend on the personal (reputation/ skills) of the therapists rather than their theoretical orientation. (547-548)

art

25-3.    According to Arnold Lazarus, who devised multimodal therapy, therapists "straddle the fence between science and (art/psychology/superstition)." (548)

**26.    Discuss what one should expect out of therapy.**

resistance

26-1. Given the very real possibility that poor therapeutic progress is due to (medication/resistance/transference), you should not be too quick to leave therapy when dissatisfied. (549)

realistic

26-2. It is important to have (lofty/realistic) expectations about therapy. (549)

# QUIZ BOXES

## KEY TERMS

| | |
|---|---|
| **Clinical/Counseling psychologists** | Specialize in the diagnosis and treatment of psychological disorders and everyday behavioral problems. |
| **Psychiatrists** | Physicians who specialize in the treatment of psychological disorders. |
| **Insight therapies** | Therapies that involve verbal interactions intended to enhance clients' self-knowledge and thus promote healthful changes in personality and behavior. |
| **Psychoanalysis** | An insight therapy that emphasizes the recovery of unconscious conflicts, motives, and defenses through techniques such as free association, dream analysis, and transference. |
| **Free association** | Therapeutic technique in which clients spontaneously express their thoughts and feelings exactly as they occur, with as little censorship as possible. |
| **Dream analysis** | Therapeutic technique in which the therapist interprets the symbolic meaning of the client's dreams. |
| **Interpretation** | The therapist's attempts to explain the inner significance of the client's thoughts, feelings, memories, and behaviors. |
| **Resistance** | Largely unconscious defensive maneuvers by the client intended to hinder the progress of therapy. |
| **Transference** | Occurs when clients start relating to their therapist in ways that mimic critical relationships in their lives. |
| **Client-centered therapy** | An insight therapy that emphasizes providing a supportive emotional climate for clients, who play a major role in determining the pace and direction of their therapy. |
| **Cognitive therapy** | A treatment that emphasizes recognizing and changing negative thoughts and maladaptive beliefs. |
| **Group therapy** | The simultaneous treatment of several or more clients in a group. |
| **Allegiance effect** | Occurs when researchers comparing different therapies tend to obtain results that favor the therapeutic approach they champion. |

| Behavior therapies | Therapies that involve the application of the principles of learning to direct efforts to change clients' maladaptive behaviors. |
|---|---|
| Systematic desensitization | A behavior therapy used to reduce clients' anxiety responses through counterconditioning. |
| Aversion therapy | A behavior therapy in which an aversive stimulus is paired with a stimulus that elicits an undesirable response. |
| Social skills training | A behavior therapy designed to improve interpersonal skills that emphasizes shaping, modeling, and behavioral rehearsal. |
| Biomedical therapies | Therapies that use physiological interventions intended to reduce symptoms associated with psychological disorders. |
| Psychopharmacotherapy | The treatment of mental disorders with medication. |
| Antianxiety drugs | Drugs that relieve tension, apprehension, and nervousness. |
| Antipsychotic drugs | Drugs used to gradually reduce psychotic symptoms, including hyperactivity, mental confusion, hallucinations, and delusions. |
| Tardive dyskinesia | A neurological disorder marked by chronic tremors and involuntary spastic movements. |
| Antidepressant drugs | Drugs that gradually elevate mood and help bring people out of a depression. |
| Mood stabilizers | Drugs used to control mood swings in patients with bipolar mood disorders. |
| Electroconvulsive therapy (ECT) | A biomedical treatment in which electric shock is used to produce a cortical seizure accompanied by convulsions. |

## KEY PEOPLE

| Aaron Beck | Developed a version of cognitive therapy, an insight therapy that emphasizes recognizing and changing negative thoughts and maladaptive beliefs. |
|---|---|
| Hans Eysenck | Wrote classic 1952 article suggesting that the recovery rate for treated and nontreated neurotics was similar. |

| **Sigmund Freud** | Developed system of psychoanalysis, an insight therapy that emphasizes the recovery of unconscious conflicts, motives, and defenses. |
| **Carl Rogers** | Developed client-centered therapy, an insight therapy that emphasizes providing a supportive emotional climate for clients. |
| **Joseph Wolpe** | Devised systematic desensitization, a behavior therapy used to reduce clients' anxiety responses through counterconditioning. |

## SELF-TEST

*Multiple Choice Items*

1.  The goal of insight therapies is to
    a.   change the patient's undesirable behaviors
    b.   intervene in a person's biological functioning
    c.   try to understand the nature of the client's difficulties
    d.   All of the above are goals of insight therapy

2.  The main reason why people who need therapy don't get it is that
    a.   it is simply too expensive
    b.   there aren't enough qualified therapists available
    c.   those who need help don't know where to find it
    d.   many people equate being in therapy with personal weakness

3.  Physicians who specialize in the treatment of psychological disorders are called
    a.   psychiatrists                          c.   counseling psychologists
    b.   clinical psychologists                 d.   psychiatric social workers

4.  Freud believed that neurotic problems were caused by
    a.   unconscious conflicts left over from childhood
    b.   recurring self-defeating behaviors
    c.   conscious conflicts with significant others
    d.   learned behaviors that become established early in life

5.  For Sigmund Freud, the most direct means of access to patients' innermost conflicts, wishes, and impulses was through
    a.   resistance                             c.   word association
    b.   transference                           d.   dream interpretation

6.  Carl Rogers maintained that most personal distress is due to
    a.   the lack of cooperation between the client and therapist
    b.   the inability of the client to follow the directions of the therapist
    c.   inadequate feedback about oneself from others
    d.   incongruence between a person's self-concept and reality

7.  In client-centered therapy, the relationship between the client and therapist is
    a.   one of equals working together on the problem
    b.   much like that of a horse (client) and rider (therapist)
    c.   the therapist directing the process through free association
    d.   one where neither plays an active role, allowing the process to unfold naturally

8.  The goal of cognitive therapy is to
    a.   identify unconscious needs and desires through free association
    b.   recognize and change negative thoughts and maladaptive beliefs
    c.   help clients think about how therapy might help them
    d.   help clients learn how to be of help to others in need of therapy

9.    A strength of group therapy is that it
      a.    has a better chance of succeeding than any other form
      b.    places participants in challenging social situations while still in the therapy group
      c.    stretches the therapy period over a longer time so that the client can make steady progress
      d.    provides the participants an opportunity to try out new social behaviors in a safe environment

10.   The subject of the recovered memories controversy involves the recovery of repressed memories
      a.    from the collective unconscious
      b.    of sexual abuse and other childhood trauma
      c.    that appear to the patient in his or her dreams
      d.    of viewing one's parents engaged in sexual intercourse

11.   Behavior therapies are based on the assumption that
      a.    behavior is a product of learning
      b.    unconscious desires lead to most psychological problems
      c.    negative self-talk is the root of most behavioral problems
      d.    insights about one's behavior are necessary for constructive change

12.   Systematic desensitization assumes that most anxiety responses are acquired through
      a.    operant conditioning                    c.    negative self-attribution
      b.    classical conditioning                   d.    observational learning

13.   Aversion therapy is considered a type of _____ therapy.
      a.    insight                                  c.    behavior
      b.    cognitive                                d.    biomedical

14.   When comparing behavior therapy with insight therapy, researchers conclude that the differences are
      a.    small, but favor behavioral approaches   c.    large, favoring the behavioral approaches
      b.    small, but favor the insight approaches  d.    large, favoring the insight approaches

15.   Antipsychotic drugs are a problem because
      a.    they work in fewer than half of the patients
      b.    patients frequently suffer overdoses
      c.    they work quickly but don't last very long
      d.    they have many unpleasant side effects

16.   Critics maintain that the negative effects of psychiatric drugs are not fully appreciated because
      a.    medical researchers don't have access to representative samples
      b.    most drugs are not around long enough to determine their long-term impact
      c.    the pharmaceutical industry has undue influence over the research on drug testing
      d.    drug testing on humans is illegal in the United States

17.   Electroconvulsive therapy is considered a type of _____ therapy.
      a.    insight                                  c.    behavioral
      b.    cognitive                                d.    biomedical

18.   In recent surveys of psychologists' theoretical orientations, the greatest proportion of respondents describe themselves as _____ in approach.
      a.    eclectic                                 c.    behavioral
      b.    cognitive                                d.    client-centered

19.   You should look for professional help for your adjustment problems when
      a.    you feel helpless and overwhelmed
      b.    those you count on to listen and help are tired of it
      c.    your life is seriously disrupted by your problems
      d.    all of the above

20.   The effectiveness of therapy mainly depends on
      a.    the theoretical approach of the therapist
      b.    the therapist's personal skills
      c.    how much the client wants the treatment to work
      d.    how well the client follows the instructions from the therapist

### *True/False Items*

T/F      1.   Most of the procedures used by biomedical therapists involve either classical conditioning or operant conditioning.

T/F      2.   It appears that many people who need therapy don't receive it.

T/F      3.   Clinical psychologists tend to emphasize drug therapies for psychological disorders.

T/F      4.   Psychoanalysis is considered a type of insight therapy.

T/F      5.   Classical psychoanalysis as done by Sigmund Freud is still widely practiced today.

T/F      6.   In client-centered therapy, the therapist's key task is clarification.

T/F      7.   Clients usually invest considerable time, effort, and money in insight therapies.

T/F      8.   Psychologists are in general agreement in accepting recovered memories at face value.

T/F      9.   Systematic desensitization assumes that most anxiety responses are acquired through classical conditioning.

T/F     10.   There is favorable evidence on the efficacy of most of the widely used behavioral interventions.

T/F     11.   Antipsychotic drugs are used primarily in the treatment of depression.

T/F     12.   Electroconvulsive therapy is rarely used today.

T/F     13.   Long-term therapy is becoming a thing of the past unless patients can pay for it out of their own pockets.

T/F     14.   Studies suggest that there is merit in combining approaches to therapy.

T/F     15.   Therapy is generally an expensive proposition.

## ANSWER KEY FOR SELF-TEST

*Multiple Choice Items*

c     1.    In addition to pursuing increased insight regarding the nature of the client's difficulties, the goal is to sort through possible solutions. (518)

d     2.    According to the 1999 U.S. Surgeon General's report on mental health, the biggest roadblock for seeking treatment is the "stigma surrounding the receipt of mental health treatment." (519)

a     3.    Unlike psychologists, psychiatrists have a medical degree with a specialization in psychiatry. (521)

a     4.    As explained in Chapter 2, Freud thought that these inner conflicts involve battles among the id, ego, and superego, usually over sexual and aggressive impulses. (522)

d     5.    For Freud, dreams were the "royal road to the unconscious." (523)

d     6.    According to Rogers, incongruence makes people prone to feel threatened by realistic feedback about themselves from others. (524)

a     7.    The therapist provides relatively little guidance and keeps interpretation and advice to a minimum. (525)

b     8.    Basically, the goal is to get clients to change the way they think. (526)

d     9.    Group therapy can provide a workshop for improving interpersonal skills that cannot be matched by individual therapy. (528)

b    10.    In recent years the media have been flooded with stories of people who have recovered long-lost recollections of sexual abuse, typically with the help of their therapists. (529)

a    11.    Also, it is assumed that what is learned can be unlearned. (532-533)

b    12.    According to this model, a harmless stimulus (e.g. a bridge) may be paired with a frightening event (lightning strikes it), becoming a conditioned stimulus eliciting anxiety. (533)

c    13.    And because of its aversive nature –the client has to endure decidedly unpleasant stimuli, such as shock or drug-induced nausea –it is the most controversial of the behavior therapies. (534)

a    14.    However, this is true mainly for certain types of disorders for which behavioral approaches are most suited (e.g., phobias). (536)

d    15.    Common side effects include drowsiness, constipation, and "cotton mouth."  Also, antipsychotics may cause a severe and lasting neurological disorder called tardive dyskinesia. (537)

c    16.    Today, most researchers who investigate the benefits and risks of medications and write treatment guidelines have lucrative financial arrangements with the pharmaceutical industry. (539)

| | | |
|---|---|---|
| d | 17. | Electroconvulsive therapy (ECT) is a biomedical treatment (typically for depression) in which electric shock is used to produce a cortical seizure accompanied by convulsions. (540) |
| a | 18. | This finding underscores the value of multiple approaches to therapy. (542) |
| d | 19. | If any of these situations apply, you should begin to think seriously about therapy. (545) |
| b | 20. | Some therapists, regardless of theoretical orientation, are just more effective than others. (547-548) |

### True/False Items

| | | |
|---|---|---|
| False | 1. | Techniques based on classical and operant conditioning are used by *behavioral* therapists. *Biomedical* approaches involve interventions into a person's physiological functioning, typically using drugs or electroconvulsive therapy. (518) |
| True | 2. | There are several reasons for this, foremost of which is that many people equate being in therapy with admitting personal weakness. (519) |
| False | 3. | Drug therapies are used by *psychiatrists*, not psychologists. (521) |
| True | 4. | Based on the work of Sigmund Freud, psychoanalysis is an insight therapy that emphasizes the recovery of unconscious conflicts, motives, and defenses through techniques such as free association, dream analysis, and transference. (522) |
| False | 5. | However, a variety of adaptations of Freud's psychoanalysis are still common. These descendants of psychoanalysis are collectively known as *psychodynamic* approaches to therapy. (524) |
| True | 6. | Client-centered therapists try to function like a human mirror, reflecting statements back to their clients, but with enhanced clarity. (525) |
| True | 7. | The good news is that studies consistently indicate that insight therapy is superior to no treatment or to placebo treatment and that the effects of therapy are reasonably durable. (528-529) |
| False | 8. | Actually, psychologists are sharply divided on this issue. Therapists are more likely to accept these memories at face value, whereas memory researchers are more skeptical. (530) |
| True | 9. | Thus, the general approach is to countercondition a relaxed response to the same stimulus. (533) |
| True | 10. | Behavior therapies seem to be particularly effective in the treatment of anxiety problems, phobias, drug problems, eating disorders, etc. (536) |
| False | 11. | Antipsychotic drugs are most likely to be used to treat schizophrenia. (537) |
| False | 12. | Actually, ECT is *not* a rare form of therapy. Estimates suggest that about 100,000 people receive ECT treatments yearly in the United States. (540) |

True    13.    Also, the goal of treatment has been reduced to reestablishing a reasonable level of functioning.  These are common criticisms of the constraints associated with managed health care. (542)

True    14.    This is why so many therapists tend to use an eclectic approach to treating psychological disorders. (542)

False   15.    Psychotherapy does not *have* to be prohibitively expensive.  Although private practitioners can be fairly expensive, community mental health centers and social service agencies can charge lower fees than most therapists in private practice. (547)